BIBLICAL AMBIGUITIES

THE BRILL REFERENCE LIBRARY
OF
ANCIENT JUDAISM

VOLUME 4

BIBLICAL AMBIGUITIES

Metaphor, Semantics and Divine Imagery

BY

DAVID H. AARON

BRILL

LEIDEN · BOSTON · KÖLN

2001

This book is printed on acid-free paper.

BS
1199
.R5
A33
2001

Library of Congress Cataloging-in-Publication Data

Aaron, David, 1957-.
    Biblical ambiguities : methaphor, semantics, and divine imagery / by
David H. Aaron.
        p.   cm. — (The Brill reference library of ancient Judaism, ISSN
1566-1237 ; vol. 4)
    Includes bibliographical references and indexes.
    ISBN 9004120327 (hardcover : alk. paper)
    1. Metaphor in the Bible. 2. Bible. O.T.—Language, style. I. Title.
II. Series.

BS1199.R5 A33   2001
220.6'6—dc21
                                                              00–069916
                                                              CIP

Die Deutsche Bibliothek - CIP-Einheitsaufnahme

Aaron, David:
Biblical ambiguities. Metaphor, semantics and divine imagery / by David
Aaron. – Leiden ; Boston ; Köln : Brill, 2001
    (The Brill reference library of ancient Judaism ; Vol. 4)
    ISBN 90–04–12032-7

ISSN   1566-1237
ISBN   90 04 12032 7

PRINTED IN THE NETHERLANDS

TABLE OF CONTENTS

PREFACE

Religions invariably seek to make true statements about the nature of reality, the nature of a god or gods, and humanity's place in this universe. Consequently, religions must address the epistemological problem of how we gain knowledge of those aspects of the world that we cannot readily experience or understand with certainty. Most often, one thinks of the transcendent realms as those most central to religious discourse. But much of our rather mundane terrestrial experience is as unknown—and, perhaps, as unknowable—as what is usually termed transcendent. The future, for instance, is very much a mystery, and in its own curious way, the past is an equally vast uncertainty. Indeed, within a given religious or political community, there can be much competition over which conceptualization of history best serves a people's sense of purpose. But that conflict over history is only possible by virtue of ambiguities confronted at every turn in the historiographic endeavor. As such, religions must address, in some manner, the problem of our world's ambiguities.

It does not matter whether we are discussing cosmic questions or pondering a decision that needs our immediate attention; the fact remains that we are constantly in a state of knowing less about ourselves and the variables relevant to our lives than we might daily acknowledge. The suppression of our ignorance surely constitutes a complex coping mechanism, which, when disabled, has crippling effects on one's psychological health. Equally problematic can be the overinsistence upon certainty in the face of so much obscurity. One's ability to handle ambiguity is undoubtedly dependent upon both psychology and culture. Individuals differ in the extent to which they suffer uncertainty. And while no western religion actually celebrates the unknowability of the universe and the nihilism that might go along with it, we should recognize that the subjects of some cultures are more sensitive than others to the limits of human knowledge.

Though not overtly the central focus, the question of how religions and scholars of religion treat the problem of ambiguity underlies this study. One may view the development of religious systems as deeply rooted in the question of how indeterminacy is resolved. Only against this backdrop can the role and purpose of metaphor be appropriately framed.

The core of this book was completed during the academic year of 1995-96, while I was enjoying a year-long leave generously provided by Wellesley College. Circumstances that I now understand to be rather typical of publishing sagas postponed its appearance for some four years. During the summer of 1998 I incorporated some additional bibliographic references, but this was done only in a casual, unsystematic manner. Except for improvements made during the editing process, the core of the book did not undergo changes after the initial writing period. I am appreciative of the financial support made available by the Hebrew Union College–Jewish Institute of Religion through the Werner and Lisl Weinberg Publications Fund and the faculty research grants that made possible the copyediting and indexing of the manuscript in its final stages of preparation.

Professor Barbara Geller of Wellesley College read very early drafts of parts of the manuscript. Professor Ray Jackendoff was also gracious enough to consider the first complete draft. The critiques offered by both of these individuals helped me rethink many crucial questions of methodology and presentation. As a result of their readings, I rewrote most of the chapters from the bottom up. I am also grateful to Professor Ellen Schauber, who served as a publisher's review reader and who chose to share with me directly her reactions and suggestions, as well as her enthusiasm for this interdisciplinary project.

During the spring of 1996, by chance, I entered into discussions with Professor Jacob Neusner, who had just begun working on a book he would later publish as *The Theological Grammar of the Oral Torah*. In that expansive, three-volume work, Neusner employed the terminology of generative linguistics to describe the structure of rabbinic thinking at its most rudimentary conceptual level. Through e-mail, we discussed the best uses of linguistic terminology to frame the ideological structure of rabbinic literature. As it turned out, Neusner's use of linguistic labels for the generative ideas within rabbinic literature proved to function as a sustained metaphor for the relationship between language and theology more generally. In this domain, his insights deserve not only attention, but adaptation for other areas of study. It was during these discussions that I first sent Professor Neusner sections from the newly emerging draft of *Biblical Ambiguities*. I wish to express my deeply felt appreciation for his sustained interest in this work and for his continued support and enthusiasm for this project, from its early stages through to publication.

The introduction to this book was reworked many times, but the most recent rendering benefited from the thoughtful reflections of Professor Susan Einbinder as well as from Professor Jerome Eckstein's insightful reading of the entire manuscript. To both I am deeply grateful. Jerome Eckstein has repeatedly explored the question of certainty, indeterminacy, and human psychology in his own philosophical quest (1981, 1991). Along the way I have been assisted by his discoveries, many of which he has shared with me in writing and in discussions over the past twenty-four years.

It is my great pleasure to express much thankfulness to Mr. Chris Rohmann, who brought innumerable improvements to this manuscript through his expert skills as an editor. He is a sophisticated reader whose ideas and questions often pushed me to articulate my thoughts more cogently.

I have undoubtedly been unable to adequately combine the collective wisdom of my teachers and readers in this work. Of course, I alone am responsible for its final form—errors and all.

Much of this book was written when my two boys were in their early stages of language acquisition. I learned more from them than they could ever imagine. Witnessing the emergence of speech is not only a joy, it is a privilege we should never take for granted. By listening to Joshua and Elisha as they learn to navigate the nuances of language and its relationship to the world about them, much of what is studied in linguistics as theory became, for me, deeply rooted in reality.

My bride, Marjorie, now knows more about ambiguity with certainty than she might ever have dreamed possible. Her support, her encouragement, and her love are ever-sustained blessings.

D.H.A.
Cincinnati, Ohio
December 1999

1.

INTRODUCTION: AMBIGUITY AND FIGURATIVE SPEECH

When we read a biblical passage that in some way involves the deity, *how do we know* whether its language was meant literally or figuratively? This study endeavors to develop a language-based interpretive strategy for understanding God-related idioms in the Hebrew Bible. In this sense, our primary focus is the character of language usage in expressions pertaining to God. However, this study does not constitute a general history of biblical God-belief. Rather, it involves an extended consideration of how semantic theory might become a factor in writing such a history, especially when it comes to interpreting metaphors.

The term "figurative" is a general designation for nonliteral speech acts, including many standard rhetorical devices such as irony, sarcasm and cynicism, allegory, hyperbole, metonymy, and of course, metaphor.[1] Each of these requires us, as interpreters, to recognize that the literal meaning of an expression is not identical to what the speaker intends us to understand. Most figurative, rhetorical devices thrive on ambiguity. This is especially true of metaphor. Ambiguity in metaphorical expressions results from uncertainty as to how the first part of a nonliteral statement is to be understood in terms of its second, or implied, part.[2] For instance, in the phrase "all the world's a stage," there is ambiguity with regard to how the world is to be understood as a stage. We might think of this ambiguity as "internal" to an expression. That is, once you recognize something as figurative, there is ambiguity involved in decoding how its parts evoke meaning. As an aesthetic element, ambiguity contributes to an expression's richness.

Besides this internal ambiguity, there is also often a lingering ambiguity as to whether something is even meant to be understood metaphorically. Given the phrase "God is a warrior," we must first

---

[1] See Culler 1997, chap. 5.
[2] Aristotle spoke of this as "transference" in his *Poetics*, chap. 21. Lakoff and Johnson (1980) call this "mapping," as will be discussed in chap. 6.

establish whether or not we should be interpreting this statement literally or metaphorically. If we determine that the phrase was meant
literally, our interpretive process is relatively straightforward. If we
determine that the phrase was meant figuratively, then we must establish possible meanings and the limits of its implications. Admittedly,
these two ambiguities—each derived from a different structural element in discourse—are often interrelated, but they are not the same
linguistic phenomenon. Although this study will recognize repeatedly
these two levels of ambiguity, the main focus will be on the problem
of how we determine whether a given statement harbors the kind of
ambiguity that gives license to a metaphorical interpretation.

The idioms to be considered are most often very simple, as far as
syntax is concerned. Many are predicate nominatives or nominative
phrases with a simple verb, for example: *God said, God is King, God is
a rock, God is an army, God is creator.* Despite syntactic simplicity, some
idioms involve more abstract concepts, such as when God *regrets* that
he had made humans on earth (Gen 6:6)[3] or when God reflects (via
Jeremiah) that it was he who (physically) *smote* the children of Judah
because of their religious waywardness (Jer 2:30), or when God *commands* laws (e.g., Exod 21-24), or when God *declares* (via the prophet) that he never *demanded* sacrifice (Isa 1:12-14; Jer 7:21-22; Amos
5:21-23).[4] Just how we categorize and then interpret these phrases—
and the many hundreds of others that are spoken by or about God
in the Tanakh—will determine how we write the history of Israelite
God-belief.

An underlying assumption of this study is that we cannot talk
adequately *about* metaphor in the Tanakh (or in any other context)
without having in place more general thoughts on metaphor and
language. This study will take as a given Jonathan Culler's methodological insight that "it is not unreasonable to expect those who take
linguistics as a model for the study of other systems to make their
own 'grammars' as explicit as possible" (1975, 24-25). A significant
portion of this book presents a theory of metaphor and word meaning, both of which are seen as essential building blocks in our assessment of biblical materials. As such, linguistics serves as both a
model and an applied discipline. The theory of semantics offered here

---

[3] See Fretheim 1984 on God's change of mind.
[4] There is much scholarly literature on the question of whether these phrases
are to be taken as literal statements or hyperbolic ones. See, for instance, Kaiser
1983, 24-33.

is actually but a single building block in a much broader theory of culture and meaning. A successful theory of meaning should not be limited to language alone; rather, it should be able to account for meaning in semiotic structures other than those exclusively linguistic, such as ritual acts, iconography, even music cognition, to name just a few. (In each area there can be both literal and figurative meanings.) Nonintegrative approaches to meaning may ultimately prove inadequate by virtue of their failure to appreciate how organically interconnected are all aspects of our cognitive structure. This cognitive structure is essentially generative in nature, allowing for the processing of a finite number of signs into an infinite number of meaningful configurations and combinations.[5]

Although cognitive theory is not the main concern of this study, our discussion will periodically assume the stand that there are aspects of language that are uninfluenced (or minimally influenced) by culture. Specifically relevant to this study is the claim that culture does not determine how metaphor works. That is, the mechanics of metaphor, just like the mechanics of most aspects of language, are fundamentally universal. This does not mean that metaphor as a linguistic phenomenon will be understood the same way in each culture; but it does mean that each culture can potentially recognize metaphor and that what causes it to be recognized is a structural element that is universal and not dependent upon culture.[6]

---

[5] On this, see Chomsky (1975), who writes that "it may well be impossible to distinguish sharply between linguistic and nonlinguistic components of knowledge and belief. Thus an actual language may result only from the interaction of several mental faculties, one being the faculty of language" (43).

[6] See Eagleton (1997, 73), who notes that we are "cultural beings by virtue of our nature." In this sense, the divide between the two may not be as extensive as many make it out to be; or, put differently, what we may regard as great divergencies might turn out to have more commonality than not. As I write these words, I am aware of research being done that contradicts the principle of the unity of human thought cross-culturally. Cultures, for instance, are said to foster different kinds of thinking patterns, some favoring logic, others favoring emotion and holistic conceptualizations, etc. Social scientists are seeing more "difference" than "similarity" when they delve deeply into the thinking structures fostered by disparate cultural groups. Undoubtedly, such learned variables will have an influence on the psychological and even the neurological development of an individual, thereby making two people from vastly different cultures quite different in very substantive ways. It remains to be seen how such research will influence the deeper structures that govern language usage and its rhetorical structures. The most fundamental aspect of the thesis being put forth here relates to the shared character of interpretive strategies, an aspect of language usage that should prove universal to all cultures as a defining characteristic of what makes language work. I will deal

Religions quite regularly deny the metaphorical meanings of figurative speech and, conversely, quite regularly make metaphors out
of literal utterances. Such acts require the violation of the most basic
rules of language. Religions, try as they will, cannot change the rules
of our cognitive structures. Insist as they may that the phrase "God
spoke" does not mean that God actually spoke the way we speak
today, their interpretations are ultimately irrelevant to the intentions
of the original writer or speaker, who may have meant to indicate
that, in fact, God spoke. (I will return to this question of "theology"
momentarily.) A full discussion of these questions regarding cognitive structure and culture cannot be undertaken by this study. Limitations on scope necessitate that we focus on statements related to
God-belief rather than cultural paradigms that are much broader.
However, in as much as God-belief cannot be torn from the broader
cultural matrix in which it functions, cognizance of the interconnect-
edness of a variety of cognitive and cultural domains will periodically emerge in the flow of our narrative. I fully recognize from the
outset that ultimately, discussions pertaining to the history of ideas
must not be worked out in isolation from these broader cultural issues.
As such, I conceptualize this study as nothing other than a building
block.

I have framed the underlying question of this study in rather traditional, binary terms. There is the danger that such a framing will
suggest that there are only two choices when it comes to expressions
and meaning: literal or nonliteral. One of the purposes of this study
is to break the binary paradigm and to employ a non-binary view
of meaning. At this early point in the book, were I to express the
question according to the "gradient model" of meaning I seek to
describe below, it would prove meaningless to the reader. By exploring a theory of semantics I hope to situate metaphor more firmly
on a continuum of meaning that is quite specifically non-binary.
During the first part of this book I will frequently use the terms
"metaphor" and "literal" in the common manner of contemporary
biblical scholarship. But as the book develops, it should become
evident that I seek to move away from this limiting, binary, either/
or conception of figurative speech, and toward a system that more
accurately reflects how we think, and reflects how the writers of
biblical literature thought.

---

with the issue of speech communities and the causes of divergent interpretations
in chapter 5.

I fully recognize that for certain schools of thought the question underlying this study is a nonissue. For instance, within the great variety of reading strategies that fall under the postmodernist's umbrella, there are those that pay no attention whatsoever to the notion of authorial intent.[7] For such strategies, the question of whether one has license to interpret a statement as metaphorical depends exclusively upon the reader, not some historical or linguistic reality that enjoys autonomy. Advocating such a "reader's response" reading strategy for Tanakh is James E. Brenneman, who writes that "truthful meaning need not derive from authorial intentions or historical background—that is, from reference points that are external to the text" (1997, 43). As Brenneman argues, all reading is essentially "community-based"; it is neither possible nor desirable to achieve some "objective" sense of meaning on the basis of some historical-critical method, since all such "truths" amount to nothing other than community-based orthodoxies. Indeed, this approach to text argues that there are no clearly intended meanings. Moreover, not only is the interpretation of texts "community-based," but even a text's compositional history turns out to be a joint project.

My perspective is quite antithetical to the "new chaos theory of Bible reading," as Brenneman calls it (27), which emerges from the ahistorical methodology suggested by "pure" literary criticism. It is undoubtedly true that a text, once written, *can* be related to in a fashion that altogether ignores the notion of authorial intent (or even denies its existence). But such an approach to text is a form of intellectual solipcism, one that chooses to ignore (or fails to grasp) the mechanics of human discourse. This is not to say that I deny the existence, in many contexts, of a persistent indeterminacy of meaning as postmodern theorists think of it; nor does it imply that I am seeking the absolute objectivity for which historical-critical methods (mistakenly) strive. In fact, as the title implies, this book is something of a celebration of ambiguity; but ambiguity as a natural and constructive element in human discourse that, rather than resulting in chaos, actually allows for fundamentally stable acts of communication which contain a significant degree of truth vis-à-vis the external world. Empty white spaces are just that—empty. As such, they should not become the subject of discourse.

---

[7] See Culler 1997 for a brief overview, or Eagleton 1996 and 1997. Advocating this position, see Taylor 1984.

Text, then, is neither an independent repository for objective meanings nor a resevoir for potentially limitless interpretations. Meaning in language does have confines, even though we can behave as if it does not.[8] Those confines may permit us to establish reasonable limits to interpretations, even as they may fail to establish certainty and univocality in most things said. We readily admit that the writing of the history of ideas must, in some sense, involve what Hayden White calls "emplotment"—the act of creating a narrative from disparate pieces of data whose significance is found only when the historian creates the overarching sense of context. But in order to make the judgments required in even the most creative of histories, one must start with a sense of how the evidence is to be evaluated. That is to say, even as we recognize the ways the individual enters into the act of history writing via the emplotment of the data, there must always be ways to evaluate which histories are closer to our experience of the world and which are altogether distorting of that experience.[9] Even subjectivities vary as to their truth quotients.

We should perhaps conceptualize texts as metonyms for their authors and their historical contexts; as such, the act of reading a text is, in a sense, the act of decoding a thought system which, in some grander sense, is part of a yet larger system (of culture, environment, biology, etc.), which transcends both its confines and language itself. The fact that its every detail cannot possibly be established should not cause us to abandon its semantic integrity. In normal acts of communication we assume that ideas are fundamentally dependent upon the people, contexts, and cultures whence they derive, just as a metonym is dependent upon the preacknowledged relationship between the sign used and the unnamed intentionality implied. The question is not whether I can *fully* grasp the original intent of an author (any more than I may be able to fully explicate the referents in a metonym); the question, rather, pertains to how I go about grasping as much as possible of that original intent while recognizing the many limits imposed by time and space and—when it comes to the literatures of antiquity—lost conventions of discourse. As a

---

[8] I will not discuss more fully the problem of discord between a speaker's intent and what a given utterance actually yields, for this concerns questions of pragmatics that are not really our concern, albeit, of great interest to the linguist. Nonetheless, we must admit that problems in textual transmission may constitute a parallel to a speaker's periodic incompetence in getting her or his idea across. On this see Chomsky 1975, chap. 2.

[9] See White 1974 and 1973.

metonym for an author, a text results from both conscious and unconscious knowledge, even as it participates in the author's own acquiescence to the conventions of his or her speech community. However, there is no way to break the text off from the author and have the result be anything more than a celebration of the reader's meaning. Reader's meaning may be amusing, but it is ultimately irrelevant to the historian of ideas. A text without authorial intent is no more meaningful than a metonym without an identifiable set of referents; or to phrase it less figuratively: a statement that altogether lacks a cultural, historical, and speaker's-oriented context is of little historical value. It is like finding a potsherd on the surface of a *tel*. Dislocated from its original stratum, it is of no value to the archaeologist.

It should be altogether clear that the linguistic theory pursued here starts with the notion of a speaker who means something in particular by what he or she says. Those are the ideas we historians of biblical thought are after. Naturally, a book of this nature can only focus on a very limited set of concerns in the sea of semantic theory. Such limitations might give the impression that other, very key concerns relevant to the interpretation of metaphor are of little importance. This is hardly the case. I am quite cognizant of the fact that most studies in semantics focus on word, phrase, and sentence meaning, and that more recently, some theorists have begun to consider how semantic theory might be extended to account for discourse, narrative, or genre. Unfortunately, these considerations, and others like them, must remain outside the confines of this study.

Some Preliminary Comments on How Metaphor Works

A thorough consideration of how metaphor works will not appear before chapter 6; however, I will put in place some of the basic assumptions of this study at the outset. Virtually all theorists accept that metaphor functions by means of indirect meaning, which is only rarely univocal. As more than one meaning is usually possible, the interpretive process requires us to rule out some senses as irrelevant to the speaker's meaning, while accepting others (or perhaps one) as most relevant. The historian of religion seeks to establish *the meaning(s) intended* by the author. Such evaluations require a process for narrowing down possible meanings to plausible intended meanings. Any such methodology must be grounded in a broader consideration of just what metaphor is, how it is structured and functions, and how it is detected independent of any biblical idiom.

Setting up such an interpretive strategy for metaphor is neither a small nor a new task. Philosophers, literary critics, and linguists alike have struggled with these issues since Aristotle. As noted, I will place before the reader in considerable detail just what my understanding is of how meaning comes about in language. Such an in-depth consideration of semantic theory is unusual for a book that is ostensibly about decoding God-related idioms in Hebrew Scriptures. Consequently, I recognize that some justification for this merging of theory and interpretation is appropriate.

During the mid-1970s, Jonathan Culler explored how such a merger might work for literary critics at large. He wrote that

> one might expect semantics to be the branch of linguistics which literary critics would find most useful. . . . What critic does not in his moments dream of a scientifically rigorous way of characterizing the meaning of a text, of demonstrating with tools of proven appropriateness that certain meanings are possible and others impossible? And even if semantic theory did not suffice to account for all meanings observed in literature, would it not, at least, form a primary stage in literary theory and critical method by indicating what meanings must be characterized by supplementary rules? If semantics could provide a description of the semantic structure of a text it would certainly be of great use to critics, even if it were not a panacea. (1975, 75)

As to the application of linguistic theory to interpretation, Culler grudgingly conceded that "semantics has not yet reached the stage where it can characterize the meaning of a text, and even the more modest goals it has set for itself have scarcely been achieved" (75). During the decades since Culler wrote this, many developments in semantic theory have taken place. Of particular relevance to our endeavor is the fact that literary theorists have employed these developments in their interpretation of a great variety of documents. In these works, scholars make explicit their assumptions regarding how meaning comes about and often delineate their understanding of how specific literary tools work within their understanding of semantics.[10]

---

[10] Among many others, see, for instance, Iser (1979), who engages the theories of Austin, Cavell, von Savigny, and others. Equally important may be how the

In contrast, biblical scholars have focused on a small cluster of
semantic theories and employed them in a wholesale fashion, usually deferring deeper questions as to their validity to the battles waged
by linguists and those literary critics willing to enter the murky waters
of semantic theory. My goal is to convince the reader that one's particular approach to language—whether explicitly defined or implicitly exercised—influences one's method for establishing cogent interpretations. Our understanding of how meaning is generated is
usually a subconscious part of our knowledge. This means that we
employ a theory of meaning—or what Terry Eagleton would call,
"an ideology" of meaning—whether we are aware of it or not.[11] By
making my understanding explicit here, I endeavor to bring into
question a great variety of assumptions held by others. My goal is
as much to cast doubt on the well-entrenched but unscrutinized
methodologies that currently dominate biblical scholarship (regarding metaphor) as it is to offer a viable alternative to the standard
approaches.

Perhaps because figurative idioms are so commonly a part of our
everyday speech acts, very few scholars feel compelled to deal with
the mechanics of metaphor and their broader relationship to semantics. When biblical scholars do employ a methodology for distinguishing literal from nonliteral statements, two approaches dominate the
field. One is based on subject matter, the other on language usage.[12]
The former is the more popular of the two and has a history going
back to the first century. The subject-matter approach argues that
metaphor is a necessary part of any literature that concerns God
because our earthbound, literal expressions could not possibly describe in a direct manner an "invisible [deity], that transcends all
human ability to comprehend it" (Von Rad 1962-65, 1:215).[13] Were
it not for metaphor, argue many scholars, little, if anything, could

---

author of the document being interpreted understood meaning to occur. While
this may often be of interest, an individual's theory may not have any relevance to
what actually occurs.

[11] See Eagleton (1996, 13), who defines ideology as "the ways in which what
we say and believe connects with the power-structure and power-relations of the
society we live in."

[12] These two do not exhaust the list of approaches. The fact is that most scholars give no thought at all as to what metaphor is or how it should be handled.
Moreover, I do not mean to propose too stringent a division between these approaches. Some scholars use both. See chapter 2.

[13] This approach, virtually an axiom of "Old Testament theology," is extremely
widespread. See McFague 1983, Banks 1994, Brueggemann 1997, 230ff.

be said regarding God.[14] According to the theologian Walter Brue-
ggeman, metaphor, because of its ambiguity, actually protects humans from the form of idolatry that results when people believe they
fully comprehend the deity. "Yahweh is hidden, free, surprisng, and
elusive, and refuses to be caught in any verbal formulation," he argues
(1997, 231). Metaphor not only protects people from believing in a
set description, it also prevents theological reductionism. Brueggemann, among many other scholars who will be discussed here, focuses on God-related nouns as metaphorical expressions that lead
one close to God but cannot "fully match the elusive Subject." All
of these beliefs about God are purportedly learned from biblical
literature.

The second major approach to metaphor employed in biblical
studies is dependent upon a theory expounded by George Lakoff.
Lakoff's approach, set forth in two books (co-authored with Mark
Johnson and Mark Turner, respectively), is undoubtedly the most
frequently cited in the exegetical literature on Tanakh.[15] Those who
follow his theories view metaphor as inexorably a part of speech acts,
arising from our cognitive structure; that is, we are *built to think
metaphorically*, regardless of the language or context. With this thesis
in place, we should expect to find metaphors everywhere and might
even be surprised should they be absent. Lakoff's theory of metaphorical meaning and its impact on interpreters of Bible will be
considered briefly in chapter 2 and quite thoroughly in chapter 6.

Both the subject-oriented approaches and those derived from
George Lakoff's work have a central point in common, namely, that
God metaphors are necessary. In one case, it is because of the way
we think; in the other, it is because of the nature of the subject matter,
God, who lies beyond speech. Upon closer scrutiny, the subject-based
methodology turns out to be just as linked to characteristics of our
cognitive structure as the linguistic theory offered by Lakoff. How

---

[14] This position is adopted by Korpel (1990), who surveys others who take the
same approach.

[15] See Lakoff and Johnson 1980, Lakoff and Turner 1989. The claim that Lakoff's
writings are more frequently cited by biblical scholars than those of any other
semanticist is based on an impression from studying the field, not a scientific sampling. Consider that in a special volume of *Semeia* (1993) on metaphor in the Bible,
Lakoff's approach to metaphor was adopted explicitly or implicitly in all but two
of the articles. See especially Brettler 1993 and Bal 1993, (the latter's title is a play
on Lakoff and Johnson's). Korpel (1990) also bases her approach on Lakoff and
Johnson, although she includes a survey of other theorists.

so? The approach maintains that since God cannot be understood *directly*, we can only speak of him *indirectly*. Thus, according to this theory, it is also our cognitive condition that necessitates speech via metaphorical images. Put differently: were it not for metaphor, God would remain an ineffable subject, perhaps altogether unthinkable.

I believe both the Lakoff theory and the theory based on subject matter are problematic. I find no evidence that God-related idioms have special linguistic status in Tanakh. Nowhere in Tanakh are we informed that literal statements about the deity are impossible because of transcendence or any other divine characteristic.[16] Biblical language, like language in all literary domains, works the same way regardless of ideational content. I will repeatedly visit the inferential arguments put forth by a variety of scholars on discrete textual examples. I will seek to show that any distinction based on subject matter is a distinction founded upon contemporary theological presuppositions rather than evidence derived from Scriptures. I will argue further that metaphor, like other forms of figurative speech, is a rhetorical device, one which cannot operate unless the subject being described is, indeed, rather well understood. In this sense, the act of classifying a phrase as metaporical may frequently turn out to be a modern-made smoke screen to obfuscate truths interpreters would rather not confront when it comes to the religion(s) of biblical literature.

Please understand that in making such a comment I am not claiming anything as to the reality of the object being defined by the metaphors. Just as we can establish whether a person is speaking of a unicorn metaphorically or literally, so should we be able to establish whether a person is speaking of God metaphorically or literally. In both cases, "reality" is fundamentally irrelevant to the nature of the utterance. What matters is what the speaker believes. Moreover, we should appreciate the complexity of such utterances, especially with regard to that area of "knowledge" known as theological. The unicorn example proves quite instructive. Umberto Eco charmingly discusses Marco Polo's sighting of a rhinoceros, which he took to be a unicorn. As Eco notes, "since [Polo's] culture provided him with the notion of a unicorn—a quadruped with a horn on its forehead,

---

[16] Richard Elliot Friedman (1995) argues that "transcendence" is a mistaken portrayal: "I am not sure that 'immanence and transcendence' are the right categories. It does not appear to me to be so much a matter of God's 'transcending' history as simply dis-appearing, becoming more and more hidden" (79).

to be precise—he designated those animals [i.e., the rhinoceroses on Java] as unicorns" (1995, 57-58). What is most instructive in this particular case, as Eco summarizes it, is that, rather than come up with a new word for a hitherto undiscovered species, Polo revised the definition of a unicorn. As Eco explains it,

> rather than resegment the content by adding a new animal to the universe of the living, he has corrected the contemporary description of unicorns, so that, if they existed, they would be as he saw them and not as the legend described them. He has modified the intension and left the extension unchanged. Or at least that is what it seems he wanted to do, or in fact, did, without bothering his head overmuch regarding taxonomy.[17]

Theological thinking is much the same. Rather than come up with a new being in the taxonomies of the transcendent, religions emend prevalent descriptions of God. Meanings, both metaphorical and literal, serve its ever-renewed attempts at defining the experience of the divine.

While we may naturally think according to basic analogical methods (comparing one thing to another), metaphor is much more than that. It is a learned technique of discourse. One need not speak with metaphor. Indeed, it is possible to mean everything one says at the most literal of levels. A culture can even eschew metaphor as a socially undesirable mode of expression.[18] Children think and express them-

---

[17] As it turns out, Eco may have told only half the story. There is considerable controversy over whether Polo ever visited the places he claims to have been. The details of this particular description could easily have been fabricated on the basis of old mythologies. The image of a unicorn with "elephant feet" dates back at least to Pliny the Elder's *Cyclopaedia Historia Naturalis*. As such, Polo's experience of confronting this creature could have been fabricated. If so, his desire to alter the definition of the unicorn involves an intentionality of considerable complexity, for now it is no longer a question of forcing the definition to conform to an experience of some rhinoceros; rather, it is a matter of overthrowing a standard mythology (perhaps even satirically), with full knowledge that one is deceiving the reader into believing that a unicorn sighting actually took place. Just what the narrator's purpose would have been remains obscure. On Marco Polo and the legends of the unicorn, see Shepard 1993, esp. 216f.

[18] This may be more regularly evident and more common with other forms of nonliteral speech. For instance, sarcasm may be considered distasteful; instances of hyperbole may be thought of as dishonest speech; repeated use of irony may make one suspicious of a speaker, etc. I will not have the opportunity to discuss all of the ramifications of culture on each of these semantic domains, but those who know several languages can certainly reflect upon the fact that imagery is often easily translatable from one language to another, while some particular images may

selves with metaphor-less, irony-less language. Prior to about the age of six, children say what they mean directly, extending the meanings of words using a variety of techniques when their vocabulary is deficient.[19] But such extensions of semantic fields are not metaphorical, they are mechanically code like. The main point is that our use of metaphor, as well as other figurative modes, is a matter of cognitive development and learned behaviors, and then a matter of choice—not an inevitable result of the way language works or the way we think, or a quality of the subject matter we wish to describe.[20]

Some metaphors appear to be paradigmatic within biblical culture: tree imagery as indicative of stability and piety, the whoring wife as an allegory for religious waywardness, natural catastrophes as divine wrath, and so forth. The most dominant of the negative images is the idol, the iconic representation of a deity. The idol has implications the whoring wife, a tree, or thunder do not. With regard to these three (and many others like them), there can be no doubt as to their metaphoricalness. But when it comes to idolatry, the multiple senses and contexts of the medium make interpretation especially challenging. Foremost is the problem of establishing the relationship between an idol and the deity. Is an idol a (prohibited) metaphor for a deity, or must the relationship be defined differently? If the idol is a metaphor, then why should such iconic metaphors be considered problematic while literary metaphors for God are acceptable?

It is in the arena of idols and icons that the interplay between metaphor and literalism is particularly poignant. The prominence of this prohibition in the Decalogues has prompted some to see it as a key aspect in Israelite theology. Thus, the idol commands a

---

not be rendered sensible outside of a given language. By considering these factors we can see how *specific images* of metaphors are often culturally dependent.

[19] See Gardner 1978 and Gardner and Winner 1979; Pinker 1984. Just the other day I witnessed this in my three-year-old. Having spent a long time in the bathtub, he noticed that the skin on his hands had become all wrinkled. "Look, my fingers are grumpy!" A metaphor? Hardly. See my comments on structural ascription in chapter 3.

[20] By "choice" I do not mean to exclude the fact that a particular individual may use metaphorical structures habitually or in conformity with certain cultural predilections. The issue is not conscious choice versus cultural habit; the issue is that we always have the *ability* to say things without these rhetorical structures. Moreover, I would fully accept that the comparative thinking process by which we construct metaphor is innate. But this does not make metaphor a necessary device of expression or thinking.

certain privilege as the quintessential counter-image in Israelite thought. Equally important is the fact that the question of aniconism develops over a very long period of time and appears to have had different meanings in discrete eras. Consequently, with regard to iconism, we are not only able to focus on the question of whether an idol was a metaphor, but we are able to trace the development of imagery that I believe moved from an early stage of literalism to a later stage of metaphorical meaning. These issues will be considered in chapter 8.

One of the most challenging conundrums in biblical studies remains the exact character of the Tanakh's compositeness, both at the level of discrete literary units and, more globally, in terms of canon. These lingering questions constitute significant complications in any attempt to write the history of Israelite belief. The connotations of words can shift significantly in a mere decade, not to mention over centuries. Identifying authorial intent in conjunction with the historical realities of an author's *Sitz-in-Leben*, while necessary, can often prove to be an elusive task. There rages a debate mong scholars as to whether the Tanakh provides true information about historical eras, or constitutes a purely literary work of fiction. This debate is undoubtedly germane to the question of authorial intent. If we keep to the (now) traditional scenario, which maintains that the J writer is tenth century and the P writer is as much as six hundred years later (with E and D in between), then we must approach the semantic fields of the different authors with considerable caution, taking care to differentiate potential nuances of meaning. If we abrogate this standard dating, following, for instance, the dating offered by John Van Seters (1983, 1992, 1994), then there are yet other implications for the intents of authors and the juxtaposition of semantic fields.

When it comes to sources, redaction, and ultimately canonization, I open up more questions than I can resolve. An earlier draft of this book included a chapter on source criticism, the redactional process and canon formation, all subjects especially germane to how one reconstructs authorial intent. It is precisely our ignorance of and about the Bible's authors—not just their worldviews, but how they went about their literary work and who they were—that makes all assumptions regarding authorial intent highly speculative. In the end, I decided to leave this chapter out, figuring that it required more space on many (only tangentially) related issues than could be afforded in this context. For the time being, I shall assume a relatively naive attitude toward authorial intent: one which allows for the separation of some more or less obvious literary layers (discrete literary units, broader narratives, redactional insertions, etc.), each of which can be ascribed to some conscious hand. In this sense, many of the textual interpretations here assume a great deal about the nature of the author,[21] assumptions which cannot be fully explicated or even justified in this context. Admittedly, it will be necessary at some point to reconsider the profound impact one's redactional hypotheses have on how we construe authorial intent. For the time being we shall work with vague hypotheses regarding authorship, acknowledging both the limitations and possibilities such a working order imposes upon us.

Contrasting Natural and Theological Language

Natural language performs its functions quite well, in most contexts. It might sound odd to speak of evaluating language's performance in this way, but there is a purpose to the consideration. Like all cognitive domains, language has its natural limits and sometimes these limits make themselves felt in blatant ways.[22] For instance, one limit regards just how exactly natural language can convey the intentions of a speaker to an audience. Assuming the competence of all parties involved, this problem of ambiguity does not derive from any inadequacy in the speaker or the audience, or in the particular expression itself. In fact, ambiguity is everywhere, but we are so accustomed to accommodating it that we hardly notice it. When Groucho Marx comments in the movie *Animal Crackers*, "I once shot an elephant in my pajamas," we might find the image humorous, but its ambiguity is only made blatant when he adds, "How he got

---

[21] And this is exactly as the Gricean principles of discourse suggest; see the discussion in chapter 5 as well as Iser 1979, chap. 3, (following Austin 1975).

[22] Other domains might be identified as vision, hearing, and smelling; and there is much evidence that musical cognition constitutes a discrete domain. Limitations are obvious. When it comes to language, our cognitive structures are well beyond those of the rest of the animal world, but in some other domains, our abilities are inferior. For instance, humans do not see in the dark as well as many other animals do, nor do we hear the same range of frequencies, or have a comparable sensitivity to and memory of odors, etc. There are also cognitive domains that do not exist in humans at all, such as echolocation.

into my pajamas I'll never know."[23] The possible interpretations of the original phrase are suddenly apparent (most of us would assume it was Groucho who was wearing the pajamas). Recognizing the prominence of ambiguity in natural speech is only a first step, but a very important one.

To think of these limitations as defects is not valuable. Consider the statement "That bicycle is defective because it cannot be ridden up a tree." We might readily acknowledge as true that the bicycle cannot climb the tree, but we would urgently point out that this hardly constitutes a defect. Bicycles were not devised to climb trees. The underlying principle is this: to judge something defective with regard to some aspect that is irrelevant to its purpose is itself an irrelevant judgment.[24]

The analogy is instructive for understanding language's limitations. In the overwhelming majority of contexts, we have no reason to use speech that is altogether devoid of ambiguity. Language accomplishes what it was created to do quite successfully, most of the time, and we function quite satisfactorily within its parameters in most instances. Demanding of language (and the cognitive structure that underlies it) absolute exactitude is quite parallel to demanding of bicycles a tree-climbing act. Rather than trying to force the bicycle up the tree, we are better off devising a more specialized apparatus for that specific task.

But in religion, the status of ambiguity can be rather different. All religions use language and all natural language involves varying degrees of ambiguity. Just as a conversation and a computer program (a non-natural language) represent language domains whose tolerance of ambiguity can be evaluated, so is religion such a domain. Particular religions can be scrutinized and placed along a continuum relative to other domains of discourse. We might expect to find that different religions deal with ambiguity in very different ways. Moreover, a given religion might tolerate high degrees of ambiguity concerning one subject, but very little ambiguity regarding something else. One might even frame the history of a religion as a history of a belief system's management of ambiguity. That is to say, a religion's internal ideological structure, beyond the specif-

---

[23] The example is provided and discussed in Pinker 1994, 102.

[24] This is similar to Gilbert Ryles' notion of "category mistakes." See Ryles 1949, 16ff. My thanks to Jerome Eckstein for leading me to this reference.

ic ideas themselves, is perhaps best revealed in its methods for accommodating, rejecting, or accepting ambiguity.[25]

Since Philo of Alexandria, theologians have used metaphor and its broader relative, allegory, as essential tools in building the thought systems of religions. I have avoided using the word "theology" throughout this study. This is because I find very little *theology*—in the formal sense of this word—in Hebrew Bible. Such a claim requires explanation. Theologies are first and foremost language games, in the same sense that philosophies are language games. This is how Wittgenstein approached it. He recognized that philosophies set up meanings for words in manners that are *not* natural to ordinary language usages. "Asked whether philosophers have hitherto spoken nonsense, you could reply: no, they have only failed to notice that they are using a word in quite different senses" (Wittgenstein 1975, 55 §9).[26] The Tanakh, with few exceptions, is fundamentally devoid of such "different senses," and hence we can assert that there is no theology that is biblical. Put differently, there are *only* biblical theologies when a religious community or scholar insists upon their fabrication. Of course, the Bible is replete with beliefs and ideologies about God, politics, social order, ritual, etc., but these beliefs and ideologies are not conveyed in language games. The lack of systematic theology in Tanakh—in this sense of a language game—has been recognized by most, but this has not stopped scholars from imposing constructed theologies upon Tanakh.[27] Scholarly attempts to describe such a theology are essentially irrelevant to the furtherance of our understanding of Israelite ideas. Ideologically speaking, it makes little sense to speak of a theology of the canon; and the canon's redactors were much more focused on the political expediencies of their documents than on God-related ideology.

Some have argued that theology proper did not exist prior to the Greeks. With some reservations, I am inclined to follow this historiography of religious thought, but I would go a step further. I would argue that theology, in the sense that it would come to be known in

---

[25] The same can be said about a scholar's approach to the text. One's willingness to entertain ambiguity, rather than constantly drive for clearly defined meanings, will have a great influence on one's interpretive strategies.

[26] Similarly, "For many words philosophers devise an *ideal* use, which then turns out to be worthless" (Wittgenstein 1982, §830).

[27] See Childs' brief survey of the history of theology writing and his bibliography (1985, 1-19). See also the surveys in Ollenburger 1985 and Brueggemann 1997.

Judaism and Christianity, was quite specifically a creation of the late
Hellenistic Era.[28] Philosophy, as it was known in ancient Greece, used
reason to make sense of our perceptions of the physical world. Theology also constituted an attempt to make sense of the world, but it
brought to this quotient a set of thinking rules (in the form of privileged documents) that was external to the average person's perceptions or reasoning ability. Until these components are present—
employment of our rational faculties, a systematic consideration of
our perceptions, and the dominance of a privileged set of documents—I would argue that a text or religion lacks theology.[29]

What differentiates a theological inquiry from a philosophical
inquiry are the ideas derived from privileged documents. These ideas
are not available from any other source (such as reason or common
experience). The philosopher can, theoretically, be open to a great
array of concepts, and then devise his or her language games based
on the perceived demands of the ideas under consideration. The theologian, in contrast, starts with a specific document that predefines
the nature of some essential concepts. Equally important is the fact
that the same document may exclude other competing ideas from
being entertained. Consider that a philosopher need not discuss God,
ever; a theologian cannot avoid the issue.

Subject limitations are hardly as significant as the more extensive
meanings and framings that derive from the privileged documents
themselves; for a privileged document not only sets up the issues of
social discourse, it may even provide the vocabulary.[30] Theology
must integrate the language of the privileged document(s) with the

---

[28] See Dalferth 1988, chap. 2.

[29] I do not mean here to create a reductionist definition of theology, claiming
that there is a set of necessary and sufficient conditions—reason, perceptions,
documents—without which there is no theology. On the contrary, I will write below
quite directly against such a method of definition. By indicating these three rubrics, I am neither defining specific characteristics nor the balance that might exist
between them for there to be theology. For instance, there is an immense amount
of flexibility in what constitutes "a privileged set of documents," just as there is an
immense variety in the way reason or perceptions are used in a philosophical system.
Thus, we have here what I will call "typicality conditions," not specific conditions
that are necessary and sufficient in and of themselves, but conditions whose exact
character floats and may vary from one instance to another. See chapter 4. However, we can still claim that there must be some set of privileged documents, along
with some attempt to harmonize them with reason (in some formal sense), before
a religious community creates theology.

[30] See Neusner (1998), who makes this a central premise in this study as he
attempts to establish the inner-thought system of rabbinic Judaism.

language of philosophical discourse. Hence, the language game is played at multiple levels simultaneously. Moreover, it is ever-evolving, based on the exigencies of a given generation and its need to provide for those exigencies on the basis of what can be derived from the privileged texts. This is not to say that "philosophy" occurs in some pure, unbounded state. On the contrary, as we have noted, philosophical discourses have their own language systems, which augment natural language. Indeed, philosophy in natural language may not be philosophy at all.[31] The same can be said of theology.

In Tanakh, there is never an appeal to the logic or perspective of some independent authoritative text. Indeed, the only authority depicted as in any sense external to the narrative is the divine voice. The concept of a canon, a set of privileged documents, must, by definition, postdate the biblical documents themselves.[32] While it is commonly accepted that numerous passages reflect cognizance of earlier documents, either by emending them or by adopting them, no single passage ever attempts to interpret a historical phenomenon, or some idea in the abstract, by harmonizing some authoritative writ with reason.[33] This is not to say that the texts are devoid of well-defined beliefs. Moreover, we can readily discern historiographies that reflect a variety of ideologies, much technical language, and many literary or legal tropes. But our concern here is the language of the Tanakh at a deeper level. How we establish which idioms are meant literally and which are meant figuratively involves a process far more complicated than the identification of broad ideologies, technical vocabularies, or recurrent imageries. None of these constitute theology, either alone or together, unless (or until) they are part of a broader language game. Whether or not we read the-

---

[31] See my comments above (n. 26) regarding Wittgenstein's suggestion that philosophers regularly use words with senses that are different from natural language usage, as in Wittgenstein 1975, 55.

[32] This is not universally accepted, and some scholars accept the existence of varying degrees of canonicity. See, for instance, Gerhard Von Rad, who writes about the textual inheritance of the Deuteronomist as follows: "the Deuteronomist had a principle of interpretation at his disposal whose legitimacy was beyond doubt—this was the word of God in Deuteronomy, which for him was almost already canonical" (1962-65, 1:341).

[33] The closest we come to this kind of scenario is the Book of Qohelet, where the perspectives of the Deuteronomic worldview are challenged head on. Though we can discern just what the target was, the author of the book stops short of explicitly identifying the literary sources behind the ideas he criticizes. See chapter 9. See Weinfeld 1972 regarding Deuteronomic thinking and Wisdom Literature.

ology into the text—in the technical sense of theology as I have defined it here—will have great import for the way we interpret what constitutes metaphor.

Because we have considered here the notion of a language game, let me introduce at this juncture the concept of *shared reading strategies*. This will be the topic of concern in chapters 2 and 6, where we will consider a variety of approaches to interpretation, all of which acknowledge the relevance of shared strategies among speakers and interpreters. According to this approach, the meaning of a conversation—or a word, for that matter—is not absolute, but is derived, instead, from an implicit set of agreed-upon rules and conventions shared by those engaged in any given speech act. Were one to enter a speech group unaware of its semantic rules and conventions, much of what would be said would remain unintelligible.

While recognizing the limitations of the comparison, we might think of a conversation's subject matter as analogous to the semantic rules of a given language. We have surely all experienced the disconcerting feeling that results when we enter a convsation already in progress, only to find the dialogue unintelligible. Of course, the individual words are all familiar, and the sentences are grammatical, but that does not prevent meaning from remaining elusive. In such a situation, simply asking, "What are you talking about?" can clarify the subject matter in a matter of moments. The baffling expressions just heard suddenly take on meaning; the shared subject matter becomes apparent.

If the subject matter of a conversation constitutes our משל, or analogy, then we must now decode how semantic rules function in our נמשל, or real-life situation. When it comes to more profound and far-reaching semantic rules, word meaning is not determined simply on the basis of a subject matter easily defined, but according to a much broader set of culturally and linguistically bound rules. Semantics involves the decoding of a complex array of interrelationships between syntactical elements, body language, vocal tonality, social custom, and broader cultural knowledge, none of which can be filled in—as the subject matter of a conversation can be—with a comment or two. The successful decoding of a speaker's metaphors will be dependent upon the extent to which the speaker and his or her hearers share an interpretive strategy. Usually, shared strategies are learned unconsciously in the same manner one acquires one's culture, or one's language itself.

But there are domains of human discourse that employ strategies that involve an array of rules fabricated to control the derivation of meanings. We might call such rules *artificial*, in contrast to those derived from natural speech acts. Their artificiality stems from the deliberate manner in which they are formed, as alternatives to the rules of natural discourse. A theology constitutes one of these artificially derived strategies (as does a computer program), in that it seeks to limit the meanings of words on the basis of some fabricated semantic system. In doing this, it attempts to bypass our natural decoding process so as to influence our consideration of context, history, and other factors relevant to interpretation. As noted, the natural ambiguity of speech acts provides for multiple interpretations. A theology endeavors to remove multiple interpretations for certain privileged meanings. My contention is that biblical language is essentially natural language, not one altogether devoid of "games," but a language that is essentially nontheological, in that it is devoid of highly construed controls on semantic variables.

Structure and Content

In the course of this book, I will endeavor to construct what I call a model for gradient judgments—that is, a method for judging statements and placing them on a "continuum of meaning." To the extent possible, considerations of biblical materials are integrated into discussions of linguistic theory. Chapter 2 introduces the concept of *gradience* and outlines the importance of *shared strategy* in acts of interpretation, biblical and otherwise. Chapter 3 provides a number of examples of how literal statements, misconstrued, influence the way we reconstruct the "theology" of Tanakh. This chapter also considers the hold that the artificial metaphorical/literal binary has had on our interpretive strategies, and introduces a category of speech acts, called *conceptual ascription*, whose goal is to account for the expressions that lie between the two extremes.

Chapters 4 and 5 develop a theory of how we conceptualize word meaning. The former considers the questions of semantics—how words convey meaning—and the problems of authorial intent, while the latter introduces principles of relevance theory. Having established concepts such as gradience and conceptual ascription which avoid the pitfalls of binary views of meaning, and having outlined

the role in interpretation of shared strategies and various conditions
of relevance, only one more piece of technical knowledge will be
necessary to complete the model for gradient judgments: how metaphor works—its mechanical and rhetorical functioning. This is the
subject of chapter 6. Chapter 7 considers in depth the metaphorical
nature of idolatry, and chapter 8 employs a theory of gradient
meaning and especially the concept of ascription to the interpretation of a broad literary motif: the biblical proscription against icons.
The final chapter will draw conclusions and reflect on the implications of this study.

2

DISTINGUISHING METAPHORS FROM
NON-METAPHORS

Matitiahu Tsevat made a point of emphasizing in his classroom and in his writings that "battle with a straw man is no battle at all." By this he meant that "in most of the nonprophetic books of the Bible, we have actuality pitted against actuality and not actuality against nonactuality." As Tsevat argues, things that are strongly or vehemently prohibited, such as magic, occult science and practice, idols, and the worship of other gods, are forbidden "precisely because they are efficacious" in the worldview of those concerned (1969-70, 124—25). The concept of "efficacy" evokes a concern with literal meanings, not metaphor. In his article on the assembly of the gods, Tsevat asks whether the Israelites believed other deities were *real* gods.[1] According to Tsevat, an affirmative answer is unequivocally required regarding most passages; that is, these passages are to be understood *literally*. But "unequivocal" is hardly a term most would apply to the majority of passages that hint at one or another form of Israelite polytheism in Hebrew Scriptures. How does one go about making the decision? What *tools* does one have to differentiate the literal from the metaphorical?

The following exercise should help concretize the issue. No one argues that the cultures of the ancient Near East (including the Israelites') did not employ common idioms and motifs. However, most scholars distinguish the use of idioms in Israel from their usage in other cultures. As such, the expression "X is Y" may be read literally in a Ugaritic text, but will frequently be interpreted metaphorically when it appears in a Hebrew text. Below are a number of verses from various documents, some Israelite, some Egyptian, some Mesopotamian. I invite the reader to try to match the texts with their origins. No doubt, with a little more context, even a novice in the field might identify their true provenance. I have purposely left out

---

[1] Tsevat 1969-70. See, for instance, Deut 4:19f.; 1 Sam 26:19; Josh 24:15; Ps 82.

words that would instantaneously align the expressions with a particular culture (for example, specific divine names or names of rulers).

This exercise has two goals. The first is to make clear for those who are not specialist in ancient Near Eastern literature just how close the expressions from different cultures really are. The second concerns the question of Israelite distinctiveness more broadly. By demonstrating the closeness of shared idioms without any cultural prejudices, I hope to illustrate just how complex (and instrumental) the literal versus the figurative decision making process can be.[2]

a) Your greatness goes out to the nation, your praise being uttered. You are exalted! you are exalted! Who can compare to you?

b) [He] is great in [the land], exalted above all peoples. They praise your name as great and awesome.

c) He is exalted above all nations; his glory is above the heavens. Who is like [him] enthroned on high?

d) You pile the disobedient land into heaps
You destroy the rebellious land which does not harken. . . .
Who can calm your angry heart?. . .
Your right hand lets no enemy escape
Your left hand lets no evil-doer flee.

e) Your hand is equal to all Your enemies;
Your right hand overpowers Your foes.
You set them ablaze like a furnace at the time of your anger;
In anger, [he] destroys them, fire consumes them.

f) You bring on darkness and it is night,
When all the beasts of the forests stir.
The lions roar for prey,
Seeking their food from God.

---

[2] Admittedly, the exercise is not perfect, in that context certainly helps shape one's interpretation. I have endeavored to choose phrases which are not made unequivocal in their original contexts. I have replaced the name of a god, whenever it is used, with the word "god" or something similar so as to hide the identities of the deities. Also, as these verses come from a variety of translations, I have endeavored to make the language uniform; for instance, the "thou" typical of translations in Pritchard 1969 has been changed to "you" so as to eliminate the impact of translators' sylistic choices. Finally, this is but a very small sampling of potential phrases which could have been used. Similarities in legal documents and in entire motifs may even be more impressive. By scanning Pritchard, one can easily get a sense of parallels by taking note of the many biblical passages indicated in the margins.

g) Although you shine on every human face,
No one sees you go.
When you set upon the western horizon,
The earth lies in darkness and death.
Sleepers lie beneath their covers,
Seeing no one around them. . . .
The lion leaves his cave, the serpent strikes
The darkness blankets the land

(h) Arise, shine, for your light has dawned;
The being of God shines upon you.
Behold, darkness shall cover the earth,
And thick clouds the peoples;
But upon you will God shine
And his presence be seen upon you.

i) You are the only one, who made what exists. . . .
We praise your might, according as you did make us.
Let us act for you, because you brought us forth.
We give you thanksgiving because you have wearied yourself with us.
Hail to You, who made all that is.
The Lord of truth and father of the divine beings.[3]
Who made mortals and created beasts. . . .

j) O God, your ways are set apart;
Which deity is as great as God?
You are the God who works wonders,
Who has made his strength known among the nations.

k) My king, if only your titanic strength were known!
Father, exalted God, if only your exaltedness were known!
Like the lion, like the muscle man were you but known!

l) Who in the skies can equal [God]?
Can compare with [God] among the deities?
A God greatly dreaded in the council of holy beings
Held in awe by all those around him.

m) What does the Lord have in his heart?
What does he have in mind?
What does he have in his pure mind?

---

[3] This word is actually "gods" in the text, however, I believe it has the same meaning as בני אלים which is found in numerous psalms. So as not to prejudice the reading, I have made this emendation to "divine beings" as the JPS translation does frequently for the parallel Hebrew idiom.

n) How overwhelmng are your thoughts to me, God
How abundant they are in number.
I count them—they exceed the grains of sand;
I end—but am still with you.

o) You cross regularly through the heavens,
Every day you traverse the vast earth.
High seas, mountains, earth and sky,
You traverse them regularly, every day. . . .
Your broad protection is caste over the lands.
Though you darken each day, your face is not eclipsed.

p) Who knows where you dwell, O my God? . . .
I am constantly in great distress: O my God, where are you?
You who have been angry with me, turn towards me,
Turn your face to the pure godly meal of fat and oil,
That your lips revive goodness. Command that I thrive,
Command [long] life with your pure utterance.
Bring me away from evil that, through you, I be saved.

q) How long, O God, will you ignore me forever?
How long will you hide your face from me?

r) Then I, justified, will behold your face;
Awake, I am filled with the vision of you.[4]

The oldest documents of the ancient Near East all appear to relate
to the gods as real beings in the same manner that we are real. They
have wills just as we have wills and what motivates them, most often,
is just what motivates us: love, hate, discomfort, hunger, fear, joy, a
desire for power, rest, or any other of the great array of ego and
physical needs we experience. These motivations and needs are
expressed regarding the divine just as they are expressed regarding
humans.[5] In the great epics and hymns of Mesopotamia and Egypt,

---

[4] (a) Eršemma 184 (Sumerian), in Cohen 1981, 60; (b) Ps 99; (c) Ps 113; (d)
Eršemma 163.2, in Cohen 1981, 126, ; (e) Ps 21; (f) Ps 104; (g) Hymn to Aton, in
Matthews and Benjamin 1991, 154; (h) Isaiah 60; (i) The Hymn to Amon-Re, Pritchard
1969, 366; (j) Ps 77; (k) Eršemma 184, Cohen 1981, 59; (l) Ps 89; (m) Eršemma 160,
Cohen 1981, 128; (n) Ps 139; (o) Shamash Hymn (Akkadian), Foster 1996, 2:534f.;
(p) "God of My Family," Foster 1996, 2:627; (q) Ps 13:2; (r) Ps 17:15.

[5] See Korpel (1990), who provides extensive lists and texts of anthropomorphic descriptions of God in both Ugaritic and Israelite texts. For other considerations of god-related imagery in Israel and the ancient Near East more generally,
see Caird 1980; Cornelius 1994; Coogan 1987; Curtis 1990; Loretz 1990; Dietrich
and Loretz 1992. See also Keel 1978 on the iconography of ancient Near Eastern
cultures. Keel draws parallels between the graphic images and the literary images.

interaction between gods and humans is related through the matter-of-fact voice of an omniscient narrator—the same voice prevalent in Hebrew Scriptures.[6] Within the literature itself, no one questions how the knowledge is imparted, whether the informing voices
from above are real or just figments in the imaginations of the writers.

The meager epigraphic remains of Arabia, Sinai, and Trans-Jor-
dan also testify to the similarities between Israelite and non-Israelite god-imagery. P. D. Miller has written:

> In most respects Yahweh appears in the texts as a Late Bronze/Iron
> Age god. He has a name and a character, anthropomorphic form,
> associations with a people or nation, a dwelling place in the heavens
> and an entourage, associations with nature, and typical roles, e.g., father,
> creator, judge, warrior, king. (1987, 212)

Despite these similarities, there remains an ongoing debate concerning
the theologically distinguishing features of Israel's beliefs and expressions.[7] The question of ideological uniqueness often centers on some
key issues (monotheism, anti-anthropomorphism, God-of-history, law-
God, etc.). When we have two fundamentally identical statements
from distinct cultures, we must establish strong contextual grounds
for interpreting them differently. The fact that one might be Israelite and the other non-Israelite is not sufficient. As Marjo Korpel notes,
when it comes to the idioms used to describe God in Ugaritic and
Israelite literature, "the general degree of correspondence is so high
that henceforth it cannot be ignored, neither in representations of
the religion of Israel, nor in studies of the theology of the Old Testament and discussions of the biblical variety of God talk" (1990,
621).[8] As this is the case, at least on the surface, it becomes an

---

[6] See Sternberg (1985, chapters 2-3; also 93 and 232), who relates to the
omniscient factor as unique to Israelite literature.

[7] A parallel debate takes place in archaeological circles. The best-case scenario
would have us coordinating the literary evidence with the material remains. The
problem is that none of the cultic artifacts described in Tanakh have ever been
located. Thus, the material remains from Judea and Samaria stemming from the
late Bronze and early Iron ages provide us with no insight as to Israelite religion
as it is recorded in Scriptures specifically. This has caused some to question whether
there is such a thing as "biblical archaeology" at all, and to recognize the elitist
character and lateness of the biblical record. See Dever 1983, 1987, 1995. On the
relationship between text and artifact, see also Postgate 1990 and Miller 1991.

[8] Korpel notes that "Ugaritic literature shares at least half of its metaphors for
the divine with the Old Testament" (621). I shall argue below that many of the
expressions Korpel rightly deems identical are not metaphors, but literal or
"ascriptive" statements. For a discussion of ascription, see chapter 3.

important task to establish whether there were differences in how such common idioms were understood.

In the particular cluster of verses I presented above, I avoided simple appositional statements such as "You are sun / You are a rock." Such statements, however, will occupy us below.[9] There is no doubt that the exercise is artificial insofar as it robs the reader of context. Such considerations, however, do not ultimately affect the purpose of the exercise. Ancient documents often leave us with such high degrees of ambiguity that context—often very meager—does not provide much assistance. Perhaps more important is the notion that my cluster of verses here is no more a "fabrication" than is a psalm composed of discrete documents from different eras, or a narrative that draws upon idioms and images from a variety of con-texts, both Israelite and non-Israelite.[10] Each of the verses above contains one or more idioms that are potentially metaphorical. Were we to move through the passages, we would have to ask ourselves the basic question with which this book began, How do we know whether the statements are indicative of a literal belief, or are met-aphorical, suggesting something not quite so direct?

Metaphor's Incongruence

Virtually all theorists accept that metaphor, by its nature, involves a kind of logical incongruity or nonequivalence. Ricoeur calls this "semantic impertinence" (1977, 95, 247). The principle is best illus-trated with simple metaphors, such as those that appear in the predi-cational form, "A is B," as in "[All the world]^A is [a stage]^B." We know that this is metaphor because the world *is not*, in any literal sense, a stage. Having identified the "impertinence," we begin seeking meanings that are different from the literal sense. Aristotle suggest-ed that we seek resemblances between the two parts of the statement. Many have followed this basic principle (see, for instance, Richards 1936) . We shall leave the discussion as to what actually takes place in the decoding process for chapters 5 and 6. Scholars have framed the question, Is A *really* B? in a manner that seeks a very simple and

---

[9] In Hebrew these types of statement are appositional; however, in English, the use of the copula ("to be") makes them predicational.

[10] Consider the relationship between the Noah story and the myths of Atrahasis and Utnapishtim. See Van Seters 1992.

direct yes-or-no answer. This process forces us to think about metaphor in terms of conceptual binaries: something either is a metaphor or is literal. I shall offer an alternative conceptualization of
meaning that replaces the binary classifications with a gradient continuum. A model for gradient judgments lies at the center of this
study. The details will be presented in chapters 4 and 5. However,
at this point, I wish to introduce what I mean by "gradient" adjec-
tivally, as well as to establish a neutral nominal form, "gradience."

The term "gradient" commonly finds usages in physics, mathe-
matics, and biology. In physics, *gradient* relates to the rate at which
a physical quantity (temperature, pressure, etc.) changes relative to
the modification in some variable (altitude, speed, distance, etc).
When I speak of gradience in meaning, I shall be focusing on the
way variables influence changes along a meaning continuum. This
continuum does not have rigid stations or discretely identifiable
points. It should be seen as fluid. Thus, instead of focusing exclusively on the question, Is that statement metaphorical or not? we can
consider whether one comment is *more* metaphorical than another
comment; put differently, we can discuss the *degree* to which a statement is metaphorical and what causes the metaphoricalness. Our
assessment of the variables causes us to place a given statement at
one point rather than another point on the continuum. Certain
variables—what we will eventually call *conditions*—cause us to read
one metaphor as more intense than another. Thus, we speak of the
continuum as gradient because we are constantly adjusting our assessment of meaning based on fluctuating variables.

I have specifically chosen not to use terms like "graded," or anything related to "graduated," because these terms may connote relative values: one is graduated from one level to another "higher"
level, and gradations are usually conceptualized in terms of progres-
sions from lesser to greater and from less desireable to more desirable. Gradience does not involve a value-oriented judgment; it is
purely descriptive. A continuum can be set up for any domain of
meaning. For instance, we can speak about the continuum of which
metaphor is part, or the continuum that allows for a comparison of
ethical judgments; or a continuum that represents gradience of beauty
in sculpture or poetry. On any given continuum we measure gradience by comparing one statement to another statement with regard
to a *series* of conditions, not just one. Each domain has its own set
of conditions. For example, the continuum for metaphor includes

the conditions of ambiguity, logic, structure, etc. Toward the "right" and "left" extremes of the continuum for the domain of metaphor, are fuzzy areas, approaching literalness on one side and meaninglessness on the other. A weak metaphor may not be easily distinguished from a literal statement; a metaphor that involves too much ambiguity may sound more like nonsense than something meaningful.

My critique of current interpretations frequently pivots on the notion that modern exegetes force biblical thought to conform to standard modes of contemporary thinking. Framing things according to either/or inquiries has resulted in rather predictable results. Biblical language—and therefore, I would argue, biblical thinking, however one may conceive of such a thing—does not operate according to the standard literal/non-literal binary that functions so prominently in modern biblical exegesis. By offering an alternative, I hope to reintroduce some of the *foreignness* in biblical thinking.

Defining the Language of Religion as Metaphor

Thorkild Jacobsen's understanding of religious language as fundamentally metaphorical has been tremendously influential. Adopting Rudolf Otto's principle of the "Numinous" (Otto 1943), Jacobsen, in *The Treasures of Darkness*, sets off on a tour of ancient Mesopotamian religions. "Basic to all religion," he writes, "is, we believe, a unique experience of confrontation with power not of this world." The "Wholly Other" is that which is "outside of the normal experience and indescribable in its terms." Simple words fail because they are limited to ideas "grounded in worldly experience." Consequently, religion is, of necessity, inextricably linked to the expression of metaphor. Jacobsen (1976) writes:

> At most, as Otto points out, it may be possible to evoke the human psychological reaction to the experience by means of analogy, calling upon the suggestive power of ordinary worldly experiences, the response to which in some sense resembles or leads toward the response to the Numinous, and which thus may serve as ideograms or metaphors for it. Such metaphors, *since they constitute the only means of communicating the experience of the Numinous*, occupy a central place in religious teaching and thought. . . . In the metaphors, therefore, all that is shared by the worshipers of an individual culture or cultural period in their

common response to the Numinous is summed and crystallized, and in the summation what is specific and characteristic in the response will stand out. For in its choice of central metaphor a culture or cultural period necessarily reveals *more clearly than anywhere else* what it considers essential in the numinous experience and wants to recapture and transmit, the primary meaning on which it builds, which underlies and determines the total character of its response, *the total character of its religion.* (3-4; my emphasis)

Jacobsen presents the development of this mode of religious expression as having blossomed in stages rather than all at once. Originally, according to Jacobsen, god-belief concerned a "situationally determined numinous." Depending upon the particular need, the object of worship might be a grain storehouse, a cloud, or a celestial luminary. With the passage of time, the numinous power came to be viewed as immanent. This development caused the ancients to "attribute form to it in terms of the phenomenon"; the idea of a particular form's function was eventually narrowed into what Jacobsen calls the "intransitive" divine figures. These figures did not make demands, but were otherwise "fulfilled in the specific situation or phenomenon" with which they were associated (9f.). Later the personalities and activities developed into the more fully "transitive" deities, those who made demands and lived out dramas that approached the imagery of daily human life, but in a *transcendent* realm. Finally, there emerged personal religion. In the literature produced in this last stage, Jacobsen notes that "the inner 'form' or 'metaphor' of the parent" is construed on the basis of child psychology. "There is a stage in childhood when parents are all-powerful and divine to the child"; it is therefore only natural that the imagery of this power relationship finds expression in the contact had by persons and their gods (161). The god as father and mother is a metaphorical expression conveying the kind of power, the kind of caring, as well as the anger and gradations of disappointment a deity might have for its subject.

Within *The Treasures of Darkness* one will not find a discussion of just what constitutes metaphor in either linguistic or literary terms. This lacuna is surprising, for Jacobsen's approach considers the "total character" of religion to be understood only through the deciphering of its metaphors. The assumptions Jacobsen brings to the study of ancient Mesopotamian religion regarding metaphor and figurative language are equally operative in biblical scholarship. My first task will be to provide a number of examples to demonstrate how attitudes toward what constitutes figurative language affect scholarly judgments. Though we shall focus on the question of metaphor, I do not mean to imply that framing things metaphorically is the only method scholars use to bypass literal meanings. For instance, though often appealing to metaphor in the process, some scholars choose to read biblical idioms clearly drawn from or parallel to those of other ancient Near Eastern cultures as having been demythologized.[11] In this manner, controversial imagery can be read without its paganistic overtones. This exegetical practice figures prominently in the writings of Yehezkel Kaufmann, Umberto Cassuto and William Foxwell Albright, to name just a few. Many have followed their examples.[12]

---

[11] This approach is found in both biblical and rabbinic scholarship, though I would argue that the latter derives from the former. Of late, there has been a contrary trend. One can contrast Urbach (1975), on how rabbinic Judaism always rids expressions and concepts of mythology, with studies by Boyarin, who sees midrash as making "manifest the repressed mythic material in the Bible's 'textual subconscious,'" thereby claiming the biblical material to have included "remnants of the suppressed [pagan] culture" (1990, 94). Also see Bal (1993), who comments on the question of how closely related metaphor and myth are for various scholarly approaches.

[12] Other schools of thought operate with altogether different premises regarding the text. Some scholars treat Tanakh as literature, thereby bypassing those questions of theology and language that occupy more historically critical thinkers. Such is the case with Meir Sternberg (1985), who describes in detail what he sees as the *rhetorical structures of faith* that were devised to assuage any concerns for the tension between the mundane, literal, human-bound language of personification and the divine transcendence it seeks to describe. While metaphor is periodically the topic of concern, Sternberg directs much greater attention to numerous other rhetorical devices of the Hebrew narrative that convey God's incomparability, omniscience, and omnipotence.

Except for a few allusions, our discussion will not juxtapose the approach to biblical literature taken by Sternberg, Alter, and a host of other contemporary writers with the thesis expressed here. My concern will be the more common treatment of metaphor and figurative speech as they appear in the writings of historians of biblical literature and theology. I mention Sternberg because of the respect I have for his work, but also to draw lines of demarcation which indicate that I feel no compunction to address the priorities he and others who take similar approaches set for themselves. We might consider their approaches to be parallel discourses, with little relevance to the concerns at hand.

A Matter of Shared Strategy

Thorkild Jacobsen's approach is essentially what I identified in the previous chapter as the subject-based explanation for the Tanakh's use of metaphor. It underlies Marc Brettler's extensive study *God is King: Understanding an Israelite Metaphor* (1989), among many other works. Brettler is one of the few scholars to approach the problem with a conscientious attempt to present a cogent analysis of metaphor.[13] *God is King* explores a single idea and its numerous corollaries (what Brettler calls "submetaphors") as they resonate throughout Hebrew Bible.[14] Brettler seeks to reconstruct the entire conceptual edifice of the phrase "God is King"—as well as others like it—against the backdrop of the biblical conception of God. The influence of Jacobsen and the function of the subject-based methodology is evident throughout Brettler's study:

> The observation of Jacobsen [1970, 164] about Mesopotamian religion equally applies to Israel: "In almost every particular the world of the gods is therefore a projection of terrestrial conditions." The earthly reality preceded and served as the basis for speculation about the divine. Thus, in cases where common imagery is shared by God and the king, I assume that human imagery has been projected upon God rather than vice versa. (1989, 15)

Brettler's claims that his methodology stems from the nature of the subject matter. Moreover, the biblical text itself frames divine imagery in such a way as to require metaphorical language.

> [Scripture] insists that God is the "incomparable one." If this claim were taken seriously on the level of language in ancient Israel, the vocabulary used of God in the Bible would be unique to him. . . . If the entire vocabulary used of God were distinct to him, he would be "incomparable," but also not grounded in human experiences, and therefore, not understandable. For this reason, biblical rhetoric uses language typically belonging to the human sphere and applies it to God. These uses may be considered metaphorical because the biblical God does not generally possess these human attributes in their usual

---

[13] A few other scholars have treated biblical interpretation against the backdrop of modern linguistics, including the problem of metaphor. See, most notably, Barr 1991, Silva 1983, 1990, Caird 1980, Korpel 1990, and Schmidt 1996, (esp. 77).

[14] The index indicates that verses cited by Brettler are culled from every biblical book except Obadiah.

form. For example, the Israelite king is crowned and is part of a dynasty; God as king lacks these qualities. Metaphor becomes a major tool, if not the major tool used to describe God in Israel. The metaphor gains its usefulness by applying ideas and terms familiar from everyday use to depict God. Furthermore, since by its very nature a metaphor "A is B" does not imply that A and B are the same in all respects, the use of metaphorical language of God does not conflict with the notion of his incomparability. (159)

Brettler contends that metaphorical expressions in Tanakh derive from the fact that language cannot literally accommodate the distinctive, transcendent nature of a deity. He speaks of the "language in ancient Israel, the vocabulary used of God in the Bible," the underlying implication being that there is a set of expressions that are semantically harmonious and that there is a cogent meaning to the concept of an "ancient Israel." With regard to Scripture's "insistence" that God is "the incomparable one" there remain many questions as to whether that incomparability makes God a species different from other beings, or whether it is a distinctiveness similar to that achieved by Marduk in *Enuma Elish*, after his ascension to power.[15] More important, the notion that Hebrew Scriptures insists upon anything as a single voice or consciousness violates the reality of the texts. As noted, Scriptures conveys many expressions about God which, according to the biblical authors, derive *directly from* God. There are passages in which God tells the people that they are not allowed to see his face, or where God says that he is angry, and that he will act in history. Thus, biblical rhetoric does not only apply the expressions of the human sphere to God, it depicts God as applying the human sphere to himself. Where are the disclaimers regarding literal meanings? It is true that the Deuteronomic writers have them; but we do not find these disclaimers in other strata of the literature.

---

[15] Tablets II-V of *Enuma Elish*, but especially tablet VI, see Dalley 1989; see also "Great Hymn to Marduk," in Foster 1996 2:521. Expressions of incomparability in Akkadian literature also relate to other gods, such as Ishtar ("who is it that could rival her grandeur?" Foster 1996, 1:69) and also see similar expressions in an 11th century psalm 1:240. This being said, see Oppenheim (1977, 194f.) regarding the difficulty of differentiating characteristics of deities in other than a superficial manner in the oldest literary strands. According to Oppenheim, individalization begins most prominently with the ascension of Assyria and its patron god Aššur. Of course, the most relevant literary evidence from Mesopotamia is that which is closest to biblical literature, namely, the so-called "Late Period," which begins with the 10th century.

Thus, to fuse the different types of expressions stemming from different eras into one big generalization does little to further our understanding of Israelite theology over the centuries.[16]

There is a much more profound question which is rarely confronted by biblical scholars who believe that the biblical God is transcendent. If humans cannot accommodate ideas about or descriptions of the deity except through figurative forms of speech, how does the human intellect manage to perceive what it is that it is supposed to describe? Hardly an original question, this is a basic problem in the history of philosophy and theology, epistemological in nature. My contention is that Bible scholars rather uncritically project postbiblical conceptualizations of language and transcendence upon the Bible, all the while assuming that the ancients recognized the same philosophical problems that occupy us. For the most part, the Bible lacks explicit statements that might confirm that the ancients understood there to be these "limits" to the powers of language, not to mention the disjunction between our perceptions and our ability to express them directly and literally.

I would maintain that the expression "God is King" was, at certain stages in Israel's history, understood *literally* and that precisely because of this, some biblical passages argued for the limitations of the conceptualization of this image. But we are moving ahead too quickly. We should first consider in greater detail Brettler's program, so that this general question regarding *how biblical language works with regard to gods and humans* does not sway our understanding of the problem of metaphor.

The notion that metaphor assumes shared intentionality was strongly argued by I. A. Richards.[17] Though there is considerable

---

[16] Gerhard Von Rad approached these issues somewhat differently: "It cannot be said that Israel regarded God anthropomorphically, but the reverse, that she considered man as theomorphic" (1962, 1:145). Von Rad bypasses the problem of literalness in God being a king, or speaking, or becoming angry, by transferring the wonderment to the human condition. We speak because God speaks—and not the other way around. But Brettler's biblical God is not identical to us (humans) in Von Rad's sense of theomorphism. Brettler approaches anthropomorphisms as metaphors which endeavor to bridge the gap between the all-too-earthly human and the altogether incomparable deity (Brettler 1989, 162 and elsewhere).

[17] See Richards 1936; for a summary of these ideas in the scholarship, see Ricoeur 1977, chapters 4-5. There are some who reject this principle. See, for instance, Kittay (1987), who indicates early on in her book on metaphor that she will "say little about individual speakers' intentions in making metaphor. Such intentions are neither necessary nor sufficient for determining that an utterance is metaphorical"

disagreement about how one measures the role of authorial intent and reader's meaning, there should be little doubt about the power of shared strategy in establishing word-meaning.[18] However, Brettler, in contrast to these approaches, emphasizes the limits of intentionality and a kind of independently derived semantics.

> For example, no "shared strategy" can make "a desk is a piece of furniture" into a metaphor or can remove "man is a wolf" from its metaphorical status. It is only because of certain semantic clashes that certain utterances in particular situations may be used as metaphors. (20)

Identifying metaphor as dependent upon "semantic clashes" is somewhat misleading, for one might assume that those "clashes" are structurally derived from something integral to the words rather than the speaker-interpreter relationship. We identify a simple predicational statement as metaphor when that statement is, in some sense, literally false. If we do not know whether the literal statement is true or false, we cannot make a judgment. Except for the category of statements which employs standard binary terms (e.g., family relational terms, such as uncle, aunt, son, daughter, etc.), our ability to determine the truth value of a statement always depends upon some form of shared strategy between speaker and audience.[19]

The amount of shared strategy required for a statement to be interpreted appropriately varies from context to context, frequently commensurate with the degree of stereotypicality in a given statement.

---

(14). The reader will be able to infer my rejection of her "perspectival theory" simply on the basis of how I shall relate to the principles of "necessary and sufficient" in the following pages. Despite Kittay's claims to the contrary, authorial intent does end up factoring into the deciphering of metaphor even in her own theory of meaning. She has simply renamed it and subsumed it within the broader notions of "context" and "field theory," both of which she portrays as factors external to the individual speaker. Her treatment of Grice and relevance theory in general is largely at odds with the approach to be presented here (see chapter 5). For a general discussion of the authorial intent issue, see Cotterell and Turner 1989.

[18] At the turn of the century, Ferdinand de Saussure presented language as a system totally dependent upon a shared social convention. See Saussure [1916] 1974 and on his influence, Culler 1975, chap. 1.

[19] I. A. Richards' *context theorem* of meaning provides a strong refutation of the notion that "semantic clashes" can exist separate from a "shared strategy." See Richards 1936. Also see Beardsley (1958, 138ff.), who situates metaphor as but one of many possible strategies and defines it as a device which states something in terms that require the interpreter to decipher *intended* levels of implication rather than literal meaning.

Moreover, there is no question that *some* information can be gleaned from a sentence without knowledge of context or authorial intent.[20] But such knowledge is generally trite or involves images stereotypical to a language community. We can, in fact, remove the statement "Man is a wolf" from its metaphorical status. Consider the possibility that "Man" may function as a personal name (like "Guy"). In such a case, the statement "Man is a wolf" would be literally true. Alternatively, the statement might be uttered by a three-year-old child, in which case it could simply be a false statement to which we would reply, "No, the man is not a wolf, the man is a human being." In other words, despite the relatively small degree of ambiguity, we are still dependent upon establishing the role of the word "man" before we can be certain that the phrase is metaphorical. Moreover, in a community that venerates wolves, the statement takes on a radically different connotation.

My son, at four, had a stuffed dinosaur whom he named Danny, and he took great pride in telling people, "Danny is a dinosaur." Once, when I picked him up from pre-school, one of the other parents saw my son pretending to be a dinosaur. She asked him what he was doing. "I'm a stegosaurus, and Danny, my friend, is a diplodocus." "Oh, really," the astonished mother replied. She promptly turned back to me and said, "I didn't know there was a Danny in the class." In fact, the statement "Danny is a dinosaur" turns out to be, for the child, a literal statement in this context.[21] However, when a colleague of mine recently said of her dissertation adviser, "Charles is a T-Rex", it was quite clear that her Charles

---

[20] This is introduced very well by Solan (1997) in the context of contemporary legal interpretation. Solan notes that certain common phrases take on meanings that are assumed by all who use them—especially in legal contexts. This, of course, is similar to the language-game theory indicated in the introduction. But it is also determined that statements, regardless of authorial intent, do usually enable us to say what something is *not*, as Solan points out. I accept this principle, but I would caution that the overwhelming majority of such intentless contexts provide us with little other than trite kinds of information and knowledge. My thanks to Professor Solan for sharing his work with me prior to its publication.

[21] Albeit, one not without complications. The statement is true in one context but false in another context. If the child had said, "Danny is my toy dinosaur," then the meaning of "dinosaur" would have been clarified. But children at this age do not regularly think with these nuances. Thus, we bump up against another instance in which literal meaning is not at hand; nor is metaphor. In what sense is my son's toy a "friend?" The language of play actually involves a category that is not literal, but elsewhere on the meaning-continuum. See the discussion of ascription in chapter 3.

was not really a dinosaur. So we conclude that, though in most contexts it would require less overt collusion, even the statement "man is a wolf" does require some degree of shared strategy for successful interpretations.[22] As it turns out, even statements which appear to be definitional and fundamentally literal may acquire metaphorical meaning by virtue of shared strategies, or they may simply be false literal statements.

Only in passing does Brettler entertain the notion that the phrase "God is King" in the Bible might not *always* be metaphorical; but even in this brief consideration, no substantive arguments are offered. Leviticus 25:55, where Israel is described as "God's servant," is identified as an instance of "reification."[23] Though sidestepping the issue as "requiring further study," Brettler argues that "it is sufficient to note that for *most people* in ancient Israel 'God is King' was not reified, and was understood as a fully metaphorical statement, and therefore did not impinge on human kingship" (24, my emphasis). How Brettler or anyone else might be able to establish what "*most people* in ancient Israel" believed with regard to any concept is a mystery. What is clear is that once a person is convinced that semantics has some independent, timeless structure, unencumbered by pragmatics, he or she can make assertions, such as those that follow, with confidence:

> There are certain instances . . . where the semantic conflict between the two elements in the metaphor is so great *that pragmatics plays no role in determining whether a statement is metaphorical.* This is the case with "God is King" since *no utterance context* can subvert the semantic clash between God and king because the ancient Israelite would have been aware that certain elements *intrinsic to kingship* could not be projected onto God. For example, Israelite kings were typically human and part of a dynasty, qualities that were inappropriate to the Israelite God. Because of the conflict between these *intrinsic features* of Israelite kingship and the intrinsic features of God, the statement "God is King" should be considered metaphorical. (20, my emphasis)

---

[22] Black (1962, 30ff.) discusses how metaphor depends as much on pragmatics as it does semantics, which is a modification of Richards (1936), who would have placed meaning totally in the realm of discourse, or what we call "pragmatics."

[23] The concepts of reification and hypostasization are closely related, in that abstract or spiritual things somehow acquire concrete or material existence. Given that these concepts are dependent upon the Greek bifurcation of the material and spiritual worlds, any attempt to see them as operative in the pre-Hellenistic parts of the Hebrew Bible strikes me as anachronistic.

In support of this claim, Brettler cites Janet Soskice, who writes: "It is *difficult to believe* that the prophets, although perhaps lacking a developed set of grammatical distinctions which enabled them to designate metaphors as metaphors, were unaware that in speaking of God as a herdsman or planter were using language not strictly appropriate to him" (1985, 77, my emphasis).[24] An argument for a position on the basis of how difficult something is to believe should be irrelevant to scholarly discourse. I know of no examples in the scholarly literature of a "set of grammatical distinctions" which enable people "to designate metaphors as metaphors"; nor does Brettler or Soskice provide any.

There is nothing "intrinsic to kingship" that forces us to see the phrase "God is King" as metaphorical. Brettler's error lies in the fact that he believes "King" must be applied identically to all realms of existence, such that unless there is a perfect match—in this case, between how human kings operate and how divine kings operate— metaphor must be at hand. This approach conforms to what some call a "feature list representation" or a "Tarskian model of truth conditions." Such approaches maintain that a word's definition (or the definition of a "concept" or "object" or "action," etc.) is based on an array of conditions which are taken to be collectively necessary and sufficient.[25] This means that for each word or concept there should be a checklist of defining conditions; anything meeting all— and nothing less than all—of those conditions meets the definition. As such, the word "dog" or "climb" or "theory" all supposedly have checklists—as would the word "king." What Brettler maintains is that "dynasty" is one of the necessary conditions for the concept "king"; and since God is not part of a dynasty, he cannot be understood to be a real king in any literal sense. Thus, "God is King" must be understood figuratively.[26]

---

[24] We cannot treat directly the implications of Soskice's approach; however, it should become evident from the following discussion that "grammatical distinctions" are altogether irrelevant to our understanding of metaphor.

[25] See Tarski 1983a; Jackendoff 1987, 128.

[26] It is not worth pursuing here in too much detail, but suffice it to point out that dynasty is hardly a legitimate condition for kingship. If it were, kingship would have to be part of an infinite regress. But new dynasties are possible, and the first king of a dynasty, by definition, could not fulfill such a requirement. Moreover, many have argued that there existed elaborate reenthronement rituals that the Israelites acted out each year during Sukkot. This, too, seems to have parallels in down-to-earth practices. See Mowinckel 1961, Volz 1912, and, for contemporary surveys of this imagery, Cooper and Goldstein 1990 and Rubenstein 1995.

The problem is that any model based on truth conditions, while appealing to intuition, is ultimately indefensible. A very limited number of concepts, such as kinship relations (uncle, niece, etc.), axiomatized terms (such as those of geometry), and jargon, may be able to comply with the requirements of necessity and sufficiency; but this set of concepts is extremely small.[27] The overwhelming majority of our expressions operate without clearly established lists of "necessary conditions" for each concept, but instead work on the basis of what Ray Jackendoff has called *typicality conditions*.[28] This compositional theory of meaning, based on a variable conditionality, does not engage conditions as necessary, but instead employs a matrix of general principles that one might describe as floating or graded.

Let us consider further the "king" example. We need not be disturbed by the fact that the word "king" is used with reference to "Philip," the seventeenth-century Wampanoag leader who fought against New England colonists; "Philip," the 4th century B.C.E. king of Macedon; "Philip the Fair," king of France at the end of the thirteenth century; and Gilgamesh, the one-quarter-human and three-quarters-god king of ancient Uruk. In each of these instances, the defining characteristics are all a bit different from one another, and those differences sometimes involve rather distinct associations, cultural motifs, and social conventions, all of which have roots in the author's intent (albeit, probably as part of a much larger cultural matrix of meanings of which an author need not be conscious). In no generic context are we obliged to interpret "Philip is king" or "Gilgamesh is king" metaphorically.[29] The fact that God might not have been a king exactly as Saul, David, or Solomon were kings is about as relevant as the fact that kingship for the Wampanoag leader was structurally and sociologically (not to mention religiously) quite different from Philip the Fair's kingship. The bottom line is that there is nothing semantically intrinsic to the statement "God is King" to bring us to the conclusion that it is either metaphorical or literal. We can only make a decision in a case-by-case manner, which means that sometimes, given the paucity of information regarding cultural

---

[27] There is even controversy over these terms, though I don't share all of the concerns. See Lakoff (1987, chap. 4.), who commits what Ryles (1949) identified as "category mistakes."

[28] See Jackendoff 1983, 121, and chap. 3.

[29] Compare the statement "Elvis is king!"

context and authorial intent (i.e., which typicality conditions may have been in effect), it may be that we are unable to make a decision.

Given the fact that most of Hebrew Bible reflects a world of henotheism, the evidence suggests that any notion of God as king of all celestial beings was understood as a literal charge of leadership. My goal is not to review the evidence in this context. I only wish to demonstrate that this type of appositional sentence may simply be literal, but it may also be ascriptive—a concept to which we shall turn in the next chapter.

This, then, is our first step toward creating a truly gradient model of interpretation. We must recognize that individual units of expression convey meaning on the basis of typicality conditions rather than necessary conditions, and that those conditions require an underlying (shared) strategy between speaker and interpreter. Both typicality conditions and the role of authorial intent must be seen as two interrelated aspects of a gradient model of judgment. Moreover, it must be understood that the variables can be constantly in a state of flux, requiring that questions as to authorial intent need to be surveyed frequently and with consistent criteria in place. Further aspects will be elucidated in subsequent chapters.

3

A NON-BINARY CONCEPTUALIZATION OF MEANING

Four hurdles face the scholar attempting to write the theology of ancient Israel. The first is the problem of establishing the best reading of our text; the second is the composite nature of a literary unit in which there are conflicting data; the third is the problem of balancing conflicting voices from disparate texts; the fourth concerns the relationship between textual evidence and the actual beliefs of the populace. In all literatures of the ancient world we find the additional problem of semantic ambiguity. Even when the reading is certain and the context clear, clarity may be elusive. James Barr (1987) noted:

> With a text of high uniformity . . . textual discussion will more frequently begin from the feeling that there is a "difficulty"; the procedure will be more independent of the existence of variant readings, and conjectural emendation will take a larger place in the discussion. (4)

Barr explicates the various methods open to resolving the "difficulties":

> [The interpreter] has to resolve his difficulties through various linguistic and literary explanations: perhaps the grammar should be recognized as an anomaly; perhaps we have a case of poetic license, an unusual meaning for a word, an ellipsis of something usually expressed explicitly, a metaphor, or an allegory with a hidden meaning. Or, indeed, the reader may just give up, and decide that he does not know the meaning and cannot know it with the data he now possesses. (3)

Barr suggests that literary explanations are just as much "conjectural emendations" as interpretations calling for alterations in the written text (30). Scholarship since Barr's study (first published in 1968) has not related to these two methodologies evenhandedly. Surely periodic speculations regarding possible textual emendations—despite a lack of manuscript support—are acceptable and encouraged; but were a scholar to move through the biblical text changing letters or word order in each and every instance of philological ambiguity with no basis in variant readings, his or her writings would be rejected out of hand. In contrast, when a scholar moves through the text interpreting phrases as figurative speech on the basis of a theological or literary imperative not blatantly disclosed by the text, we only rarely seek a comprehensive justification for the approach offered.

Unfortunately, Barr himself periodically practices this type of "literary emendation" when making judgments as to the significance of various biblical images. In his study of theophany and anthropomorphism, Barr comments that the "frequent expressions about God's ears or nose, his smelling or whistling, are not seriously anthropomorphisms in the sense of expressions trying to come to grips with the form, the *morphe*, of God"; in other words, these are not literal descriptions (Barr 1960, 30). No support is given for this judgment. Rather, Barr dismisses the evidence by arguing, "These expressions provide a rich vocabulary for the diversity of the divine activity; but for the more precise and particular question which the word 'anthropomorphism' should suggest, the question is what form, if any, God may be kown, there is a danger of exaggerating their importance" (30). It is not surprising that statements entailing anthropomorphism engender the greatest amount of controversy. We shall return to this issue repeatedly.

The Problem with Mythology

One subtle form of literary emendation is the claim that a narrative, idiom, or literary figure has been demythologized. This occurs when scholars, troubled by the mythological implications of the words at the literal level, opt for a less mythological rendering that conforms better to their view of Israelite belief. Often, a given motif is judged "mythological" in the non-Israelite context while the Israelite parallel is thought to be nothing other than a demythologized "remnant." Periodically, these judgments are attached to literary-structural choices. An example of this practice can be found in Miller and Roberts's fine essay on the ark narratives in 1 Samuel 5. There we read about Yahweh's defeat of Dagon in a relatively simple prose form. The authors reflect upon the passage as follows:

> These verses present us with the ancient mythological motif of the battle of the gods and the victory of the divine warrior Yahweh. Only in

this case, the motif appears in a prosaized, non-mythological context. We do not have here a poetic recounting of divine victory as in the early poetry, but rather a carefully structured prose narrative, the heart of which is in this episode in 1 Sam 5 and the events that grow out of it. The prose narrative character of the story presumably contributes to the way in which the divine battle is reported, that is, the Philistine discovery of what happened to the statue of Dagon. In this period one would expect a recounting of the actual battle in mythopoeic, poetic form rather than prose. But the battle lies behind and is to be presupposed in this prose narrative. The incident of these five verses is rooted in Canaanite mythology—more so than usually acknowledged—but at the same time, in typically Israelite fashion, it is "demythologized," both by the way in which the report of the battle comes to us and by the fact that the intent of the mythological cosmic battle is lost. Here it is not life against death, fertility against sterility, order against chaos, the young god against the old god. It is Yahweh against the gods of Israel's enemies and ultimately it is Yahweh overcoming the enemies themselves. (1977, 72)

The crucial issue here is quite simply, What constitutes demythologization? We are asking whether literary structure does, in itself, constitute a good reason to posit a demythologized interpretation. Let us summarize our quandary as follows: We have a prose story about an ark placed in a room with an idol. We find the idol toppled over. The narrator informs us that this is the work of the god of the ark. This theme is unequivocally about competition between gods. Is this a mythological rendering, or a demythologized account of the story?

In claiming that this is a demythologized rendering, Miller and Roberts point not to thematic content but to literary-structural elements. When they consider the *meaning* of the story they are compelled to speak of it as "rooted in Canaanite mythology—more so than usually acknowledged"; but then they focus on the absence of a "mythopoeic, poetic form" and argue that the prose contributes to the way in which we are to understand this whole report. The authors suggest that "in this period one would expect a recounting of the actual battle." By the words "in this period" Miller and Roberts have in mind "the period of religious crisis between the disastrous defeat at Ebenezer and the much later victories of David" (74). They argue for this date of composition because of the story's theological message. The story is essentially a theodicy. The theological problem of God's power "has been posed by an historical event, the Is-

raelite defeat at Ebenezer and the shocking loss of the ark" (74). No
one would write such a story in the post-Davidic era, reason the
authors, simply because the defeat of the Philistines would already
have demonstrated Yahweh's superiority.

While it is certainly possible that the current story derives from
oral traditions dating back to the pre-monarchic era, it is highly
doubtful that the literature as we now have it actually has such origins.
Unfortunately, there is no objective evidence to allow us to date any
biblical passage to a pre-monarchic period. Beyond that, the dating
of a story on the basis of some *theological* relevance to a given historical event is extremely tenuous. When we consider that the entire
Exodus episode can be read quite successfully as an extended allegory for events relevant to the monarchic and exilic periods, we
should cringe at the notion that certain narratives make sense only
in the context of real historical episodes.[1] That is, the radical message of the biblical conceptualization of history is that the past is best
explained via literature—and fiction, at that. Literary tastes change,
as does a people's conceptualization of its origins.

For the most part, the Canaanite literatures that describe the divine
battles in mythopoeic and poetic forms and which are used in contrast to Israelite writings, were penned during the fourteenth and
thirteenth centuries b.c.e., at least 500 years prior to what most see
as the earliest biblical literature and as much as 900 years prior to
the standardized literary structures that took hold sometime during
the Second Commonwealth.[2] There is no question whatsoever that
much of biblical literature differs from more ancient Canaanite literatures in a great variety of ways, one of which is structural. But it
should be recognized that "myth" is being defined according to the
earliest structural paradigms, in which "myth" is indeed most fre-

---

[1] The problem of whether one can relate the biblical text to history has been
questioned by many, including Morton Smith 1971; Lemche 1988, 1994; Thompson 1974, 1995; Davies 1992, 1995; Van Seters 1976, 1983, 1992, 1994; Dever
1983; 1987, 1995; Finkelstein 1988, 1994 J.M. Miller 1991. Brettler (1995, 6), who
speaks of the dissolution of the former consensus on this issue and indicates that
no new consensus has yet to be found. See also Ahlström 1986 as well as his essay
on the travels of the ark (1984).

[2] I do not mean to state that the Bible does not contain old materials stemming from the tenth century. I mean only that if discrete passages did exist at that
time, they were not yet integrated into anything we might recognize as the biblical
narrative, and consequently are of little relevance. It is the juxtapositioning of the
various mythological concerns that produces the construct we think of as ancient
Israel.

quently couched in what most scholars consider poetry. We are left
to ponder why the literature regularly appeared with the structures
that it did. To wonder such a thing, we must presume the existence
of more than one way to express myth. And so we ask further, Could
the Canaanite author, in writing about Baal, have exercised an option
to tell his story in prose? Unfortunately, we do not have such literary creations from the Mesopotamian or Canaanite world. We might
then wonder, If they *were* to have written their mythology in prose,
what might it have looked like? Would they have told the story the
same way, only with a different structure? Or would a different structure have forced upon the myth a different meaning?[3]

I do not have a solution for this conundrum. In the absence of a
solution, I am hesitant to evaluate the *meaning* of choices that pertain to literary structure. It seems to me that we are missing essential conditions of relevance. No matter how we slice it, we are still
left with a story about a divine confrontation in which the ark constitutes the object of divine power. If that is not myth then I do not
know what is. The fact that the way the story is told is unequivocally different from the way older combat legends were told in the
fourteenth century B.C.E. may prove to be a valuable observation,
but I am not certain how we may go beyond that observation. Certainly the imagery is less dramatic and the amount of verbiage used
to convey the episode far less in quantity than in Canaanite paradigms. But we should still find it difficult to attach meaning to such
differences, given the great disparity in time and our complete ignorance regarding those rubrics that governed the stylistic and structural choices of the Canaanites. If we consider the possibility that
the entire Torah narrative constitutes one complex, extended myth
(a fictional invention), filled with miraculous incidents of divine intervention into human history, none of which could possibly have
taken place, how are we to evaluate the claim that Israel preferred
to demythologize its history? That the manner of telling is in some
sense *different* is beyond doubt; what that difference *means* remains
to be evaluated more cogently.

I cannot help but find irony in the fact that the scholars who view
a prose narrative as "demythologized" consider it to be, somehow,

---

[3] There has been considerable debate over how to define poetry in contrast to
prose when it comes to biblical literature. On this, see Kugel 1981 and for a summary of the issue, Weitzman 1997.

safer than a mythologized poetic narrative. Many theorists write of
the power of prose as deriving from the credible way it is perceived
to represent reality. As such, the passage about Dagon in 1 Samuel
should come off as more matter-of-fact than a highly stylized and
embellished poetical account, one which might otherwise be dismissed
as *mere* mythology of ambiguous significance. In contrast, this rather traditional historiographic rendering could prove to be at once
the sign and the proof of reality, convincing the reader of Dagon's
existence.[4] So the charge of "demythologization" turns out to be a
double edged sword, cutting reality however the bearer might wish.

In the case of the ark narrative, we were dealing with a judgment
that regarded a broad motif. But similar judgments must frequently
be made with smaller literary units, idioms, and even words. There
is no doubt that, just as metaphors can lose their resonance, so can
they lose their mythological connotations. The question is, How do
we go about evaluating their mythological resonance in a given
document? Such judgments are made quite frequently in the scholarly literature without the disclosure of methodological principles.
Consider the following discussion by Frank Moore Cross (1973):

> In Canaan, Ba'l and his mythology tended to take over the epithets
> and especially the functions of king and warrior. On the contrary, Israel
> was free to use the *language of kingship and war in its image of Yahweh and
> his retinue*, although it *exposed the faith* of the nation to the inroads of
> syncretism, notably the absorption on the myth of Ba'l's battle of
> creation. (190, my emphasis)[5]

Cross's analysis separates the free use of language with regard to
kingship and war imagery from Israel's *real* ideology. According to
Cross, while Israelite religion "in its first lusty and creative impulse
absorbed mythic elements readily into its language of faith and into
its cult," these expressons were transformed for the "service of Yahwism" (190). However, something changed in the ninth century:
"Israel had become vulnerable to a less wholesome syncretism, and
in fact the religion of Yahweh began to give way to the popular cult
of Ba'l" (190-91). As for the reliability of Tanakh for establishing

---

[4] See Barthes 1989, 127-48, and Hayden White's extensive discussion of this
issue and related themes (1987).

[5] On Yahweh, kingship, and war imagery, see Cross 1973, chapter 5; Weinfeld
1978a, 1978b, 1986. Brettler (1993) provides a detailed philological commentary
on four psalms with warrior terminology.

chronologies, Cross is mostly silent on the issue; he tacitly accepts the literary chronology presented within the text and relates to the depictions of syncretistic tendencies as historical rather than literary flourishes. This perspective on chronology and historicity still dominates the scholarly literature,[6] but as we have noted, some scholars are now questioning this approach, arguing that "Israelite religion" is better recognized as a creation of the biblical redactors who worked many centuries after the "events" described in the narratives.[7] Moreover, narratives constitute literary constructs that have less to do with *what happened* than they do with what the author wished for us to think happened.[8] For the time being, we will sidestep the problems of dating and historicity that permeate Cross's work (and much biblical scholarship), accept his surface reading of biblical history, and ignore the question of whether there was, in fact, a ninth-century crisis concerning syncretism.

Cross's reconstruction suggests that originally the use of the mythic expressions associated with the Canaanite gods was somehow inert, devoid of the problematic overtones normally thought to accompany pagan expressions regarding deities. In other words, the language was taken figuratively. A given expression used for El or Baal literally, when adapted by Israelites, would not have had the same mythological (and implicitly polytheistic) connotations. These expressions (by then centuries old) would regain their original pagan connotations in the ninth century, thereby posing a threat to the establishment religion. Cross writes that "mythical elements in the old language of Yahwistic tradition were no longer harmless, but were used as conduits through which to introduce the full, sophisticated mythology of Canaanite Baʿl" (191).[9]

We are seeking to establish the methodological basis for arguing that originally Israelite belief *was* different from the literal connotations of the very many kingship and war images that permeate its

---

[6] For instance, Gary A. Rendsburg (1996) argues that the Genesis author "was a royal scribe in Jerusalem, who lived during the reigns of David and Solomon in the tenth century B.C.E., and whose ultimate goal was to justify the monarchy in general" (50).

[7] See p. 46 n. 1 above. On dating and other issues, see Vervenne 1996.

[8] On this, see White 1973, 1974, and Eagleton 1996b, on literature as ideology.

[9] Cross postulates that some incursion of Canaanite ideology and practice might have occurred because of Zadok's priesthood, as Zadok may have been a Jebusite (210). No textual support is offered.

literature. Cross does not explicitly indicate the reasoning behind his interpretation. Nonetheless, he insists that this awkward relationship between an expression's mythical connotation and its culturally acceptable one is present even in the language of the prophets:

> It is not coincidental that the language of theophany and the imagery of revelation derived from the mythology of the storm god largely fell out of use, beginning in the ninth century, and including the two centuries to follow, in prophetic Yahwism. The prophets chose another language, other imagery with which to describe their intercourse with Yahweh, drawn as we have seen from the concept of the messenger of the Council of 'El. So far as we are able to tell, the prophets did not attempt to suppress in systematic fashion the old hymns and traditions which used the *uncouth language* of the storm theophany. The attack was on Ba'l and not on the notion that Yahweh controlled the elements of nature. Nevertheless, they used *a refined or purged language* of revelation, because Yahweh, so to say, no longer used the storm as a mode of self-manifestation. The revised prophetic language was also, of course, a *traditional language of revelation,* narrowed and specified by the evolution of the prophetic office. (191, my emphasis)

In Tanakh, the division between "prophetic language" (endemic to "prophetic Yahwism") and the language of other literary forms is quite arbitrary. Numerous psalms are identical in literary form to passages in the prophets and many narratives in prophetic and non-prophetic passages are also indistinguishable. Indeed, it is impossible to conceive the prophets' relationship to language usage as independent of some more general Israelite literary or cultural preference. Some argue that the so-called Literary Prophets are themselves constructs, patched together from a massive database of literary fragments, only rarely constituting a cogent whole.[10] More problematic is the division between language that *really* reflects what the prophets believed and language that is "uncouth" or indicative

---

[10] The lack of cogency and historical realia in much of the Literary Prophets, when paired with the frequent use of stereotypical images and common motifs, should push us to reconsider the compositional history of the documents, not so much in terms of redaction, but in terms of their *Sitz-im-Leben.* Are we to believe that there was a prophet Isaiah, who spoke such poetry, which, on the surface, has no *clear* and *compelling* relationship to any political or historical events underway? or, alternatively, are the prophets literary constructs consisting of highly stereotypical materials? See, for instance, Peckham (1993), who discusses the micro-units of the prophetic literature. On the canonization of the prophetic corpus, see Barr 1983; Barstad 1993.

of archaic notions no longer central to Israelite ideology. As Cross would have it, the prophetic language is itself a form of circumlocution. The language of the prophets is "unsuppressed," despite the fact that (according to Cross) it must be seen as containing expressions whose literal meanings and imagery the prophets rejected as too syncretistic.

Appositional Phrases

Similar distinctions figure prominently in Mark S. Smith's study *The Early History of God*. Smith, however, makes the terminology of metaphor and literal speech overt. For instance, on the solar imagery in Psalm 84:12, Smith comments: "While this language is figurative, it assumes that the divine could be described in solar terms. Psalm 84 also reflects the larger context of the Bible's application of solar language to Yahweh" (Smith 1990a, 115).[11] It is unclear just what Smith meant to say here about the relationship between Israelite assumptions as to how God *can* be described and the role of figurative speech. If the language were not figurative, would something else have been assumed about the appropriateness of the description? Does Smith wish to comment on one's ability to describe God figuratively? or on the appropriateness of such a description (implying that one is permitted to describe some things figuratively and other things not)? One gets the impression that Smith means to say that only by virtue of the fact that the language is nonliteral could people use solar imagery to refer to God. But he does not explore how we might determine the way the ancient Israelite interpreter heard these phrases. Nor do subsequent comments clarify the ambiguity, despite an extensive consideration of sun and storm imagery as metaphors in Hebrew Bible. Consider the following:

> The combination of solar and storm imagery and iconograhy in Mesopotamian sources and biblical texts raises an important issue. By combining two types of natural phenomena, Psalm 50:1-3 and Ezekiel 43:1-5 suggest that the divine nature is beyond identification with a single natural phenomenon. In effect, Yahweh is equated metaphorically with natural phenomena, but also has power over and transcends

---

[11] Also see Smith 1990b.

these natural phenomena. Like Ningirsu and Marduk, Yahweh is "supernatural." (117)

Here Smith makes explicit the notion that the biblical language equates images metaphorically. We are to understand that the equation can be metaphorical (rather than literal) only by virtue of the fact that God transcends natural phenomena.[12] If two things are really to be equated (where "A *is* B" is true), then their juxtaposition in an appositional phrase does not result in metaphor. Conversely expressed: if one has a metaphor, then the two parts of the appositional phrase *cannot* be truly equal. Thus, if "Yahweh is sun" equates God metaphorically with natural phenomena, we would expect that God is *not* ontologically identical to sun.[13] The two verses Smith refers to read:

> Devouring fire preceded Him; it stormed around Him fiercely. (Ps 50:3)

> And there, coming from the east with a roar like the roar of mighty waters, was the Presence of the God of Israel, and the earth was lit up by His Presence. (Ezek 43:2)

As I read them, neither passage meant to *equate* Yahweh *metaphorically* with natural phenomena. Rather, their goal is to demonstrate how natural phenomena serve God. Surely the psalm imagery can be read quite literally, such that fire and storm (personified?) were understood to have actually accompanied the deity. The Ezekiel passage is more complex. The phrase "Presence of the God of Israel" (כבוד אלהי ישראל) and "the earth was lit up by His Presence" (הארץ האירה מכבדו) are indeed problematic.[14] The difficulty begins with this word כבוד, invariably translated as "presence" when it speaks

---

[12] As noted, the Hebrew structure of the phrases now being considered is appositional, but the normal English form, "A is B," is usually described as "predicative." There are, of course, other kinds of metaphor that do not use this syntactic structure at all.

[13] By using the term "ontological" I wish to convey the notion of identity, as in a predicational statement that uses a form of the verb "to be" between two nouns. I am concerned here with the beliefs of the utterer, not what John Searle has called "brute reality." Searle indicates that we can speak of a subjective ontology, such as that which is "socially constructed reality." I would submit that God-belief is such a socially constructed reality, but the point here does not concern the character of the belief, only the utterer's supposition when the statement is made. The utterer believes that statements about what God is, do have some correspondence to the "brute reality" of the world. See Searle 1995, especially 190ff.

[14] See Mettinger 1982a.

of God being somewhere, and "glory" when the context involves people proclaiming *kavod* to or about God.[15] The usage of this word clearly has a long history, as is evident from its extensive distribution in Tanakh. I would argue that the common usage of the English word "presence" for this Hebrew word is a distortion of the nuances the word had in different contexts for various generations. The appearance of the term in construct with other nominal forms helps us reconstruct the evolution of its meaning. On the one hand we find כסא הכבוד (1 Sam 2:8) with the altogether simple surface meaning of "seat of honor." In contrast, consider its usage in Jeremiah as the Throne of God.[16] The phrase וימירו את כבודם בתבנית שור in Psalm 106:20 is often translated, "They exchanged their glory for the image of a bull" (JPS), but one recognizes from the context that what was exchanged was the deity, quite literally, and not "their glory." Whether this is a euphemism or simply a code word remains to be determined.[17]

This is not the place to review all of the evidence regarding this term.[18] My main point is that the usages reflect a wide spectrum of meaning, such that any judgment as to metaphoricalness must be rendered with caution. I am not inclined to use the word "presence" as a translation of כבוד in any verse, for this term harbors highly charged theological connotations in later religious contexts. In some strands of literature, *kavod* appears to be indicative of the physical being of the deity. Consider the JPS translation of Numbers 14:22, "none of the men who have seen My Presence and the signs that I have performed in Egypt and in the wilderness. . . ." What could the ancients have meant by "seeing a Presence?" In Exodus 33:18 we have a series of terms that stand for the divine body. In this case, טוב and כבוד are used in a parallel fashion. First, Moses requests, הראני נא את כבדך (JPS, "Let me behold Your Presence!"). Why would

---

[15] See, for instance, 1 Chr 16:24, ספרו בגוים את כבודו "Tell of his glory among the nations" (JPS)

[16] Jer 17:12 כסא כבוד מרום מראשון.

[17] It should be kept in mind that metaphor and euphemism are not the same, though the latter may employ the former. Moreover, this particular passage has both a euphemism and a scribal emendation used to deflect the rebellious action from God directly. Thus, the third-person plural pronominal ending stands in place of a singular pronominal ending (כבודו), which would have made God the explicitly intended object. On this phenomenon, see Fishbane 1985, chap.3; on this pslam, see Dahood 1968, ad loc.

[18] See Mettinger 1982a and 1988.

someone standing in the presence of some else request to see their "presence"? A few verses earlier in the chapter (v.11) we read, ודבר יהוה אל משה פנים אל פנים כאשר ידבר איש אל רעהו ("Yahweh spoke to Moses face to face as one person speaks to another"). God responds that he will cause his טוב, his "goodness" (v.19, JPS) to pass before Moses; but when the כבוד (v.22) moves by, Moses is shielded, by the palm of God's hand (כף), from seeing God's face. If in these very verses we can be rather blunt about God having a hand and a face, then why do we insist on the abstractions of "Presence" and "goodness" when translating the terms כבוד and טוב? Whether etymologies should factor in is difficult to say (as they are often irrelevant to a given usage). In many of these contexts the word *kavod* functions in Hebrew as a euphemism—a figurative expression—for God's body, and nothing more metaphysical than that.

Smith does help us understand a profound aspect of the development of Israelite god-belief when he introduces it as a complex process of "convergence and differentiation of deities" (1990a, 161).[19] He summarizes his approach on such matters in the chapter "Portraits of Yahweh," where he postulates that a number of rhetorical devices allowed for the emergence of the Israelite concept of God. There is much instructive in his discussion. There can be no doubt that the texts, as we have them, contain just such rhetorical efforts. However, our goal might be to discern the threads of older materials (and meanings) that might have escaped the revisionist efforts of the redactors.

To achieve convergence, Smith argues that paradox is sometimes used as a rhetorical device. On the one hand, we find expressions that attribute both solar and storm language to Yahweh, yet "at the same time, Yahweh transcends such manifestations" (161). Likewise, "Yahweh embodies both male and female, both El and Asherah," and yet, God is not both male and female, but "transcends the human finiteness inherent in both of them" (162).[20] In such cases, Smith sees

---

[19] In Smith's writing, this process is depicted as "the development toward monotheism." One problem with Smith's book is that no attempt is ever made to segregate sources on the basis of their temporal context. In any given discussion, passages might be taken from Genesis, Deuteronomy, Deutero-Isaiah, the Book of Ruth, or Proverbs. For a different approach, see Thompson (1996), who discusses what he calls "inclusive monotheism."

[20] In support of this concept Smith cites Psalm 27:10: "Though my father and mother abandon me, Yahweh will take me in." It strikes me as a long stretch to see this as a declaration of transcendence. See Smith's otherwise thorough treatment of the evidence in his chapter 3.

the paradoxes as polemical. Metaphor is yet another rubric in the process of convergence and differentiation, while serving as a ready solution to some of the biblical "paradoxes."

> A further process underlying the development of convergence and differentiation was *the creation of new contexts for metaphorical expressions* that functioned originally in polytheistic settings. Yahweh is called a "sun" (Ps 84:12) and described as "rising" like the sun (Deut. 33:2). Although this solar attribution was thought to have been taken *too literally* (at least according to Ezek. 8:16), solar language functioned to convey aspects of Yahweh *without reducing* Yahweh to being the sun . . . . Some originally polytheistic motifs were changed into forms deemed compatible with monotheistic Yahwism. One dramatic example of this alteration is the female figure of Wisdom in Proverbs 1-9. In addition to her other components, she perhaps included some features of Asherah. The representation of the divine presence as "glory" (kāvōd) or "name" (šēm) constituted alternative strategies for expressing divine presence. The background to the divine "name" and "face" of God is to be found precisely in the Canaanite milieu of the other deities. While these terms in both Canaanite-Phoenician and Israelite contexts expressed divine qualities, in Israel these terms lessened the anthropomorphism that characterized older descriptions of the deity more in continuity with Israel's Canaanite heritage. (162, my emphasis)

Leaving aside this broader question of methodology, let us turn to the specific example Smith employs in this context. As I read it, the Ezekiel passage under consideration (8:16) does *not* relate to a metaphorical understanding of Yahweh as the sun at all. The verse describes "about twenty-five men, their backs to the Temple of Yahweh and their faces to the east; they were bowing low to the sun in the east." That their backs were to the Temple of Yahweh conveys their spurning of the deity who dwells there. What Ezekiel witnessed was precisely the transgression of the edict which forbids the worshiping of *other* gods (Exod 20:3, 34:14, etc.). The verse must be understood in the context of the literary tour of religious abominations conducted by God for the prophet in this passage. A few verses before the incident on the Temple Mount, God shows Ezekiel the seventy elders of Israel secretly employing idols in (private?) cultic rituals (בחדרי משכיתו Ezek 8:12). Those idols are not idols of Yahweh and the worshiping of the sun is not an overly literal understanding of any Hebrew liturgical expression. There is nothing here indicating that the sun is being equated to the deity who occupies the Temple. Rather than reading the text as indicating Ezekiel's concern with a literal association of Yahweh with the sun, we should see him as distressed over their insolent (and opportunistic) polytheism. The sun is some other deity, parallel to the *maskit*-idols: the expression "god is sun" is being rejected on the literal level as polytheism. Essentially, the verse has nothing to do with expressions such as that found in Psalm 84:12.

We are seeking a way to establish whether, for instance, the figure of Wisdom in Proverbs represents an alteration of an Asherah consort-type figure rather than a literal depiction of a consort with a different name. If we argue that this must be the case because monotheism precludes other than a figurative Wisdom-Deity, then we have chosen to ignore the immediacy of the language in favor of some other cultural knowledge. On the surface, this is surely the way language works; that is, broader cultural knowledge (among other kinds of knowledge) allows us to establish the presence of incongruity or anomaly in a statement. But with ancient literatures a variety of cautionary checks and balances must be put in place before we can assume a sufficient understanding of the context to make our judgment. For instance, how does the dating of Proverbs influence our understanding of Asherah/Wisdom imagery in Israel? The burden is upon us to *demonstrate* that the meaning of the imagery applied to Yahweh is *different* from the meaning of the imagery applied to pagan deities, even though the words used in this imagery are identical in both cultures.

Moreover, we might also consider how it is that we have determined that the imagery in pagan contexts was literal! There is irony in the fact that Jacobsen had argued that all of the pagan materials regarding the gods were to be understood metaphorically. Smith and others appear to reject that premise, thereby asserting that pagan religion was essentially literalist while Israelite religion was essentially metaphorical (here, demythologizing) when it came to language usage and literature more generally. This must be seen as a key underlying assumption if we are to take the Israelite material as having been "demythologized." For if demythologization was necessary, then, minimally, the Israelites "missed" the metaphorical meanings of their pagan neighbors.[21] To sustain this approach, one would have to

---

[21] Please note, I am not agreeing with Jacobsen's position; I am only emphasizing that Jacobsen's approach has received widespread support and that implicit in any argument about demythologization is the notion that the pagans were literalists while the Israelites were nonliteralists.

demonstrate that the conception of deity was different enough in
Israel so as to foster the types of comparisons we have in Smith, Cross,
and others (see below). The distinctiveness would allow Israelite
expressions—often the same word-for-word expressions as those
found in pagan contexts—to be interpreted figuratively, and therefore (for some authors) intellectually superior to the polytheistic myths
of Canaanite and Mespotamian theology.

The whole notion that "polytheistic motifs" were at one point
"deemed compatible with monotheistic Yahwism" derives from the
conviction that Scripture is *a priori* a document of monotheists who
believed in a deity quite differently from the surrounding peoples.
The contemporary pagans come out of this as simpletons who believed everything literally, that stones and storms were gods, that
magic works, and that kings hear directly from their patron deities—
as if Israelites did not believe such things. But the evidence does not
support these assumptions, as will be discussed below. What is true,
and what Smith and others show so very well, is that Israelite literature eventually came to concentrate on a single deity with mini-
mal concern for that deity's relationship to the other gods who are
periodically mentioned but remain unnamed. This distinguishing
factor has indeed reached us as the primary victory of the generations who redacted the text. That victory is witnessed in such semantic
phenomena as the identification of a place with God's name rather
than with God directly. The religion emerging from the vestiges of
uncensored materials demonstrates that one generation's metaphor
is another's literal proclamation of faith.[22]

Psalm 84's sun "metaphor" includes numerous compound phrases serving as military appellatives. Prominent among them are the
expressions יהוה צבאות in vv. 2, 4, and 13, and יהוה אלהים צבאות in
v. 8.[23] Scholars have discerned that ancient Hebrew did not normally
include names in the construct form.[24] Combinations of nouns that
appear to serve as names should be read as straight appositional

---

[22] Job, which attacks the very foundations of the Deuteronomist's worldview,
employs polytheistic imagery, baroque anthropomorphisms, and unfiltered mythological motifs, especially in its climactic chapters. Surely it must be integrated in
this context as being at least as representative of Israelite thought as those expressions preferred by the DH editors. See my discussion in chapter 9.

[23] The latter occurs only six times in Scriptures; see Tsevat 1965, 50 n.11.

[24] See Tsevat 1965; Eisfeldt [1950] 1966; Mettinger 1982a, 1982b, 1988. See
Smith (1990a, 86f.) on the issue of names in construct state with reference to the
Kuntillet 'Ajrûd inscriptional evidence.

clauses (statements of predication). Matitiahu Tsevat suggests reading יהוה צבאות as either "Yaweh, the Army," or "Yahweh is the Army." Tsevat believes these appellations derive from the earliest strands of Israelite literature—the period of the Judges—when the militarization of the deity was of ideological significance. Later usage in the Psalms and in prophetic literature—at a time when the military imagery may have been less relevant—saw the diversification of this originally personal nomenclature. Other terms are cited in support of this interpretation, such as יהוה רבבות אלפי ישראל ("Yahweh, the myriad of Israelite soldiers," in the Ark Song, Num 10:36) and instances where "shield," "troop," "tower," "refuge," and "wall" all serve in nominal statements (Tsevat 1965, 56).[25]

Psalm 84:12a reads כי שמש ומגן יהוה אלהים חן וכבוד יתן יהוה ("Sun and shield is Yahweh God, grace and glory does he bestow [upon the blameless]").[26] I would prefer to render חן וכבוד יתן יהיה as "God will make his beneficence manifest for [the purpose of saving] the blameless," reading the words חן וכבוד as a conceptual unit (perhaps even a hendiadys of sorts) conveying the effects of God's physical presence, or in this case, intervention.[27] In other words, those who are blameless are given the privilege of being in God's (physical) presence.[28] Historical intervention is precisely what is meant by "sun and shield," two forces that will make or break the Israelites under seige. The lack of a determining article moves us to distinguish between "God is *the* sun" and "God is sun" and between "God is *the* shield" and "God is shield," as Smith indicates (1990a, 115).[29] Adopting Tsevat's hypothesis, we might opt to see both phrases as akin to יהוה צבאות (the difference in the syntax is necessitated by the literary duple). How are we to interpret "God is army," metaphorically or literally? As noted, Smith argues that literal understandings of the statement "God is sun" were rejected and were thought only

---

[25] See Brettler 1993; Seow 1989, 11ff.; Mettinger 1982a and 1982b, 1988; Schmidt 1996. For a discussion on a variety of construct forms, see Cross and Freedman 1975, especially 68ff. regarding Jacob's blessing (Gen 49).

[26] This reflects the JPS translation, though I have altered the syntax to reflect the Hebrew word order more closely. "The blameless" is derived from the last part of the verse, להלכים בתמים.

[27] The word *kavod* occurs elsewhere paired with terms related to God's characteristics, physical and psychological, especially strength; see Ps 63:3 לראות עזך וכבודך in contrast to Ps 21:1 et alia; Ps 62:8 for a string of such terms; Deut 5:21.

[28] Similarly, see Ps 24:3-4.

[29] The use of "our shield" in v.10 is difficult to understand; it does not seem to refer to God, but stands opposite "your anointed" in the parallelism.

"to convey aspects of Yahweh *without reducing* Yahweh to being the sun" (162, my emphasis). What, then, of the other nominal part of this literary duple and the other military images in the psalm? My sense is that the warrior deity, Yahweh, was understood quite literally to be an army (in addition to commanding celestial troops) and to be a shield—again, literally, in the sense that he shielded Israel from its enemies. Smith is right, however, in saying that these phrases do not *reduce* God to army and shield. Rather than call this a paradox which derives from an evolved imagery, I believe we have to create a new taxonomy for biblical expressions, one which can appreciate the mindset of the biblical speaker without ascribing to him unintended nuances that lead to distorted reconstructions in contemporary biblical theologies.

Yahweh *is* a warrior god in the most literal sense of a combatant; anything less would render him impotent to make the Israelites victorious in battle against their enemies (and their enemies' gods). Yahweh is a shield in the most literal sense of a protective device; anything less would leave Israel undefended. First let us establish why *God is sun, God is army, God is shield* are not metaphorical. Anticipating the more thorough discussion of what constitutes metaphor below, I take note of two characteristics common to these expressions: (1) *real* actions, not figurative ones, are required of God as established by the context; and (2) there is no incongruity or anomaly implied by the predicational statements. While the appositional phrases do not convey ontological identity via reductionism, ontological identity is *not* the only alternative we have to metaphorical meaning.[30]

Theory of Functional and Structural Ascription

We must differentiate a third category of expression beyond "literal" and "metaphorical," one which uses appositional (or predicational) statements to equate things *literally* without insisting upon ontological identity.[31] Today, were someone to step in front of a loved one to shield him or her from an aggressor's gunfire, that person would

---

[30] Those who maintain a stringent decompositional theory of semantics will not agree; see page 5f. for a consideration of this problem.

[31] I do not mean to limit this category to appositional statements exclusively. But since the discussion thus far has concentrated on them, I am addressing this common category in this context.

become the loved one's shield—quite literally. Of course, the protector would not have been physically transformed by the act, but the functional and structural roles played in that situation would make that person a "shield." Put differently, the person's identity (in this case, as a shield) is context dependent. Likewise, we can think of terms such as "branch," "tail," and "head." A river has branches which (on a map) appear structurally identical to the branches on a tree; a comet has a tail; a tennis racket has a head. These words are not metaphorical usages. Indeed, we shall see that one might wish to classify them as simple extensions of basic structural terms. But in each case, we have understood the "structural" identity of branch, tail, and head in the context of an object that does not have any one of these things in the sense that a tree has branches and a dog has a tail and a head.

Similarly, I am suggesting that God *is* sun, in that God does everything the sun does (shines, rules the skies, etc.); God *is* army, in that God literally brings about the defeat of foreign aggressors. In such statements, God is not to be distinguished from army, or sun, even though God is not ontologically identical to the sun or to an army of chiefs and foot soldiers.

I am proposing a category of expressions I shall call *conceptual ascription*, of which there are two kinds: *functional* ascription and *structural* ascription. They are defined as follows:

> Functional ascription occurs when there is a simple predicational phrase, *A is B*, where B is not ontologically identical to A, but A fulfills the proper function of B.[32]
> Structural ascription occurs when there is a simple predicational phrase, *A is B*, where B is not ontologically identical to A, but A is perceived to have the same structure as B.[33]

Conceptual ascription differs from metaphor in two distinct characteristics: except insofar as A is not ontologically identical to B,

---

[32] The "proper function" of a thing is definable only in context. The next chapter will treat the problem of word definitions more fully.

[33] Gregory L. Murphy (1996) explored what he calls "the structural similarity view," which he presents as "an alternative hypothesis" to the rubric established in the Lakoff and Johnson (1980) model. Though my own understanding of this issue and terminology had been worked out before Murphy's article appeared, I wish to recognize the many similarities between our positions. His concerns are more focused on defining metaphor than mine will be here, and his break with Lakoff and Johnson is not quite as complete. I first saw Murphy's work in a prepublication form in 1994.

statements describing their "identity" entail no incongruity or anomaly such as is contained in metaphor. And since functional and structural identity involve the literal meaning of the predication, there is little ambiguity. This is because significant functional or structural characteristics of B are found in A, except that A is not ontologically B. Metaphors move beyond the simple meanings of terms by pointing to something that derives from the creative combining of otherwise independent semantic domains. This naturally results in a considerable degree of ambiguity. As James Fernandez puts it: "A metaphor is a predication upon a subject of an object from a domain to which the subject belongs *only by a stretch of the imagination.* In that sense metaphor makes a false attribution" (Fernandez 1974, 123, my emphasis).[34] Imagination is little used in conceptual ascriptions and its decoding process, for the need to resolve ambiguities is virtually absent. If you serve as a shield, you are fulfilling that function, simply and literally. Moreover, ascriptive statements will be part of a broader cultural knowledge of how the world works. Thus, for the native hearer, not only is there no ambiguity, but an ascriptive statement's meaning will be, in some sense, common knowledge.

Let me approach the concept of ascription from yet another angle. In Wittgenstein's *Remarks on the Philosophy of Psychology* (1980) we find the following passage:

> "The words 'the rose is red' are without sense if the word 'is' has the meaning of 'is identical with.'" We have the notion that if someone would try to say the words "the rose is red" with these meanings for the words, he would actually get stuck while thinking it. (Just as, one cannot think a contradiction, because it is as if the thought falls apart.)
>
> One would like to say: "You cannot mean these words this way and still attach a sense to the whole [statement]" (1:50, §246).[35]

---

[34] I had thought to name this category of speech "functional / structural attribution" rather than "ascription," but chose not to because of the multiple connotations carried by the term "attributes" when theologians speak of God. For linguistics, "attribution" works as well and is more commonly used.

[35] This is my translation. The text reads:

> "Die Worte 'die Rose is rot' sind sinnlos, wenn das Wort 'ist' die Bedeutung von 'ist gleich' hat." Wir haben die Idee, daß der, wer versuchte, die Worte "die Rose ist rot" mit diesen Bedeutungen der Worte auszusprechen, beim Denken steckenbleiben müßte. (Wie auch, daß man einen Widerspruch nicht denken kann, weil der Gedanke einem sozusagen zerbricht.) Man möchte sagen: "Du kannst diese Worte nicht so meinen und noch eine Sinn mit dem Ganzen Verbinden."

Here Wittgenstein identifies an aspect of predicative statements that is yet more elementary than what we have considered thus far. Given the simple statement "the rose is red," no one thinks—or is able to think, for that matter—that "rose" and "red" are somehow identical.[36] Something happens in our decoding of the sentence that allows us to recognize how the predication takes place. In terms of language structure and meaning, I claim that the statements "the rose is red," "God is sun," and "God is army" all function identically.

Conceptual ascription is but one step along the way to a more nuanced understanding of meaning. Our goal is to develop a semantics that approaches meaning as gradient. Rather than forcing concepts into rigid categories, we should recognize a continuum of various types of meaning. Conceptual ascription provides a middle way between literal language and metaphor. In the process, we are not forced to make unsupportable statements about demythologization or belief shifts. There are scholars who have done this intuitively, though they may not have developed a terminology to frame their discernments. Let me briefly provide three examples. It should be apparent how, in each case, the concept of conceptual ascription, or other categories yet to be developed, would have benefited their textual analysis.

Jon D. Levenson (1993a) questions the meaning of those biblical expressions that depict the God-Israel relationship as that of father and son:

> The status of Israel as the first-born son of God is both metaphorical and *more than metaphorical*. It is metaphorical in that Israel, however delineated, is descended from a line of human fathers and not from the union of a god and a woman. . . .
>
> Yet there are dangers in interpreting the statement that Israel is YHWH's first-born as purely figurative. One is that kinship language in ancient Israel, as in many tribal societies, can express relationships that are other than biological. . . . To us, these convenantal uses of familial language seem to be straightforward metaphors, but that is only because our culture makes a sharp distinction between biologi-

---

[36] This is assuming that in the language now being used, everyone understands that the word "rose" refers to a flower, not to the name of a color. Admittedly, this is more complex than it might first appear, for as Wittgenstein discusses elsewhere, there is a problem in understanding what it means to imagine colors. See Wittgenstein 1977.

cal and other types of relationship and attributes greater reality to the former: "blood is thicker than water." Ancient Israel, following a different convention, could comfortably see a father and a son or two brothers in people who were known to have no blood relationship. *To call such usage metaphorical is to presume anachronistically the primacy of biology in Israelite perceptions of kinship.* That Israel is the first-born son both of Isaac and of YHWH poses a problem for us, but it posed none, so far as we can tell, for the biblical authors. . . . To call that sonship a figure of speech is to fail to reckon with the import of the biblical story. (40-41, my emphasis)

Levenson does not succumb to the general tendency to opt for one of the two standard paradigms, metaphor or literalism. He recognizes that the latter—implying biological fathering—is altogether impossible, while the former does not quite explain the meaning of his texts, in that it bypasses the character of this imagery. To avoid the common pitfall, Levenson appeals to a restructuring of the biblical conceptualization of kinship as pertinent to a nonbiological domain. Such a restructuring may indeed prove valuable in describing the culture's use (and understanding) of these terms. As it turns out, the tension Levenson senses would be quite well served by the concept of ascription. Father-son language in Hebrew Bible is fundamentally *ascriptival*, in both functional and structural ways, and for most of these expressions, metaphor is not involved. In this case, the functional ascription regards how one comes into the world (God as creator) and the structural ascription regards the attribution of authority to whomever it is that occupies the hierarchical station of "father" within a clan. Both are meant quite literally in the manner that ascription is closer to literal than it is to any figurative mode of expression. When we fail to recognize this, we guarantee a distortion of the biblical concept.

Another example can be found in Jacob Neusner's discussion of incarnation imagery in rabbinic literature (1988a and b). For the most part, Neusner's presentation on metaphor is rather standard. He initially approaches the literature with the subject-matter methodology as we reviewed above in chapter 1:

There is no language referring to God that is other than metaphoric, so far as I know, since given the nature of that being to whom we refer—defined as the Creator of the entire universe, for example—we can at best appeal to things in this world that we think stand for that being, that God beyond all this-worldly comparison or charac-

terization. I surely break no new ground in simply treating as axiom
the fact that when sages speak of God, the very definition of their speech
beings with metaphor. (1988a, 36)

Neusner starts out replicating the standard approaches, but then when
confronted with the evidence, he veers off the standard path. In
suspecting that there is something "different" about this form of
metaphor Neusner provides an alternative model. Like most writers
on this topic, he finds himself trapped within the standard terminology
and conceptualization of figurative language, while sensing that
something more is needed. Neusner argues as follows:

> The reason that the Torah was made flesh was that the Torah was
> the source of salvation. When the sage was transformed into a salvific
> figure, through his mastery of Torah, it was an easy step to regard the
> sage as the living Torah. . . . In the Talmud of the Land of Israel, the
> rule of Heaven and the learning and authority of the rabbi on earth
> turned out to be identified with one another. The first stage in the
> incarnation of the Torah in the person of the sage is marked by that
> *identification.* Salvation for Israel depended upon adherence to the sage
> and acceptance of his discipline. *Both God's will in Heaven and the sage's
> word on earth constituted Torah.* (1988b, 214)

Neusner sees the concept of Torah as having been expanded from
its original "written" definition to its more inclusive "written and oral"
definition. He readily incorporates the notion of "identity" in his
construal of the relationship between the two parts of the appositional idea—the sage is Torah (or "constituted" Torah). The identity, however, causes a problem. The human being is not exactly a
scroll, nor is the scroll identical to the abstract notion of Torah.
Neusner sees the process as involving the imagery of incarnation.
The question is, Are we to interpret it as literal or metaphorical?
"Incarnation . . . was far more specific and concrete. It is represented by the claim that a sage himself was *equivalent* to a scroll of the
Torah—a material, legal comparison, not merely a symbolic metaphor" (1988b, 214, my emphasis).

Speaking directly to the problem of categorization with the words
"not merely a symbolic metaphor"—words that have the same function as Levenson's expressions cited above,[37] Neusner defines the
problem directly and explicitly: "The scroll of the Torah is realized

---

[37] Levenson (1993a, 40) indicates that there are "dangers in interpreting the
statement as purely figurative."

in the person of the sage. The conception is not merely figurative or metaphorical, for, in both instances, actual behaviour was affected" (1988b, 215). It is the very visceral nature of the "identity" (sage=Torah) that forces him to dismiss the notion of metaphor as being inappropriate.

In this case, conceptual ascription works perfectly as an accurate description of what it is that Neusner means by the incarnation of Torah. The identity of sage and Torah manifests itself in both functional and structural ascription. The sage, like the Torah, is the source of salvation; and ultimately, the sage, like the Torah, is the subject of interpretation. Indeed, the sage's dictum *is* Torah.[38]

Elliot Wolfson's work on the role of anthropomorphism in Jewish mystical literature can provide a third example with a slightly different approach. Wolfson recognizes that the binary classifications of metaphorical and literal do not accurately describe the literature under consideration, and he forges a new terminology to accommodate another realm of meaning. In his study of incarnation in Jewish texts, Wolfson criticizes the stereotypical depictions of Judaism's rejection of corporeal imaging of the divine as "grossly oversimplified." Drawing on his consideration of certain liturgical formulae and reflections derived from a variety of medieval thinkers, Wolfson concludes that divine embodiment was not contrary to Jewish doctrine. The tradition contains many passages that speak of God standing before the Israelites at the Red Sea or upon Sinai; in each instance, clear physical attributes are ascribed to him. Wolfson argues: "This does not mean, however, that the rabbinic texts that speak of God's body are to be deciphered as merely allegorical or metaphorical" (Wolfson 1996, 139). But if they are neither allegorical nor metaphorical, are they to be taken as simple literal comments? The answer is quite clearly negative; simple literal meaning causes great conflicts in the conceptualization of the deity, not only with regard to the specific passages Wolfson considers but within the tradition taken as a whole.

To solve the dilemma, Wolfson devises a set of terms to classify the meaning of those texts that relate to incarnation. Wolfson borrows adjectival and nominal forms derived from the Hebrew דמות

---

[38] Neusner has moved into non-linear models of thinking in a more comprehensive way in a number of more recent studies. See for instance, Neusner 1996, which relates to rabbinic thinking as "paradigmatic" with respect to history writing, rather than simply propositional and linear.

first coined by Henry Corbin: "imaginal" and "imaging." By the "imaginal body," Wolfson means a kind of incorporeality that is somehow part of the symbolic conceptualization of the deity. "Through the images within the heart, the locus of the imagination, the divine, whose pure essence is incompatible with all form, is nevertheless manifest in a form belonging to the 'Imaginative Presence'" (Wolfson 1994, 8). Wolfson grasps "the imaginal [as] an intermediary realm wherein the imaginative forms (or archetypal images) symbolize the intelligible in terms of the sensory" (62). Imagination as sensory; an imaginal body of an otherwise imageless deity: paradoxes, to be sure. Wolfson had to reject the standard binary approaches to meaning because the texts themselves had rejected them. However, his consideration of "imagination" (in this technical sense) relates not only to mystical sources; he locates its roots in the corpus of rabbinic literature proper:

> The function of the imagination is to say one thing in terms of another and thereby conjoin that which is inarticulate and that which is verbally circumscribed within a semantic field. Imagination is the faculty through which one opens the boundaries of the phenomenological horizon by producing symbols that express the inexpressible in such ways that there is perfect agreement between the symbol and what is symbolized. (62)

While the phrase "one thing in terms of another" is reminiscent of metaphor, Wolfson ascribes to the sources a different conceptualization.[39] The underlying philosophy of language in these rabbinic texts requires sensitivity to a form of speech that, according to the writers, enables humans and God to bridge a metaphysical gap. Wolfson recognizes that the meaning of the mystical sources was not *simply* metaphor, but something else. Mystical language in general involves a violation of standard semantic structures.[40] Frequently, it engages paradox.[41] The logical incongruity or anomaly in metaphor

---

[39] Whether or not this is actually an instance of "ascription" would require a fuller discussion. The primary point here is that the binary, metaphor/literal, is not exhaustive.

[40] On the metasemantic usages of Hebrew, see my forthcoming essay, Aaron 1999.

[41] See Ricoeur 1977, 95 and 247, where Ricoeur sees the "semantic impertinence" of metaphor (what I am calling incongruence or anomaly) as causing "a metaphorical interpretation whose sense emerges through non-sense." Sense can come from nonsense only when there is a shared strategy among advocates of the

is not as strong as that of paradox, but paradox is undoubtedly just beyond metaphor in its degree of ambiguity. In the context of some forms of post-Hellenistic Judaism (though certainly not all), such utterances are viewed as the results of literary and intellectual creativity. Wolfson maintains that they should be studied as "essentially a dimension of language [whose] most basic structural feature [is] semantic innovation" (62). Thus, the innovation here involves using paradox to convey sense (itself a logical conundrum). Of course, paradox is nonsense; but in religious traditions, it is frequently a privileged form of nonsense.[42] Hence, a terminology for such speech acts had to be devised.[43]

Ascription is but one of a number of semantic categories that can free us from artificially limiting approaches to meaning in Hebrew Scriptures (or for that matter, any other literature). One's understanding of the way language works will directly influence the way one goes about the task of interpreting and writing the history of ideas. Put differently: our interpretations are fundamentally structured by our suppositions about how language works. Whether those suppositions are conscious or unconscious is irrelevant. If we employ a standard, stereotypical conceptualization of semantic categories, we can only interpret within their limiting boundaries. If we establish a model that responds to the natural elasticity of our conceptual structure, and how that conceptual structure is manifest in language, then perhaps we can avoid forcing texts into the language games of contemporary theological biases.

---

nonsense. Those outside the shared strategy cannot resolve the logical tension into meaning.

[42] Ricoeur (1977, 95) posits that "attributions that appear to be 'non-sensical' can make sense in some unexpected context." Furthermore, he claims that "the power to create new contextual meanings seems to be truly limitless." Employing I. A. Richards' contextual theorem, this is theoretical, and in terms of history, pragmatically correct. There are religions that base their "meanings" on glossolalia, much of which is complete nonsense. (See, for instance, Is 28:9, and Lindblom 1962, 200f.) But this pushes the notion of a semantics of metaphor too far. The fact that one can sit and find "meaning" in a blade of grass or the shape of tea leaves only testifies to the willingness of some individuals to abandon the rules of semantics by creating their own system of symbolization, which, at a certain point, resembles what Wittgenstein called "private language."

[43] On the notion that religious language involves expressions that are useful, regardless of how ambiguous their meaning or how logically inconsistent they might be, see Ramsey 1963; Tracy 1975, chap. 6.

4.

TOWARD A MODEL FOR GRADIENT JUDGMENTS

In this and the following chapter, I will focus on a theory of how we conceptualize word meaning. As noted in chapter 1, my goal is to build an interpretive strategy that will allow for more accurate assessments of ancient utterances while improving our description of how ancient belief systems functioned. I am presenting a semantic theory as part of the interpretive strategy because I believe the two to be inseparable. In the Introduction I argued that one's conception of how language works implicitly functions in how one interprets. This is the case whether one employs the rubrics of a language game (such as a theology) or natural speech.

In the previous chapter I outlined a category of literal meaning called *conceptual ascription*. It serves to break the standard binary approach to appositional statements. At a certain level, this constituted putting the cart before the horse, for one arrives at the notion of conceptual ascription not by analyzing would-be metaphors but by understanding something about the way words convey meaning. It is not the purpose of this study to merely replace a binary categorization with a tripartite one. The principle of gradience implies a *meaning continuum*, not discrete semantic categories.

The theory of interpretation presented here, decidedly nonbinary, is derived largely from Ray Jackendoff's work on semantics and cognitive structure (1983, 1987). Jackendoff believes that language production and interpretation involve cognitive processes that should not be analyzed in isolation but, rather, in concert with other cognitive processes. Thus, the notion of "meaning" in language is not divorced from how we establish meaning in other contexts (music, art, vision, spatial relations, etc.). This principle is important for two reasons. First, methodologically speaking, it keeps us honest. To make claims about how language works without verifying their legitimacy in terms of parallel cognitive processes proves methodologically unsound. If I were to say that a waving hand signalled to me that we should now walk across the street, but I could not identify whether the hand belonged to a police officer, an infant, or an animated billboard, you would find my confidence in my interpretation absurd. In contrast, it is not commonplace to question our confidence in judgments regarding metaphorical meaning, even though scholars are frequently unable to establish key concerns with regard to a statement's original context.

The second reason it is important to employ an integrated approach to cognitive structure is because religion is ultimately about human experiences in a great variety of domains and not just the interpretation of texts. Frequently, the writers of texts are describing visual or auditory experiences. We need to understand how they make the transference of information from vision or audition to language. Can that transference be made literally, or must it engage metaphor or some other form of nonliteral expression?

This study will assume Jackendoff's perspective without providing a history of the literature on the subject.[1] While it will be necessary to provide a working terminology, I shall endeavor to minimize the highly technical character of the linguistic side of our discussion.

How Preference Rules Work

As discussed in chapter 2, the most popular theories of word meaning are often based on one form or another of truth-conditional semantics.[2] The approach strikes us as intuitive, and its genealogy can be traced as far back as Aristotle himself.[3] Sometimes these approaches are called "feature list representations." Frequently the theory of truth conditions is associated with Alfred Tarski's work,

---

[1] The exception will be an extended consideration of Lakoff and Johnson 1980; see chapter 8. For a survey of competing theories, see Schauber and Spolsky 1986, who regularly contrast their thesis with other linguistic approaches and literary theoreticians. See also the fine surveys by Cotterell and Turner (1989); Traugott and Pratt 1980; Hawkes1977; and Culler's important work (1975, 1982).

[2] As noted, there are various names for this approach. A. J. Greimas spoke of "an invariant core." See Culler's fine discussion of how this aspect of Greimas's theoretical approach to semantics (in consort with others) ultimately introduced insurmountable complications (1975, 7).

[3] This principle functions in a number of contexts in Aristotle's writings, though as Günther Patzig puts it, one must abstract it from his practice rather than derive it from specific definitions. See the discussion on "logical necessity" in Patzig 1969, especially chapter 1.

and hence called the Tarskian truth conditions.[4] Despite numerous attacks on the theory, this approach is still very popular today—covertly, if not overtly.[5] Truth-conditional semantics maintains that for any given concept—whether it is of a thing, an event, or an abstract idea makes no difference—there is a checklist of yes-or-no questions that pertain to what is essential to the concept. As such, when you experience a certain object, you begin a cognitive process that establishes whether the object under question fulfills affirmatively all of the necessary "yes" judgments in a litany of characteristics.[6] (Usually this process takes place unconsciously.) If the object exhibits sufficient and necessary characteristics to identify it as the thing in question, then one can confidently assume the identity of the object and employ the appropriate lexical item. For example, if you were looking at my table, and someone asked you, "Is that a *table*?" you

---

[4] See Tarski 1983a and 1983b. In the latter article, Tarski's concluding comments are of particular interest in the current context. Tarski was concerned that his treatment of artificial "formalized languages" would be judged disparagingly by philosophers who concern themselves with natural, colloquial languages. "In my opinion the considerations of §1 prove emphatically that the concept of truth (as well as other semantical concepts) when applied to colloquial language in conjunction with the normal laws of logic leads inevitably to confusions and contradictions. Whoever wishes, in spite of all difficulties, to pursue the semantics of colloquial language with the help of exact methods will be driven first to undertake the thankless task of a reform of this language. He will find it necessary to define its structure, to overcome the ambiguity of the terms which occur in it, and finally to split the language into a series of languages of greater and greater extent, each of which stands in the same relation to the next . . . [as] a formalized language stands to its metalanguage. It may, however, be doubted whether the language of everyday life, after being 'rationalized' in this way, would still preserve its naturalness and whether it would not rather take on the characteristic features of the formalized languages" (267). Thus, for Tarski, there is a certain hopelessness with regard to a semantic theory for natural language, but ironically, this may be by virtue of his conceptualization of truth conditions—a truly unmanageable theoretical approach to meaning.

[5] See Barsalou (1992), who makes these theories a primary target of his article; also Lakoff 1987, Jackendoff 1983. Wittgenstein's work is largely counter to this approach as well.

[6] See Traugott and Pratt (1980, 99ff.), who set up a series of lists in a binary fashion and then bring together semantic features that they claim indicate how words have meaning. If your semantic features include *male, adult, human, animate, abstract, vegetable*, etc., you would simply go down the list and check off some as "yes" and some as "no." As is quite typical of books from the seventies and eighties, semantics receives much less atention than other areas of linguistics. Consider that their chapter on syntax is allocated 55 pages, while semantics is discussed in a chapter of 37 pages, most of which has very little to do with a theory of meaning and a great deal to do with lexicology, language usage (as in synonymy, homonymy, etc.), and even metaphor.

would answer affirmatively because you would have determined that the object under consideration allows for an affirmative answer to each of the characteristics deemed necessary and sufficient for allowing an object to be defined as "table."

The seemingly self-evident nature of truth-conditional semantics derives from the fact that there are a number of words for which the theory appears to adequately explain meaning. For instance, relational terms (such as uncle, bachelor, widow, father), states of being (such as pregnant, present versus not-present), mathematical terms (such as parallel, triangle, greater-than),[7] or jargon that remains unique to scientific or even literary communities: all such concepts *can* be defined on the basis of a checklist that identifies necessary and sufficient conditions.[8] We classify these concepts as binary: object Z either is or is not the thing under consideration. Either two lines or planes are parallel or they are not, either you are pregnant or you are not, either you are a bachelor or you are not.[9] If a given object or state of being does not fulfill all of the necessary and sufficient conditions, then we determine that the object or state of being is not the thing being considered. Thus, under no circumstance can Mary (a woman) literally be an uncle, nor can John (a man) literally be pregnant, nor can line α and line β merge if they are parallel (assuming a Euclidean model of geometry).

This is not the appropriate context for a thorough exploration of just why this particular approach has proven so durable. However, the psychological underpinnings of this conceptualization are, in themselves, worthy of study. Religions frequently adopt this mode of binary classification as it might regularly be determined by an authoritative structure which is itself binary (you either are or are not an authority). The most we can say here is that such a theory of

---

[7] Of course, there may be mathematical systems in which terms are used differently, or in which valid theorems suddenly prove invalid. See Hofstadter 1979, 88-102, on Euclidean geometry, among many other discussions of different mathematical systems throughout the book.

[8] There is some debate even with regard to these cases. See Lakoff 1987, 34ff.

[9] We are not here concerned with the problem of polysemy, where "bachelor" can refer to a college degree rather than marital status. We are also not concerned with the question of how we might establish the very moment a certain state of being is definable, for instance, in terms of pregnancy, when conception takes place: does the very second of fertilization constitute pregnancy, or does pregnancy mean the implantation of the fertilized egg? None of these issues are related to the problem of word meaning per se, though they have interesting implications in terms of the ambiguity factor.

meaning strikes most people as plausible and, in some sense, this plausibility is wishful thinking. It would certainly be more efficient if meaning were to function according to binaries, with all variables allowing only for black-and-white distinctions. Many daily experiences suggest that such a meaning theory functions well. But the kind of meaning satisfied in a binary theory is basically trite; and the number of instances in which the theory breaks down greatly exceeds those that are satisfied. Most concepts involve complex judgments, and their definitions involve a certain degree of ambiguity. Because truth-conditional theories pivot on the two notions of *sufficient* and *necessary*, they cannot account for borderline cases very well, if at all. Once something has met the sufficient and necessary conditions, it cannot be less like one thing and more like another.

But perhaps more important, as Ray Jackendoff points out, the stringent notion of a list of essential characteristics fails to reflect the *cognitive structure* that underlies our fundamental construal of meaning. For ultimately, word meaning is but one aspect of a much larger cognitive system that allows us to *understand* our experiences of the external world. The way we understand words is related to the way we understand spatial relations and auditory, visual, and olfactory stimuli. Indeed, every act of structuring data from the outside world and every act of generating meaning (i.e., organizing the outside world) takes place according to an underlying cognitive structure. And that underlying structure is gradient. It involves categories with shifting parameters. It involves methods for accommodating ambiguity not as a defect but as a natural part of our thought processes and our experience of the world. Jackendoff's integrated approach to cognition (one facet of which is language-related semantics) provides a model for analyzing the meaning of statements that relate to visual and auditory experiences as well. Word meaning is better understood, according to Jackendoff (1983), as derived from

> a large heterogeneous collection of . . . conditions dealing with form, function, purpose, personality, or whatever else is salient. Taxonomic information . . . also plays a role. As the importance of information for individuation and categorization drops off (as weighting, observability, or frequency of occurrence decreases), it shades toward "encyclopedia" rather than "dictionary" information, with no sharp line drawn between the types. (139)[10]

---

[10] Jackendoff posits a set of primary and more complex concepts which under

Let us consider a couple of examples. Were an alien to arrive from outer space and ask for a definition and example of a "dog," what definition would you offer and which example (token) would you show: a Chihuahua, an Irish wolfhound, a beagle, a poodle, a Labrador (white, black, or brown)?[11] Consider how confusing it would be to explain that the Chihuahua and Irish wolfhound are both dogs (of the species *canis familiaris*), but the fox, wolf, coyote, hyena, and jackal are not. Another example: when my son Joshua was four and a half years old, he learned that a praying mantis, a butterfly, an ant, a tick, and a dragonfly are all considered insects, but a spider is not. He could not see any rhyme or reason for this categorization; it was, after all, counterintuitive.

I purposely employ the dog and insect examples because I know that someone will immediately point to the fact that biologists may have no problem defining which creature is an insect and which is not, which creature is a dog and which is not. This is ultimately irrelevant to our concern, however, for scientific classifications are not natural parts of language creation but highly specialized instances of jargon. Since ancient times, humans have had words for dogs and insects, just as they have had words for chairs, and no one ever mistook an ant for a dog, or vice versa. The means for classifications available to the twentieth-century biologist were not available to the ancient Israelites, yet they still managed to create a word for dog, and to use it functionally without ambiguity.[12]

We know a "dog" when we see one.[13] And yet, the diverse crea-

---

lie word meaning, but I do not believe it is necessary to get into quite that much detail in order to indicate the central thesis in this context. The issue is discussed in a very accessible way, however, in Jackendoff 1992.

[11] It is interesting to note that the American Heritage Dictionary (3rd ed.), which uses illustrations copiously, has no graphic for "dog" or "cat," but does have a picture of a horse. In contrast, Webster's Collegiate Dictionary (10th ed.), which has very few illustrations, represents a dog with the picture of an Irish setter.

[12] Now that we are today able to alter the genetic make up of an individual token, it is fair to ask whether an altered mouse is still a mouse.

[13] Jackendoff separates [TYPES] from [TOKENS] of a genus, where the word "dog" is a [TYPE] and our neighbor's beagle is understood to be a [TOKEN] thereof. I will use these terms periodically, but more loosely, without the brackets that serve as part of Jackendoff's symbolic representation when sentences are diagrammed algebraically. There is the question of how children *learn* this ability to classify according to types. Anyone who has ever read picture books with a very young child will have experienced a child's ability to identify a dog and a cat, and other images, despite the great variety of breeds, not to mention variations in the artistic renderings.

tures we call "dog" have less in common in terms of appearance than certain types of dog have in common with other species. Appearances, and the way social convention classifies those appearances, is what matters here; for it is on the basis of seeing dogs that one learns to use the vocabulary. Could we establish a list of necessary and sufficient conditions? Four legs might be necessary, but they are so for innumerable other creatures. Fur is necessary, in a way, but then, the fur of a Newfoundland, a poodle, and a Chihuahua hardly look alike. Tail does not work; nor does the type of ears, the shape of the face, or for that matter, even the sound they make: one might say they all bark (though there is quite a range in what constitutes a "bark"), but no one argues that a dog that does not bark is other than a dog. What we see happening is that the characteristic(s) we think we can identify as necessary actually involve a great array of variation, so that ultimately, we have an ever-expanding set of conditions rather than a finite list. Of course, this does not mean that everything, by extension, is ultimately a dog, or that the word "dog" is meaningless. However, as fewer common characteristics are present and more alternatives become salient, categorization tends to be based on negative rather than on positive identifying attributes (it is γ because it is not δ). I wish to show here the amount of lexical ambiguity that there can be in a relatively simply term, such as "dog." The concern becomes far more complex when it comes to terms such as "god," "love," or "evil." Ironically, postbiblical religious systems, sensing this built-in ambiguity, frequently limited such terms in an artificial manner (i.e., theologically), thereby eliminating some of these problems. That fact should not influence our interpretive strategy.

A truth-conditional theory of language cannot account for either the degree of ambiguity or the fact that we manage to function quite well in spite of it. As Schauber and Spolsky (1986) express it, the reality is that our

> ability to accommodate new, variable, contradictory, and endemically insufficient data is the basis of the interpretive competence that people exhibit every day. That necessary and sufficient conditions for the creation of meaning are not usually available does not prevent all understanding; thus, a model of interpretation must account for the emergence of meaning without satisfying such absolute conditions. (7)

Not only can we do away with the notion of necessary and sufficient characteristics, but we need not even be able to establish an awareness of an exact reference for comprehension to be successful. "I took my dog to the vet." "A beautiful tree stands in our yard." "I wrote the paper on my computer." You do not need to identify a particular "dog" or "tree" or "computer" in order to understand. If you happen to have a particular picture in your mind, the token you imagine does not have to accord with the reality described by the speaker for a meaningful exchange to occur. Whether it was a terrier or a collie, a pine or an oak, a Macintosh laptop or a mainframe's terminal makes no difference; understanding was successful despite the ambiguity.[14]

In his preference-rule model, Jackendoff solves this issue of ambiguity in semantics by acknowledging that, by their nature, concepts other than those most linguists acknowledge to be binary contain a certain degree of indeterminacy. Meaning derives from judgments concerning conditions that are satisfied *in varying degrees* rather than in absolute, necessary measures. How much fuzziness is permissible in a given instance depends upon the context and function of an expression or an object (1983, 115-117). This constitutes a fundamental change in the common attitude toward the value of ambiguity in both language and our cognitive structure. Fuzziness is not a failure of human thought and communication but a natural by-product of the *way* we think.[15] Our proclivity, however, is to approach ambiguity as a pejorative aspect of inferior speech. Jackendoff calls for a reassessment:

> The moral is that fuzziness must not be treated as a defect in language; nor is a theory of language defective that countenances it. Rather, . . . fuzziness is an inescapable characteristic of the concepts that language expresses. To attempt to define it out of semantics is only evasion. (117)

In our examples of the insect and dog, above, we noted the ambiguities encountered when establishing characteristics that allow us

---

[14] When there is significant circumstantial evidence or knowledge of related facts, an educated guess may prove accurate. However, it is still just a guess and the specific information ultimately adds nothing to the communication that was intended. Scholarship quite frequently fails to discriminate between information that should be "filled in" (implicature) and information that is irrelevant.

[15] There is a discrete field of study that treats "fuzzy logic," a term coined by Lofti Asher Zadeh in 1962. See Zadeh 1975 and Kosko 1993 for considerations of "fuzzy logic" in the contexts of linguistics, artificial intelligence, decision analysis, etc. Fuzzy logic may not be the best name for the kind of thinking I am discussing, but I introduce it here because the most common term used in literary contexts, "indeterminacy," carries with it a variety of theoretical implications.

to identify a species. Similar exercises are frequently conducted in the realms of color, temperature, and spatial relations—things that most people naturally think of as involving continuous, graded domains. Final judgments as to whether a word is appropriate for a given object (or vice versa) take place according to *typicality conditions* (rather than necessary conditions), conditions that one might describe as "floating" rather than being fixed according to a sufficiency set. It is hard to say just what takes place cognitively when one uses the word "dog" without a specific instance of a dog in mind. In most cases, if someone says, "I took my dog to the vet," comprehension regarding the important actions takes place without any typicality conditions being violated or even accessed. Our identification of the most important action also takes place according to the preferencing of conditions. Thus, the fact that the word "dog" may not spark any specific image in the person hearing the sentence is not as important as understanding the role the dog had in motivating the speaker's intent. But what if the person added, ". . . but I had to wait for my husband to come home with the truck because she wouldn't fit into our station wagon"? In such a case, our most typical set of conditions regarding "dogs" would be violated, pushing the conditions of "size" well beyond one's common understanding of dogs. The violation of our typicality conditions also causes a shift in our focus when it comes to establishing the most important conditions of relevance. The dog's unusual size may eclipse the whole issue of the veterinarian. It is the *context* that causes the readaptation of the embraced conditions. Assuming that all of the exchanges here are truthful and literal, we now have a new characteristic. If a truth-conditional theory of language were in effect, we might be forced to argue: "You've got it wrong! By definition, anything that big cannot be a dog."

Our principle of typicality conditions, then, acknowledges not only that words can have a broad (gradient) span of meanings, but also that our parsing of a sentence—as a larger semantic unity—involves the weighting of conditions according to our perception of authorial intent. Since we do not assign equal weightings to all parts of a sentence, we are not bothered by all ambiguities equally. This aspect of the preference-rule theory is especially important for our consideration of biblical literature. Frequently what differentiates interpretations of biblical passages are the distinct weightings given by scholars to the discrete parts of a sentence or a story. But since our ability to assess the conditions of relevance is often so limited, we have very little opportunity to check the validity of our weightings against some unambiguous indicator of authorial intent.

To summarize, we can point to three aspects of the preference-rule theory of semantics that provide us with significant advantages over the more common truth-conditional approaches:

1. Typicality conditions are in a speaker's and audience's heads rather than being part of the object or concept being defined. That is, we accrue such conditions with experience, and we organize them conceptually.

2. For adequate communication to take place, the speaker and the audience must have about the same conditions in their heads. (This implies that their experiences of the world must also have a great deal in common.) Exact overlap is neither necessary nor relevant, but there must be enough in common for basic mutual comprehension to take place.

3. More than anything else, typicality conditions allow for a great deal of flexibility and accommodation. Even the rules for preferencing conditions need not be identical in two people for them to have some effective communication. However, the more diverse the preferencing rules are, the greater the divergence will be in the way two individuals understand something.

The last point is especially important. Different communities can have different sets of typicality conditions for any given thing. There might be just enough overlap for the people to think that they are communicating, when in fact, interpretations do not agree in enough instances to allow for truly successful interchanges. How much agreement there must be is itself a variable, depending upon the given concept and its role in the exchange. Thus, preferencing structures are themselves quite flexible. Even the relative importance of a given concept must be factored into our understanding of how the preferencing of conditions will affect the outcome of our interpretations. Frequently, historical change causes drift in the salience of various conditions in a community's use of concepts. Diachronically speaking, such shifts in salience among conditions can be so great that a given word takes on a radically different meaning. We could read an entire eighteenth-century book thinking that "officious" meant "haughty or meddlesome," whereas the author had in mind "courteously dutiful." This is not a case of polysemy, but a gradual shift in how typicality conditions are preferenced.

The Assumptions Regarding Authorial Intent

Among the typicality conditions that factor into every act of interpretation is an interpreter's assessment of the speaker's intent. When a person speaks or writes a thought and another hears or reads it, the interpretative process involves a set of assumptions that leads the interpreter to think, "She meant this by that comment."[16] As is the case with anything written today, behind all ancient documents there lies intent. We shall operate on the principle that an intentionless, sensible utterance is not possible; that is, such a thing is an oxymoron.[17] The typical circumstance is that the author's meaning is just what the interpreter understands. We expect the perspectives of the two to coincide as best they can, given the natural limits of language, and we consider this identity of understandings to be the most cognitively desirable state of affairs.[18]

For all intents and purposes, the author-reader construct is an extension of the normal speech act. The change in medium does cause certain shifts in various aspects of the evaluation process, but those shifts derive from the medium and are not part of the assumptions shared by those engaged in the communication act. The causes of these shifts are obvious. For instance, a reader cannot hear the tonal innuendoes that someone speaking integrates into the speech act. The written word can span centuries and numerous speech communities but the spoken word is spontaneous and momentary to one speech community.[19] On the other hand, spontaneous speech does

---

[16] This notion of "meaning" involves, first, the evaluation of the individual words, and then, as noted, the act of ascribing variable amounts of significance to the discrete parts of the statement.

[17] I am not here considering the issue of trances or altered states of consciousness which can produce utterances that may make sense but are not intended. This requires an entirely different consideration of religious phenomenology, though I would maintain that a general consideration of semantics is relevant to it as well. At the edges of religious institutions are those who would maintain that the most profound utterances are those which bend the rules of ordinary language. These include mystics and charlatans (often indistinguishable).

[18] See Erving Goffman's notion of social and natural framing (1974).

[19] Sound recordings may present another set of problems, while film and video may prove yet more complex. These are all issues of theory that remain to be worked out and are fundamentally irrelevant to our present context.

not permit the careful choice of terms and the reworking of sentences so that they might convey concepts as clearly as possible. One of the functions of socialization and education is to enable people to hone their skills as speakers and writers.

The privileging of authorial intent is not without controversy on two levels.[20] First there is the theoretical debate, then there are the post facto assumptions of biblical scholars who bypass our extremely sketchy knowledge of compositional contexts in order to come up with thorough theologies. The controversy centers on the question of whence meaning derives: does meaning derive from the author, the text, or the reader? This "project" (the deconstructionists actually avoid the word "theory") of questioning *Whence meaning?* relates not only to literature but to thinking and values in general. In seeking a new path toward meaning, the deconstructionists sought to transform the basics of western logic. Central to this project was the flat rejection of literal, authoritative, or obvious meaning (Ellis 1989, 79). "Deconstruction is not a theory that defines meaning in order to tell you how to find it. As a critical undoing of the hierarchical oppositions on which theories depend, it demonstrates the difficulties of any theory that would define meaning in a univocal way: as what an author intends, what conventions determine, what a reader experiences" (Culler 1982, 131). The issue that occupies the centerpiece of this study is for the deconstructionist a nonissue, for, quite simply, if there is no such thing as literal meaning that is essentially identical with author's meaning, one's decision-making processes must be concerned with something else. Even those who do not go as far as this with regard to authorial intent and context may be bothered by the fact that a text may appear to have many "meanings" the author was not aware of and therefore could not have intended.[21]

---

[20] For a fine summary of many of the issues discussed here, see Cotterell and Turner 1989. They contrast E. D. Hirsch (1967, 1976) with Stanley Fish (1980), among other writers. See Culler (1982, 110ff.). Early in her study, Kittay (1987, 14) dismisses the importance of authorial intent altogether.

[21] The issue of multiple meanings to a single phrase is discussed in Austin 1975. Authorial intent is part of a governing context which allows typicality conditions to be assessed. For Austin, meaning is somehow distinct from the state of mind of the speaker, but wrapped up in conventional procedures of interlocution. In effect, the speaker's state of mind does not function as an operative in the interpetive context, for it must be subordinated to the broader conventions of discourse. Obviously, the position taken here is at odds with Austin's. Austin introduces a distinction between *performative* and *constative* speech acts, a taxonomy I find essentially irrelevant to questions of semantics and authorial intent as we are now con-

I am very much in agreement with John Ellis when he argues that deconstruction "does not advance serious thought or inquiry but gives an impression of profundity and complexity without the effort and skill that would be required to make a substantial contribution to the understanding of the matter under discussion" (Ellis 1989, 7). The preference-rule model has no problem dealing with the question *Whence meaning?* simply because its system of gradient judgments can take all sources of meaning into consideration without needing to boldly demark beginnings and ends. That there exists such a thing as "reader's meaning," or that a text might provide a person with a "meaning" the author never intended, does not controvert the need to make rules about the appropriate borders of literary criticism. Instead, what we need to recognize is that there are multiple perspectives for establishing meaning, and that one perspective may have nothing to do with and be irrelevant to the next. Moreover, just because there are cases in which authorial or contextual meaning is, in fact, impossible to ascertain with a comfortable degree of certainty, we are not obliged to declare all forms of meaning equal, or give up on meaning altogether.[22]

The fact that there is such a thing as reader's meaning is ultimately irrelevant to the historian of religion who is attempting to write the history of ideas in ancient Israel. Once that is agreed upon, rules of interpretation must be put in place. Context always provides a narrowing of choices, even if it can only rarely allow for a complete elimination of ambiguity. The fact that some ambiguity may exist in very many speech acts ultimately has little impact on our ability to speak with meaning and to interpret meaningfully. By rooting this ambiguity in our conceptual structure rather than in texts, we may begin to contextualize the natural ambiguity in all speech acts.

What, then, is "intent"? Often, intent is confused with the conscious expression of ideas. I have tried to establish here that typicality conditions need not be conscious, or even well delineated at any given moment, despite the fact that communication functions quite naturally according to them. The hiddenness of intent is highlighted in the following passage in Wittgenstein's *Remarks on the Philosophy of Psychology:*

---

cerned with it. Moreover, we should point out that he has simply created one more binary taxonomy, which by its very nature, is doomed to fail.

[22] Of course, giving up on meaning and interpretation altogether is not the deconstructionist's goal, as Culler explains (1982, 132).

> When I see the milkman coming, I fetch my jug and go to meet him. Do I experience an intending? Not that I knew of. (Any more, perhaps, than I *try* to walk, in order to walk.) But if I were stopped and asked "Where are you going with that jug?" I should express my *intention*. (Wittgenstein 1980, 1:38, §185)

Surely most speech takes place in the manner of fetching one's jug when seeing the milkman, or walking here and there. We do not sit and figure out in advance just what our intention is before uttering it.[23] Moreover, the remarkable thing about the human speech act is that we are virtually *never* conscious of how we go about structuring a sentence as we express it; indeed, we are only rarely conscious of our ideas as we endeavor to articulate them.[24] Because of this, there is much ambiguity regarding meaning and intentionality. Since we are not conscious of meaning—that is, we have no explicit awareness every moment of what we mean or what we think—some would argue that there might be meanings in our statements of which we are not aware. One might think of writing as considerably more deliberate, but it is not necessarily the case. We do not regularly think about our thinking; we do not regularly say, "What am I meaning and how do I find the words?" and then undertake some conscious reflection of what happens when the words are found. Indeed, the same is true of the interpretive framework we regularly employ, as Erving Goffman writes: a person "is likely to be unaware of such organized features as the [interpretive] framework has and unable to describe the framework with any completeness if asked, yet these handicaps are no bar to his easily and fully applying it" (Goffman 1974, 21). The fact that the process is fundamentally hidden relates more about our cognitive structure than it does the ability of an individual to fundamentally articulate what she or he means. And ultimately, the hiddenness should not factor into our assessment of how language generates meaning.

When it comes to biblical literature, many scholars ignore these basic principles and provide us with extraordinarily detailed descrip-

---

[23] See Wittgenstein's comments on the relationship between intending and thinking something out, as a simultaneous event which is then linked to verbal expression (1980, 1:35, §173).

[24] We are especially conscious of the speech process when we are not fluent in a language, or, to express it conversely: if we are routinely conscious of how we form a sentence (syntactically), we are not competent speakers of a language.

tions of which beliefs dominated at the time of composition and which myths had been rendered ineffective. The methodology by which they are able to determine such things with such confidence and clarity remains hidden and in this case, hiddenness is a liability.

5.

TYPICALITY CONDITIONS AND RELEVANCE

Literatures from the ancient world present a great array of problems for the modern interpreter. I am not concerned here with the stability of textual versions, but rather with the semantics of ancient languages. Successful interpretations are dependent upon our evaluation of conditions of relevance. If we prize the value of authorial intent as a major determining factor in the meanings of statements, then it is legitimate to inquire as to how well we know the author of a given passage and all that might be relevant to his thinking. How important is authorial intent for establishing the meaning of a statement? How can we determine whether we are sufficiently integrating authorial intent into our interpretations? In chapter 7, I will deal quite directly with this question in terms of biblical authorship. Before that discussion, however, we need to put in place some additional theoretical considerations that relate to preference rules.

We should start with the well-rehearsed principles now commonly attributed to Paul Grice, but frequently elaborated upon in the literature that concerns relevance theory.[1] Grice was essentially concerned with the relationship between intention and effect in common speech acts. To say that Ploni meant something by saying X is roughly equivalent to saying that Ploni intended the utterance X "to produce some effect in an audience by means of the recognition of

---

[1] See Grice 1957, subsequently discussed and expanded in 1961, 1969, 1971, 1975, 1978, 1981, and 1982. See the discussion in Sperber and Wilson 1986, 21-38, and the extensive bibliography there of those who have discussed Grice's presentation. See also Searle 1969, 42-50, for a critique of Grice and some suggestions regarding competence that improve Grice's approach. Also on Grice, see Black 1972-73; and Kittay 1987, 221ff., for a critique I find altogether unconvincing regarding the relationship between Grice's principles and "private language." See also Chomsky (1975, 60-77), who deals with the concept of "speaker's intent" at a more complex level, indicating that there are even times that language is not used to communicate. For the most part, these categories of speech acts are irrelevant to our discussion because of the nature of the literature under consideration. Howeover, Chomsky's discourse on speaker's intent is instructive in that it deals with the question of what happens when a given utterance does not end up yielding the meaning that the speaker wants it to yield.

this intention" (Grice 1971, 58, also 1957). There is a whole series of assumptions implicit in such an exchange. Taken together, Grice calls these assumptions the "cooperative principle":

> Our talk exchanges . . . are characteristically, to some degree at least, cooperative efforts; and each participant recognizes in them, to some extent, a common purpose or set of purposes, or at least a mutually accepted direction . . . at each stage, *some* possible conversational moves would be excluded as conversationally suitable. We might then formulate a rough general principle which participants will be expected (ceteris paribus) to observe, namely: Make your conversational contribution such as is required, at the stage at which it occurs, by the accepted purpose or direction of the talk exchange in which you are engaged. (Grice 1975, 45)

Grice has included within his conceptualization of conversation a considerable degee of indeterminacy. The qualifying terms "characteristically," "to some degree at least," "to some extent," and then "a rough general principle" all function in this context as part of Grice's recognition that ambiguity is a built-in feature of all speech acts, and that necessary and sufficient rubrics do not pertain. Naturally, there are limits to our tolerance of ambiguity—those will be discussed below—but for the time being, let us assume that the ambiguities are such that communication is still readily possible.

Grice posits a set of nine maxims as part of the cooperative principle of conversations.[2] While their specifics need not concern us here, their general function has been described by Sperber and Wilson (1986):

> This account of the general standards governing verbal communication makes it possible to explain how the utterance of a sentence, which provides only an incomplete and ambiguous representation of a thought, can nevertheless express a complete and unambiguous thought. Of the various thoughts which the sentence uttered could be taken to represent, the hearer can eliminate any that are incompatible with the assumption that the speaker is obeying the co-operative principle and maxims. If only one thought is left, then the hearer can infer that it is this thought that the speaker is trying to communicate. Thus, to communicate efficiently, all the speaker has to do is utter a sentence only one interpretation of which is compatible with the assumption that she is obeying the co-operative principle and maxims. (34)

---

[2] See Samely 1992 for a integration of these maxims into an interpretive approach to Midrash.

Two of Grice's postulates are particularly worthy of note in the context of interpreting Hebrew Scriptures: (1) we assume that the speaker does not say what he believes to be false, and (2) a speaker does not state that for which there is a lack of adequate evidence. While these function as the underpinnings of our daily conversations, we might be hard-pressed to determine whether this is true of the biblical writer. Certainly we read Scriptures with the belief that the writer tells us the truth. But about those things the writer speaks of, is there ever truly adequate evidence? Given the number of statements attributed to God, are we ready to assert that the authors were as convinced of the evidence underlying them as they were of the evidence underlying statements attributed to Abraham? Is there any difference between the two? Obviously, what constitutes "adequate evidence" cannot be determined according to an absolute standard. But we must begin somewhere, and it is altogether appropriate to start by seeking those cooperative principles that govern biblical "conversation."

Interpreters seek as much stability as possible in both the realm of word meaning and the realm of these unspoken but implied meanings. Problems of interpretation frequently result from ambiguities that diminish our powers of implicature. By "implicature" we mean those acts of weighting, those acts of preferencing, that allow us to evaluate the relative importance of various implied conditions relevant to meaning.[3] For every utterance there is meaning that is derived from unspoken contextual pieces of information. These pieces of information are evaluated according to typicality conditions, just as words are in natural speech. Consequently, contexts that provide less than optimally stable conditions for interpretation might be described as resulting from one of the following three scenarios:

1. The speaker's communication did not sufficiently allow for irrelevant interpretations to be eliminated from the realm of possible meanings.

2. The hearer did not have enough knowledge of relevant-to-meaning fctors to eliminate irrelevant interpretations from the realm of possible meanings.

---

[3] "Implicature" is the term used in relevance theory, but it is fundamentally identical to what Monroe Beardsley (1958, 125) called "secondary signification," dependent in turn on "contextual connotation."

3. Both (1) and (2) combined to varying degrees.

The less knowledge we have of relevant-to-meaning factors, the more difficult it is to evaluate semantic structures. This sounds like a simplistic truism, and yet, as we have already seen, scholars regularly "interpret" without considering the stability of their interpretive context. One of the assumptions of the cooperative principles is that, generally speaking, interlocutors are equally competent in the language they use to communicate.

Having bypassed the issue of reader competence up until now, we should introduce it as one of the other possible reasons for misinterpretation. Normally, competence would be assumed as a basic principle, but since the corpus under consideration is ancient literature, we should be especially attuned to how difficult it is to establish stability, especially with regard to conditions derivable from implicature alone. Competence is admittedly gradient, so it is hard to say when it is that a hearer simply lacks knowledge of a few key relevant-to-meaning factors and when a whole range of conditions are altogether beyond his or her grasp. The incompetence I have in mind is not that of the novice student of the ancient languages who makes anachronistic or poor judgments because of a lack of experience. Rather, I mean that level of incompetence that derives from our inability to grasp certain crucial pieces of cultural information that functioned at the time the texts were composed.

In many cases, these pieces of information may be lost forever, but in certain instances, we believe we can reconstruct them using the principles of convergence. Convergence is basically the coming together of all those variables that enable us to make decisions regarding meaning. The weighting of the variables occurs naturally in each instance of communication. But when we know that some variables are missing, we may push toward a stable meaning by making certain *assumptions* based on whatever relevant variables present themselves. All too frequently in Tanakh, authorial intent is one of those missing variables that we *reconstruct* through the convergence of other pieces of evidence. In some respects, this is normal procedure. Language's natural ambiguities regularly force us to adjust and readjust our understanding of the discrete variables of a statement. This is especially the case with extended narratives, where we must allow for reassessments (reweightings) to occur when new variables influence our evaluation of previously established ones. But with time, we tend to allow distinct approximations to take hold as more or less fixed constituents in our construal of meaning. Upon moving to the next item in a narrative, we factor in the approximation as a fixed variable, virtually ignoring its characteristics as an approximation. The process reveals what we might consider an algorithm of semantic approximations.

Examples of this phenomenon are many in the interpretive literature. For example, Jacob Milgrom (1990) asks the question, Did God dwell in the ark?[4] Once he has arrived at a conclusion (in Milgrom's case, the conclusion is that God does not *literally* dwell in the ark), subsequent discussion involving the ark naturally follows from the initial inference. The interpretive strategy blindly perpetuates this algorithm of approximation. If our attitude toward language embraces the principles of preference rules, we are more likely to factor in each additional piece of information in such a way as to cause a reevaluation of our initial preferencing of conditions. Thus, instead of using an algorithm that factors in approximations as stable meanings, we will constantly be adjusting our approximations. If this is not our procedure, an estimation factored in as a heavily weighted condition will foster a false confidence in the stability of the semantic fields we are interpreting.

Erving Goffman's term "framing" is useful in this context. Goffman calls the set of rules used by an interpreter to attribute meaning to a given experience (a statement heard is just such an experience) a "frame." We might describe the mind as constantly asking itself, "What is going on here?" Each moment requires quick computations to establish which frame—which set of interpretive tools—will provide the optimal interpretation. The frames are fundamentally clusters of relevant-to-the-moment concepts. Relevance is based on the fundamental belief that "the world can be totally perceived in terms of either natural events or guided doings and that every event can be comfortably lodged in one or other category" (Goffman 1974, 35).

As Goffman describes it, we are constantly glancing at different things in life and in very quick order making judgments as to appropriate frames. The process is facilitated by the fact that most experiences do fit into *typical* patterns. (In part, this fact is what leads people to place their confidence in truth-conditional theories of mean-

---

[4] See my more extensive discussion on the meaning of the ark in ancient Israel in chapter 8.

ing.) We ascribe meaning without always verifying our basic assumptions because we could not possibly function if we were to direct our attention to each and every aspect of our interpretations. In fact, we end up accepting the meaning of certain factors exclusively on the basis of past experience, and we frame things based on those experiences. Thus, any given moment looks like a lot of other given moments simply by virtue of the fact that we carry over conjectures from past assessments into what we expect in the future.

Herein lies a certain danger. As interpreters of literatures from the distant past, we are burdened by the task of framing expressions uttered in a world about which we have very limited knowledge. To do this with a sense of historical integrity, we must first endeavor to avoid framing according to what we expect. Naturally, every scholar's goal is to convince the reader that his or her framing is identical to the author's conceptualization of reality. The challenge, first and foremost, is not to frame the alien in familiar (contemporary) terms, but to allow conditions of significance to emerge from the text, to the greatest extent that we can.[5]

Admittedly, the distance in terms of time and cultural structures makes the act of determining preference rules particularly tenuous. The principle of convergence in interpretation can become a kind of self-fulfilling prophecy. But using the convergence of conditions to fill in missing pieces is at once necessary and risky. We constant-

---

[5] Gadamer (1988) speaks of the interpretive process as an inevitable "circle of understanding." He describes the search for meaning in texts (with particular attention to those of antiquity, especially Plato) as follows: "All correct interpretation has to screen itself against arbitrary whims and the narrowness of imperceptible habits of thinking, training its sights 'on the objects themselves' (which for philologists are meaningful texts which for their part again treat of objects). To let oneself be determined in this way by the objects is obviously no one-time 'scout's honor' resolution, but really 'the first, permanent, and final task.' For it is a question of fixing one's gaze on the object through all the diversions with which the interpreter constantly assails himself along the way. Whoever wants to understand a text, is always carrying out a projection. From the moment a first meaning becomes apparent in the text he projects a meaning of the whole. On the other hand it is only because one from the start reads the text with certain expectations of a definite meaning that an initial meaning becomes apparent. It is in working out this sort of projection—which of course is constantly being revised in the light of what emerges with deeper penetration into the meaning—that the understanding of what is there consists" (71). This essay, which originally appeared in 1959, exhibits the influence of Heidegger (in fact, the essay was originally written for a Festschrift in honor of Heidegger's seventieth birthday), but also shares much in common with the way Goffman will discuss framing.

ly adjust our estimations regarding certain questionable features (in Goffman's language, we constantly reframe) and these adjustments have reciprocal effects upon all the other constituents in our interpretive exercise. But there are limits to the efficacy of even our best efforts at convergence. The tendency is to become ever more tolerant of lesser degrees of semantic or implicated stabilities. As a result, most interpretations look a great deal like previous interpretations by virtue of the fact that we adopt those aspects of previous conjectures that functioned well for us (or others) in another context. This principle of convergence works marvelously in everyday speech, but it may very well be our downfall in the interpretation of ancient texts.

Despite this caution, ambiguity does not normally preclude strong interpretations, apparently because our logical powers of implicature (estimating, approximating unknown variables) are substantial.[6] Moreover, we get a great deal of practice; it is natural. Sperber and Wilson (1986) describe the process as follows:

> We are assuming that all the hearer can take for granted is that an utterance is intended as an interpretation of one of the speaker's thoughts. This does not mean that whenever an assumption is expressed, the hearer has to compute all its logical and contextual implications and sort through them one by one to find out which subset of them are implications of the speaker's thought. In the framework we are proposing, this wasteful maneuver is quite unnecessary. If the speaker has done her job correctly, all the hearer has to do is start computing, in order of accessibility, those implications which might be relevant to him, and continue to add them to the overall interpretation of the utterance until it is relevant enough to be consistent with the principle of relevance. At this point, the sorting will have been accomplished as a by-product of the search for relevance, and will require no specific effort of its own. (234)

When considering ancient literatures, we are caught in a bind by

---

[6] Goffman notes that we require a conceptual apparatus to deal with what he calls "slippage and looseness" (1974, 35). When we cannot establish a cause-and-effect relationship, for instance, we are left without a clearly applicable frame for understanding why something happens. Nature itself may be given responsibility for "meaning," but we also have what Goffman calls "fortuitousness," which is our framing of an event as having come about "incidentally." This involves the notions of coincidence, happenstance, accident, and so on. Language must also allow for such a framing device. We should be able to say, "Her words came together coincidentally to mean X, even though she meant to say Y."

the very natural structure of this process. As Sperber and Wilson see it, determinations of relevance start with the basic relationship of the speaker and hearer, where the interpreter's strategy is to establish relevance based on his or her understanding of that relationship. When such a great distance of time separates us from the speaker, these judgments of relevance become highly unstable. This is the case with all types of meaning, but metaphorical expressions, which, by their nature, involve a higher degree of ambiguity than literal statements, will involve yet greater instability. This is because the speaker's intent is not communicated with the literal meaning of a sentence but by virtue of the fact that there is a discontinuity between the literal meaning and the speaker's intent. In such cases, implicature (or convergence) is more important than otherwise.

Scholars often eliminate the factor of ambiguity and put stable suppositions in its place. Earlier we pointed out that in many speech acts particular tokens of a said type are not identified. Thus, words like "computer," "dog," and "tree" can all be used without a specific kind of computer, dog, or tree being defined. This kind of speech act involves the implicit recognition that the particular token is irrelevant to the conveyance of meaning. When it comes to writing the history of God-belief, these gaping silences are somehow interpreted by scholars as calls for speculation. Consider the following example. When Moshe Greenberg elucidates the burning bush episode, he considers why God chose to appear to Moses in a burning bush. According to Greenberg, "the choice of fire as a divine element . . . flows from its manifold God-like characteristics." Greenberg teaches that God's passion is "often expressed in similes of fire" as well as in his "destructive power," for which "fire provides an analogy to God's dangerous holiness." Moreover, "purity . . . and illumination . . . are further points of comparison." In conclusion, Greenberg instructs that "the mysterious texture of fire—its reality yet insubstantiality, its ability to work at a distance—must have contributed to its aptness as a divine symbol" (1969, 71).

This is a remarkable cluster of images, with simile (a cousin of metaphor), symbol, and straight comparison all figuring into Greenberg's explanation of why God would be depicted as a bush on fire. However, absolutely none of these ideas are derivable from the text itself. Greenberg approaches biblical materials as if there functioned a principle of intertextuality similar to that popularly ascribed to rabbinic literature.[7] That theory would maintain that every aspect of Scripture can be used to illuminate every other aspect of Scripture, regardless of the genre, context, or intent of the compared passages. In creating theological meaning, Greenberg ignores the most simple aspect of the narrative, namely, the fundamental absurdity of a burning bush that is not consumed. Upon seeing the phenomenon, Moses thinks, "I must turn aside to investigate this remarkable sight; why doesn't the bush burn up?" (Exod 3:3). Greenberg bypasses the fundamental curiosity of this event while transforming the entire concern into one of theological symbolism. "Moses was startled, not by any shape in the fire," claims Greenberg, "but by the unburnable quality of the bush." Whence this concern for a "shape in the fire?" Verse 3:2 informs us that "an angel (מלאך) of YHWH appeared to him in a blazing fire out of the bush."[8] The verse clashes somewhat with the overall character of the event and this might lead us to speculate that it is an editor's interpolation, added by someone who was a bit squeamish about direct appearances of the deity.[9] Such insertions are not unusual.[10] The notion that Moses would have looked for a human (or angelic) form is relevant only if we embrace the current narrative as a unified whole. If we accept the composite nature of the text, we accept that the character himself would not have been looking for "any shape in the fire." That is, we have a choice to write the theology of the story

---

[7] See Boyarin 1990.

[8] For a similar, though more thorough consideration of the use of "angel" in this and other passages, see Mendenhall 1973, 56-66. He concludes that "the *mal'āk* thus designates something in human experience which is identified with the action of deity. It is a manifestation that is tied to time and place and the capabilities of human senses, but its effects can be recognized and felt elsewhere" (61). My approach will clearly be quite different, understanding "angels" to be the preferred euphemism of a particular stratum of text.

[9] Childs 1974, 72 calls it "an interpretative superscription to the entire description which then follows."

[10] Gen 22:11, 15; 31:11; Josh 5:13-15; Judg 13; even in the Hagar story, Gen 21:17f., although it may have a different purpose there. See Mendenhall 1973, 56ff., for a discussion of many relevant passages. In some contexts, this character is called by the technical phrase *angelus interpres*, playing an especially important role in Zechariah and Daniel. However, in Genesis and here in Exodus, the angelic figure is inserted as an intermediary whose primary purpose appears to be to distance the deity from the action. This can be posited by virtue of the fact that within the same narrative, it is not the angel that acts or speaks, but God directly. In contrast, the *angelus interpres* constitutes a late literary trope, one that perhaps evolved out of the earlier preference for euphemisms introduced by some schools of thought.

that contains the angel image or the story that does not contain the angel image.[11] Greenberg has opted for the former, which means that the meaning of the angel image must be integrated now into the flow of the narrative. He tells us that the angel of YHWH (מלאך יהוה)

> here, as everywhere, refers to a visible manifestation of YHWH, essentially indistinguishable from YHWH himself, . . . except that here the manifestation is not anthropomorphic but fiery. There is, then, no special difficulty in the shift from "angel" to YHWH in verses 2 and 4. The shift from YHWH to 'elohim in verse 4 is strange. . . . Since 'elohim is a general term for all celestial beings, angels included, perhaps it is used here to refer to the mal'ak [angel] who was in the bush." (70)

In a footnote, Greenberg explains yet more deliberately his understanding of the anthropomorphisms in this passage. "Since, as will be noted below, the burning bush revelation adumbrates the later theophany at Sinai, something may be suggested about the former from Moses' insistence with regard to the latter that 'you heard the sound of words, but you saw no image [Deut 4:11]'" (70). Finally, summing up his consideration of this whole encounter, Greenberg explains the dialogue initiated by this scene as part of a broader theme of God's "anthropotropic" character. YHWH is "turned toward man," in that he is "concerned with, accessible to, and considerate of men." But since there are such differences between the nature of man and the nature of God, Greenberg posits that "the first condition of such dialogue is God's willingness to adjust himself to the capacities of men, to take into consideration and make concessions to human frailty. Such divine forbearance is evident throughout our story" (93-94).

All of this theology is derived from the mere image of an unconsumed, burning bush. If Greenberg could show that there operates in Scripture a hermeneutic that allows for so complex a set of images to derive from a one-time occurrence, then there may be some justification for this interpretation. But basically, what we have is an attempt at implicature which draws upon all sorts of possibilities and then presents them as informative fact. Greenberg's reconstruction

---

[11] Of course, we could do both. Moreover, writing the theology as if the angel image is essential to the text could also assume that the angel was added but that as interpreters we should concern ourselves only with the final, redacted form of the text.

of the theology constitutes a convergence algorithm of great complexity, arrived at without any attempt to establish relative weightings of conditions.

Greenberg (and his readers) would have been better off had he left many of the ambiguous issues alone. The burning bush image is, conceptually speaking, rather isolated; it does not constitute a biblical leitmotif in Tanakh (unlike the recurrence of divine throne scenes, splitting waters, storm imagery, bringing to life one who has just died, combat with primal forces in nature, etc.), nor does it appear as the adaptation of some non-Israelite literary image. As far as the story goes, there appears to have been no intention for a reader to exercise implicature with regard to any other matrix of meanings. The story is simple, direct, and unique in its content. Though we moderns might be bothered by them, the ambiguities are not begging to be clarified in some intertextual collage of images.

What we see here, as in so many theological commentaries, are interpretations that violate the most basic structures of language and expression. No author whose writings are now in Exodus could possibly have had the selective view of imagery that Greenberg has as a student of the canonized Scriptures. Greenberg's weightings of variables relevant to implicature are determined more by the history of canonization than by anything internal to the burning bush narrative. We can also assume that a great many images that were available to the biblical writer and that functioned as part of his cultural vocabulary are now altogether lost to us. In a sense, the misweighting of conditions goes beyond a misconstrual of the evidence, for one cannot even verify whether the conditions of relevance actually constitute verifiable evidence. By preferencing a particular matrix of images to explain the burning bush, Greenberg yields an interpretation that proves irrelevant, simply because the semantics of the narrative are stabilized with data whose relevance is so very dubious. In such a context, our struggle for convergence is little more than a grasping at straws.

On the Problem of Scholarly Disagreement and the Hierarchy of Weightings

There are a number of ways to frame disagreements over the interpretation of a given text. One might be able to establish that different interpreters occupy distinct interpretive communities. In many instances, the community that governs one's interpretive strategies is clearly identifiable. For instance, adherence to the beliefs of a particular religious community may cause a person to maintain a particular perspective regarding the meanings of texts. Other interpretive communities are less easily identified or defined and, theoretically, may involve as few as two people or as many as an entire nation when it comes to certain domains. Schauber and Spolsky (1986) distinguish interpretive individuals or groups on the basis of what they call their "conditions of significance":

> These conditions embody the hierarchy of interpretive values, or weightings, of a community or of an individual. They are not, as some critics have thought, identical to the whole of the interpretive system itself. Rather, they are the conditions that, for each genre of a text, define the relationships of texts to the values of the reader or of the community as a whole. (20)

We seek to differentiate miscomprehension that results from incompetence and disagreement that results from disparate conditions of significance. Failure to understand an author's intention may result when conditions relevant to meaning are ignored, missed, or simply unknown by an interpreter. Two people may accept the same conditions of significance, but one might simply be incompetent to make cogent decisions.[12] This is not just disagreement, but a breakdown in the interpretive system. We previously noted a number of reasons why an interpretation might fail. They involved the inability to make judgments concerning relevant-to-meaning conditions. But an inability to understand and disagreement regarding the correct interpretation are not the same thing. Disagreement can be attributed to one of two scenarios:

> 1. People who accept predominantly the same conditions of relevance give different weights to various conditions. Thus, their interpretations vary according to the way those particular conditions influence the overall interpretation.

> 2. The sets of conditions of relevance employed by two people are themselves radically different. Consequently, interpretation derives not sim-

---

[12] Using Goffman's terminology, we might say that two people frame things in the same manner, but one is unable to employ the rules encompassed by the frame chosen. This is frequently the case when an event or document elicits strong emotional reactions.

ply from different weightings, but from distinctly different conceptualizations of the event or text under consideration.[13]

In the first scenario, ambiguities natural to language and its many cultural contexts may make complete agreement impossible; but all interpretations that result from different weightings of predominantly the same conditions of relevance will occupy a continuum that exhibits the conceptual relatedness of the various interpretations. That is, two interpretations that result from different weightings of the same conditions of relevance will nonetheless appear conceptually related. On the other hand, when the sets of conditions of relevance maintained by interpreters are predominantly different, one senses such a profound disjunction in the character of the interpretations that there might appear to be very little hope for useful discourse.

Two illustrations might help us concretize the way varying conditions of relevance result in disparate interpretations. Many scholars have drawn attention to the ways in which Judaism has been framed in scholarly discourse according to Christian historical and theological preferencings. The vocabulary of western theology is, by and large, Christian in its origins. The artificiality of employing contemporary theological language in describing ancient biblical or rabbinic beliefs is usually overlooked, simply because the discordance between the preference rules of the ancient world and those of the modern world is never sensed. The modern scholar abrogates ambiguity in the interest of semantic and philosophical stability.[14]

But a similar kind of clash can be seen within Judaism, such as when the factors of prophetic revelation are deemed irrelevant by rabbinic hermeneutics. A blatant example of this is found in an often cited passage in the Babylonian Talmud (*Baba Metzia* 59b). A halakhic dispute is described in which Rabbi Eliezer alone supports one position while the entire rabbinic assembly is sided against him. To sway the beliefs of the audience, R. Eliezer calls upon divine proof through various forms of miracles and, eventually, a direct communication from God. The heavenly dispatch goes so far as to say, "Why

---

[13] For instance, in contemporary literary criticism there are those who do not believe authorial intent to be at all significant when interpreting, and there are others, such as E. D. Hirsch, who believe that interpretation which does not assume authorial intent as a fundamental condition is not interpretation at all, but "authorship" (Hirsch 1976, 49).

[14] See Levenson 1993b; Neusner 1988c, introduction, discussing Montefiore, Moore, and Urbach, among others.

do you dispute with R. Eliezer, seeing that in all matters the hala-
kah agrees with him!" At that moment, Rabbi Joshua rises and
rebukes the revelatory process by citing a biblical verse, "It is not in
heaven" (Deut 30:12), meaning that in matters of interpretation, the
sages pay no heed to heavenly voices. The passage constitutes an
exposition on relevance theory but ironically twists the most common weightings of natural language (where authorial intent is among
the most prominent of conditions) for the weightings of a theology
(in this case, a language-game that ignores authorial intent—specifically, God's original legal intent). The rabbinic process of ascribing meaning to the biblical text is founded upon the notion that there
are conditions of relevance that are preferred over authorial intent.
Thus, we have here a conscious reframing of the biblical text, one
that makes explicit how certain conditions are to be factored into
the act of interpreting.

Since we are dealing with a gradient continuum and not a list of
necessary or sufficient conditions, it is difficult to establish just *how
many* conditions of relevance must be shared for interpretations to
be close, or at least conceptually related. This is to say that the
measure of "predominance" will shift depending upon the character of the issues under consideration and the weightings of the conditions of relevance that are held in common by interpreters. The
issue of how different the variables must be before we identify two
distinct interpretive communities is itself a gradient judgment. That
people within a single domain might still disagree when it comes to
the meaning of a text points to the fact that their weighting of different typicality conditions vary. Just because two people do not agree
on an interpretation does not mean that they belong to discrete interpretive communities. Because the community does not have necessary and sufficient conditions for defining itself, but only gradient
more-or-less conditions, it is altogether understandable why disagreements regarding the strength or weakness of interpretations exist.

But the case in the talmudic text just discussed does not involve
a variation in weightings. The conflict between R. Eliezer and R.
Joshua (who represents the majority view) arises from such distinct
approaches to meaning that we can confidently say the two men were
members of distinct interpretive communities. In this case, a single
condition—divine revelation, the very condition of relevance that has
almost exclusive prominence in R. Eliezer's hermeneutic—is rejected
by the Joshua camp as irrelevant to meaning. What makes the

instance so noteworthy is the fact that the talmudic exposition is so explicitly focused on those aspects that separate the distinct paths to meaning.

Sometimes, rather than being pushed away by disagreement, one may be lulled toward another interpretive community by virtue of the appeal of its significantly different weighting of various conditions. This is the whole purpose of scholarly discourse. We engage in the promotion of a particular weighting of certain conditions (certain approximations) in contrast to another person's weighting. This does not mean that in cases when indeterminacy is high, we can always articulate what it is we find attractive in a given argument. However, it does mean that, consciously or not, when we accept an interpretation (an argument for a certain meaning) we are basically accepting the weighting of typicality conditions offered by the proponent of the argument.[15] Of course, the *amount of agreement* reached within a given speech community is not indicative of an interpretation's verity.

Most of us are able to occupy multiple interpretive communities, not only at various points in our lives but even simultaneously. Those of us working in the academic discipline of religion witness this fact frequently—in colleagues, if not in ourselves. The words of the Amidah or the Sermon on the Mount or the ninety-nine names of Allah are all factors in a scholar's attempt to write the history of religious belief, but they may become meaningful in an altogether different sense in the synagogue, church, or mosque for the very same individual. The difference in meaning should be ascribed to humans' ability to segment their lives according to interpretive strategies (i.e., different frames), though, of course, some people do this better than others. We should also recognize that we naturally communicate best with those who are already a part of our interpretive community, or close by, and little meaningful dialogue is possible with those who stand too distant from us.

However, even in those systems of interpretation we utterly reject, we are nonetheless able to distinguish stronger from weaker interpretations on structural grounds. That is to say, an interpretive

---

[15] I do not want to get into the very complex scenario in which different sets of weightings actually result in the same conclusion, just as 6+4 and 5+5 both add up to 10. One could examine this in the political arena, where groups with virtually antithetical principles may share certain political views despite the immense differences in their weightings of factors of relevance.

strategy has its own logic or grammar, and one can learn the grammar of another interpretive community without adopting it as one's own. The importance of this fact should not be overlooked. Empathy is not simply an emotional trait, but an aspect of our cognitive structure. We can manipulate our own framing of contexts in order to better understand, and even master, the meanings of other cultures (which are nothing other than distinct domains), though we ourselves might not originally belong to that domain. This is not only because of our capacity for basic empathy but also because of the non-rigid dividers between domains. Here too, we need to conceptualize domains of meaning as occupying a gradient continuum rather than being separated by impenetrable walls of steel.

These concluding comments all refer to a best-of-all-possible worlds scenario. That is, the optimism that we can master the conditions of significance in disparate speech communities is a gradient optimism and not a misinformed hope for the unattainable. And of course, I am talking about contemporary speech communities—in this case, scholarly discourse—and have not focused exclusively on the question of mastery when it comes to the cultures of antiquity. Admittedly, then, multiple levels are underway in this discussion. There is the question of how scholarly agreement takes place, and then there is the question of how scholarly agreement may relate to truth. But there is an intersection between these two questions, and that is whether scholarly agreement can take place with regard to how much truth is ascertainable. That discussion requires us to step back even further, to question how we go about weighting our weightings. Aspects of this concern will occupy us in the next chapter.

6

METAPHOR AS A GRADIENT JUDGMENT

In previous chapters we spoke of metaphor as a rhetorical device, one founded on a strategy shared by the speaker and the audience. In this chapter, I wish to explore the mechanics of metaphor more closely. My goal here is to expose the underlying cognitive structure that functions when we make decisions regarding literal and nonliteral meanings. By making our thinking patterns explicit, I hope to clarify two stages of our interpretive processes. The first is the way we decide *whether or not we can make a decision* as to what kind of language we are dealing with; the second stage is the actual computational process that decides where on the continuum a given statement falls. I will begin this analysis with a critique of the most influential contemporary theory of metaphor, and then offer an alternative approach.

Metaphor and Gradience

The question of what makes something metaphorical and how we distinguish literal from nonliteral expressions has been the subject of thousands of studies over the past half century.[1] Commonly cited are the works of I. A. Richards that focus on the conception of interactive metaphor, and Max Black and Paul Ricoeur, both of whom build upon many of Richard's insights.[2] But no work has been as influential on biblical scholarship as that of George Lakoff and Mark Johnson, whose short book *Metaphors We Live By* (1980) is cited with unparalleled frequency. Lakoff expanded his theory of metaphor into the realm of literary criticism more directly with Mark

---

[1] See Shibles 1971, which lists more than four thousand titles; for titles after 1970, see Noppen, Knop and Jongen 1985 and Noppen and Hols 1990.

[2] See Richards 1936; Black 1962, 1979a/b; Ricoeur 1970, 1974, 1976, 1977, 1978. See Mac Cormac 1985 on linking metaphor to our cognitive structure, as well as Kittay 1987. For an overview of metaphor theory and its application to biblical scholarship, see Korpel 1990.

Turner in *More Than Cool Reason: A Field Guide to Poetic Metaphor* (1989).
The fundamental ideas of these two works are accessible and easily
applicable, which is no doubt partially responsible for the immense
impact they have had on numerous disciplines. Few historians of
religion, however, have actually scrutinized the validity of their
concepts.[3] I shall offer here a consideration of the thesis presented
in both Lakoff and Johnson and Lakoff and Turner. The concept
of metaphor in both of these works is identical, though there are some
differences in terminology. The critique that follows will treat the
two books as a theoretical unit, to be referred to as the Lakoff-
Johnson-Turner Thesis (LJTT).[4]

Lakoff and Johnson argue that "primarily on the basis of linguistic evidence we have found that most of our ordinary conceptual
system is metaphorical in nature" (1980, 4).[5] They continue:

> The most important claim we have made so far is that metaphor is
> not just a matter of language, that is, of mere words. We shall argue
> that, on the contrary, human *thought processes* are largely metaphorical.
> This is what we mean when we say that the human conceptual sys-
> tem is metaphorically structured and defined. Metaphors as linguistic
> expressions are possible precisely because there are metaphors in a
> person's conceptual system. (4-6, emphasis original)

Because the LJTT equates metaphor with a cognitive process, the
authors proclaim that "it could be the case that every word or phrase
in a language is defined at least in part metaphorically" (1989, 119).
Despite the qualifier "it could be the case," one gets the impression

---

[3] This is the case despite the methodological rigor applied in other fields tan-
gential to the study of religion. See, for instance, Howard Eilberg-Schwartz's extensive consideration of biblical metaphors in *The Savage in Judaism* (1990). The author
spends almost a third of his book discussing anthropological theory. However, because
"the concept of metaphor led to a reconceptualization of the entire question of
totemism" (117), a consideration of metaphor is central to the book's purpose. When
it comes to setting the stage for treating metaphor as a subject, only one work is
cited: "Recent theoretical and ethnographic literature has shown that metaphor
not only infuses thought but that language itself is metaphoric at its root (Lakoff
and Johnson 1980)." This position goes unquestioned.

[4] Many of my comments here will parallel concerns expressed in Jackendoff
and Aaron (1991).

[5] This work is virtually devoid of footnotes referencing other scholarship; its
bibliography cites a mere twelve works. I believe Julian Jaynes (1976, chap. 2), as
a non-linguist, completely anticipates Lakoff and Johnson in maintaining that
metaphor is what allows for the expansion of language and understanding in general. But also, see Paul Ricoeur's extensive work on the subject (e.g., 1976 and
1979).

from these books that this principle is a basic assumption in the LJTT: human thought processes, and consequently all complex word meaning, are essentially metaphorical (yet another example of a convergence algorithm). The cognitive process is one that transfers the meaning of one term to another: "The essence of metaphor is understanding and experiencing one kind of thing in terms of another" (1980, 5). This is true of all metaphorical expressions: conventional, poetic, figurative, and literal. Metaphor, as built into our conceptual structure, allows us to *express* and *understand* one thing in terms of another thing.

The LJTT treats metaphor as the mapping of conceptual organization from one domain, the *source domain,* to another, the *target domain.*[6] Elements of the source domain are usually expressed in a text, whereas the target domain may or may not be explicitly there. Even so, the target domain is what the metaphor is really about.[7] For example, in Shakespeare's phrase "All the world's a stage,"[8] the source domain is the conceptualization of the theater, as evoked by the term "stage"; the target domain is life in general, as evoked by "all the world." According to Lakoff and Johnson, each metaphor of this sort can be sloganized into a simpler nominal-predicative sentence. In this case, the authors suggest LIFE IS A PLAY. In both *Metaphors We Live By* and *More Than Cool Reason,* numerous examples of basic or generic metaphors are provided: ARGUMENT IS WAR, TIME IS MONEY, HAPPY IS UP, SAD IS DOWN, UNDERSTANDING IS SEEING, LOVE IS A JOURNEY, and so forth.[9]

According to the LJTT, permeating our language are these generic or basic metaphors, upon which yet more complex expressions

---

[6] Varying uses of the word "domain" in this study were unavoidable. The reader is already familiar with it from the previous chapter. The sense here is fundamentally the same, but the perspective has shifted. In the previous chapter we were speaking about domains in terms of large groups of interpretive rules—cultures, areas of discourse, communities of discourse, etc. Here the LJTT looks upon each family of concepts, perhaps, as a separate domain. One might think of the "domain" in the previous chapter as a macro-analysis, whereas the LJTT is concerned with a micro-analysis.

[7] There are various terms used for the different parts of metaphors, each with some unique characteristics, but ultimately, they refer to the same structural elements. Richards (1936, 23) speaks of the "tenor" and the "vehicle." Black (1962, 28f.) speaks of the "focus" and the "frame." Ricoeur (1978) discusses the "metaphier" and the "metaphrand." Lakoff and Johnson do not discuss the need for their terminology against the backdrop of the terminology developed by others.

[8] *As You Like It,* act 2, scene 7.

[9] These conceptual building blocks, or basic metaphors, are always represented in uppercase letters in their work; the same convention will be adopted here.

are based. Indeed, "metaphors are so commonplace we often fail to notice them" (1989, 1). The authors claim that most "conventional metaphors" have as their source domains "grounded" concepts; these are concepts that are known directly. "We conventionally understand these [grounded] concepts not by virtue of metaphoric mappings between them and different conceptual domains but rather by virtue of their grounding in what we take to be our forms of life, our habitual and routine bodily and social experiences" (1989, 59). Examples of grounded concepts are departures, journeys, plants, fire, sleep, days and nights, heat and cold, possessions, burdens, locations, rocks, trees, arms, and legs. Though grounded concepts are not exclusively derived from physical experiences or states of being, most of them are. Indeed, the authors claim that we "typically conceptualize the nonphysical *in terms of* the physical" (1989, 59). More complex or less conventional metaphors involve clusters of the conventional metaphors. Thus, their complexity is derived from the compound nature of their construction.

One aspect of metaphor is its "ability to *create* structure in our understanding of life" (1989, 62).[10] This occurs when we map the schema of one domain onto another. Consider the metaphor LIFE IS A JOURNEY; Lakoff and Turner explain it as follows:

> The metaphor LIFE IS A JOURNEY is thus a mapping of the structure of the JOURNEY schema onto the domain of LIFE in such a way as to set up the appropriate correspondences between TRAVELER and PERSON LEADING A LIFE, between STARTING POINT and BIRTH, and so on. (1989, 62)

This "mapping" exposes the conceptual activity involved in decoding a metaphor. In the LJTT, metaphor, by mapping otherwise unconnected domains onto one another, can create *new meaning*. Metaphors do this by highlighting certain features while suppressing others, and by allowing for inferences.[11] Metaphors also relate to the

---

[10] Neither Lakoff and Johnson nor Lakoff and Turner make any effort to place their thesis in historical perspective; thus, the unsuspecting reader might think it is altogether original. On the notion of creating new meaning, see Aristotle, *Rhetorica* 1410b,13f. The same thesis is adopted by Mac Cormac 1985.

[11] Lakoff and Johnson actually list five different ways in which metaphor creates new meanings, but three of them are virtually indistinguishable from the point about highlighting or suppressing, and the fifth, which relates to cultural learning and the gaining of knowledge about something unknown, is irrelevant to metaphor (1980, 141-42). There is some improvement on this topic in Lakoff and Turner

truth value of statements. Though the authors reject objectivism explicitly (1980, 159f.), they do not entertain the question of whether a metaphor created by a person who is an objectivist must be interpreted differently. In general, the question of how personal philosophy might influence the metaphoricalness of a statement is not directly addressed. Indeed, the whole issue of authorial intent is ignored.[12]

One of the problems with the books espousing the LJTT is that they unfold through a long string of examples provided by the authors. There is very little description or analysis separate from these examples. For some readers, this may make coming to terms with the central thesis quite easy, because the examples help the thesis appear intuitive; but the lack of close readings leaves the question of the LJTT's validity altogether unexamined. To demonstrate the danger of unscrutinized examples, let us look at one very simple example used by the LJTT, an exposition on the concept IN. Lakoff and Johnson are attempting to demonstrate that IN is a grounded aspect of many metaphorical expressions. They start by listing three common usages:

> Harry is in the kitchen.
> Harry is in the Elks.
> Harry is in love.

> The concept IN of the first sentence emerges directly from spacial experience in a clearly delineated fashion. It is not an instance of a metaphorical concept. The other two sentences, however, are instances of metaphorical concepts. The second is an instance of the SOCIAL GROUPS ARE CONTAINERS metaphor, in terms of which the

---

1989, 67ff., although as Jackendoff and Aaron (1991) note, the whole issue of creativity is problematic. Incidentally, Aristotle wrote (*Rhetorica* 1410b), that when a poet calls old age "a withered stalk," he is indeed conveying something new about old age. Thus, according to Aristotle, the metaphor creates knowledge that otherwise might not be found.

[12] This is especially salient in their chapter on "The Myth of Objectivism and Subjectivism" (chap. 25), where the authors argue that "truth is always relative to a conceptual system, that any human conceptual system is mostly metaphorical in nature, and that, therefore, there is no fully objective, unconditional, or absolute truth" (185). So much for an individual being able to articulate exactly what they mean! It is also relevant that Lakoff and Johnson understand myths to be "like metaphors. . . necessary for making sense of what goes on around us." This particular chapter exhibits a rather binary approach to meaning, as well as a salient lack of awareness of far more sophisticated and nuanced theories of meaning.

concept of a social group is structured.[13] . . . The word "in" and the concept IN are the same in all three examples; we do not have three different concepts of IN or three homophonous words "in." We have one emergent concept IN, one word for it, and two metaphorical concepts that partially define social groups and emotional states.

From the outset we find a problematic notion: that a preposition constitutes a "metaphorical concept." Normally, the metaphorical connotation of a statement emerges from the two (or more) things that are forced into a relationship (usually in an appositional phrase, but not exclusively). By definition, a preposition indicates the relationship between things; but it is the things *brought into relationship* that convey the metaphorical meaning. Thus, the term (here the target) of importance in each instance happens to be a prepositional phrase (in the kitchen, in the Elks, in love), but not the preposition independently.

In most languages, prepositions have an enormous range of connotations, and most are spacial terms, "grounded" in some physical experience.[14] But the notion that a physical definition is *the* grounded one, and that all other meanings are metaphorically derived, is difficult to defend. By establishing an essential (i.e., grounded) concept of "in," the authors have determined that *only* the grounded concept is original, or basic; all other uses are nonoriginal, nonbasic, and therefore metaphorical.[15] With prepositions, most of which are, in some sense, spacial, the approach seems intuitive. But for more complex terms, establishing which meaning is grounded becomes a problematic endeavor. For instance, did the concept BECOME originate in the realm of space ("He became big") or in some cognitive domain ("He became smart") or the domain of states-of-being ("He became well")? How about terms of possession where it is difficult to see any relationship between spacial, conceptual, or event-related verbs. For example: "I kept the book on the shelf" (spacial); "I kept the money," or "I kept thinking about her" (conceptual, see Jackendoff 1983, chap. 10). Indeed, these ambiguities can be found

---

[13] The full classification of "Harry is in love" is conspicuously missing from the summary. One would assume that EMOTIONS ARE CONTAINERS must also underlie this "metaphor."

[14] Of course, not all languages use prepositions, so the focus of the LJTT is too specific here to the English structure.

[15] Similarly, see Lakoff 1987 on the word "over," (416-461), but especially on the metaphorical senses, 435ff.

in every category of our lexicon—verbs, nouns, prepositions, etc. The LJTT engages us in a somewhat hopeless regression for "first meanings" or grounded experiences.[16] While the authors admit that not everything is grounded in spacial concepts, they argue that *most* things are. Even if the philologist were somehow able to accomplish the impossible historical research of determining the groundedness of concepts, there is nothing to indicate that every person will learn a particular word usage first. What if some philologist proves that "keep" is grounded in a spacial-possession experience ("keep the book on the shelf"), but I can show that my son first heard KEEP as a temporal-event experience, "Do you want me to keep singing?" For my son, is "keep the book on the shelf" the metaphorical usage, or is "keep singing" the metaphor derived from the grounded sense? Such an inquiry is useless, and tells us nothing about metaphor itself.

Eve Sweetser has discussed the etymologies of "metaphors of perception," adopting the LJTT outright. She happens to provide an example of a grounded concept as it appears in Tanakh. She notes that the root meaning "hear" (שׁמע, shəma‘) "is used to mean 'obey' or 'understand' or 'listen/heed,' and in fact is often translated into English by one of these other English words" (1990, 42f.). For Sweetser, the word שׁמע, when used to mean "understand," is being employed metaphorically.[17] "It is probably the case," Sweetser concludes,

> that hearing is universally connected with the internal as well as the external aspects of speech reception. Inasmuch as speech is the communication of information or of other matter for the intellect, hearing as well as sight is connected with intellectual processing. It is thus not surprising that "I see" should mean "I understand," but that Fr[ench] *entendre* "hear" should also etymologically be connected with understanding. (43)

Let us consider the logic of this argument. In citing Gen 11:7, Sweetser maintains that the phrase "so that they may not *understand* each other's speech" is a correct but metaphorical rendering of the Hebrew לא ישׁמעו אישׁ שׁפת רעהו. Sweetser adds:

> This is God speaking, in the Tower of Babel story. He is not intend-
> ing to stop their hearing by affecting their ears, but rather their inter-
> nal "hearing"—understanding—by confusing their language. But the
> Hebrew text has the verb "hear." (43)

This explanation, typical of explanations that employ the LJTT, is
tautological. The Hebrew does not have "the verb 'hear'"; the
Hebrew has the verb שמע. The fact that some lexicologist decided
to make "hear" the chronologically primary meaning of שמע is an
accident of history, not an etymological fact. The word שמע as a lexical item should not be defined as "hear" exclusively; and its *wordfield*, as Wittgenstein called it, should not be identified as a set of
"metaphors." The word שמע means "understand," just as the word
ראה sometimes means "understand"; these are not instances of metaphor, they are instances of wordfield extension. The fact that cognitive processes are associated with the perception of stimuli only
speaks to the fact that human beings intuited that epistemological-
ly, sight and hearing are identical to certain cognitive functions. That
Sweetser bifurcates intellectual "understanding" from perceptual
"hearing" is perhaps informative, but ultimately arbitrary. The Hebrew quite specifically does not bifurcate these two "meanings"; the
ancient Israelite would engage an assessment of typicality conditions
so as to derive the meaning of שמע in each and every instance.[18] There
is no basis for insisting that שמע "originally" meant "hear," to the
exclusion of an array of other connotations that are conveyed by it
in biblical Hebrew.

The error made by Sweetser is identical in form to that made by
the LJTT when discussing IN. "Harry is in the Elks" does not indicate a metaphor of "containment," but rather containment in a literal sense. If the Elks is a group, then one can very *literally* identify
its confines (they meet at such and such a place, have thirty-nine
members who have lunch together at Mel's Diner on Thursdays, and
they support the following charities, etc.). My sense is that the concept of "membership" would turn out to be one of those concepts
which does have at least one necessary condition, namely, falling
within predetermined limits (for instance, those who pay dues and
those who do not). The grounded meaning of "in" might simply be
defined as "a preposition that situates a subject A within the defini-

---

[18] Consider Jackendoff on the verb "see" (1983, chap. 8).

tional limits of B, whether B be a physically, intellectually, or temporally defined thing."

Another problem with the LJTT is the intersection within metaphor of literal and figurative language. According to the authors, "Harry is in love" and "Harry is in the kitchen" are both literal, despite the fact that one statement is a metaphor and the other is not. To deal with this problem, the authors note that conventional metaphors and nonmetaphorical statements (simple sentences) are understood as true or false in the same way. "The only difference is that metaphorical projection involves understanding one kind of thing in terms of another kind of thing. That is, metaphorical projection involves two different kinds of things, while nonmetaphorical projection involves only one kind" (1980, 171). As it turns out, nonconventional metaphors (they are the "creative" or "new" metaphors) present no added interpretive problem, because all new metaphors are themselves made coherent by their underlying generic metaphors. By breaking the new metaphors into their conceptual parts, one ends up decoding a series of conventional metaphors. According to the LJTT, what differentiates literary from nonliterary (i.e., generic) metaphors is the newness; and newness, in turn, defines the degree of creativity. The more a metaphor is used, the more "generic" it becomes.

How, then, do we know what a person believes when a statement is uttered? If a person says, "Harry is in love," there is no inclination to doubt it. Yet when Brettler read the statement "God is King," he decided there was reason to doubt it, for according to Brettler, this is not literal speech, it is metaphor.[19] In this case, the literal truth value of the statement is questioned, while in the other case ("Harry is in love"), the literal truth value is accepted outright. As noted, I believe Brettler made an incorrect judgment: both statements, "Harry is in love" and "God is King" are equally literal, and I maintain that neither are metaphorical.

A number of times in the LJTT, the authors disparage the charge that they have simply redefined metaphor. They are right to be sensitive to this issue. We have already noted in passing that their definition of metaphor is ultimately functionless in the hands of either the literary exegete or the philologist; moreover, I believe it

---

[19] In this way, Brettler broke out of the LJTT theory, though I am not sure he saw the implications of his methodology with respect to the LJTT's concept of metaphorical meaning.

distorts reality. The LJTT basically extends the concept too far. By defining metaphor as an aspect of conceptual structure, the authors rob us of important tools for differentiating subtle nuances in language *usage*, as well as cognition. Consider it similar to having only one word for all living things. What the LJTT has labelled "metaphor" is nothing other than what linguists for some time have discussed as instances of lexical extension, the very essence of how words can expand their semantic fields. But this is a matter of choice, not conceptual structure. We do not need to have metaphor in any given expression, and there are many instances in which we actively forbid it (such as the legal profession and other professional domains). Frequently idioms arise, neologisms are formed, which have nothing whatever to do with metaphor.[20] The fact that there is a great deal of metaphorical speech has to do with how a culture tolerates or even encourages this type of linguistic development. But the LJTT fundamentally confuses a variety of possible choices with one overarching conceptual issue, which they call metaphor.

This tendency may derive from the common pattern of bifurcating language into metaphorical and nonmetaphorical speech. I suggest that a gradient approach will reveal a much greater variety of linguistic and cognitive phenomena. To define all instances of semantic accretion (the expansion of a word's possible meanings) as literal and nonliteral "metaphor" is fundamentally a redefinition of the term. What makes semantic accretion possible is best explained in terms of conceptul structure and our ability to abstract functional and structural similarities between objects or actions. I do not mean to deny that we learn by comparing one experience with another, but "metaphor" should be saved for a more distinctive rhetorical

---

[20] Consider the origins of the term "kick the bucket," meaning to die. We might think of this as a metaphorical idiom, but several hypotheses as to its origin point to very literal circumstances. One etymology derives from the practice of farmers who, when leaving the farm for an extended period, would leave an animal tethered to a post or beam with a bucket of food sufficient to last until the owner returned; if the animal were to kick the bucket, scattering the food out of reach, it would starve to death. Another refers to a man standing on an upturned bucket preparing to hang himself, which he accomplishes by kicking the bucket from under his feet. Yet another version, also agrarian in origin, suggests the fate of a cow that, while being milked, kicks the milk bucket over, enraging the farmer. None of these derivations is the least bit metaphorical. See *The Shorter Oxford English Dictionary on Historical Principles*, 2 vols. (Oxford: Oxford University, 1973) 1:246, "bucket," sb.[2]; and the *Dictionary of American Slang* (New York: Crowell, 1960) ad loc.

strategy, one that involves a process of decoding and mapping.[21] Thus, my rejection of the LJTT has to do with the fact that it treats the continuum as a single set of fundamentally indistinguishable kinds of speech acts.

Incongruity and the Continuum of Meaning

Metaphor, like all concepts, must be understood as a series of points on a line understood to represent the gradient continuum of meaning. Figure 1 contains a single graph line, which is shaded from white to black in a graded manner. The words below the graph line connote degrees of ambiguity, while above the graph line are words connoting types of meaning. "Ambiguity" is a general term for an array of more specific kinds of fuzziness. For instance, semantic fuzziness exists when particular lexical items cannot be clearly understood; syntactic fuzziness derives from a lack of stability in sentence structure. The words above the line represent types of meaning that start with simple, very stable binaries and move farther to the right to include literal meaning, conceptual ascriptions, simile and its close relative, simple metaphors.[22] Moving toward the right we encounter expressions employing higher degrees of ambiguity, such as more intense metaphors, irony, sarcasm and other forms of speech which involve varying degrees of incongruity. At the extreme right lies obscurity and then nonsense; types of statements whose ambiguity is so great that meaning cannot be ascertained. We have already noted that some religions make ready use of statements which most of us would define as nonsense, by interpreting and insisting on their (usually hidden) meanings. Thus, we must accept that paradoxes and other kinds of statements which confound our ability to make sense of the conditions of relevance can fit into a semantic rubric, but never as "literal" speech.

---

[21] While I would not insist that this process be conscious, I would argue that the more intense (or complex) the metaphor, the more conscious the thinking process turns out to be. But this is precisely because I am approaching consciousness as that aspect of our cognitive structure that solves the conundrums of ambiguity— regardless of the cognitive domain. See Jackendoff 1987.

[22] Aristotle differentiates a simile from a metaphor on the basis of the former's nonappositional character, adding, "and just because it is longer it is less attractive." Thus, for Aristotle, the structural character influences the aesthetic value. I would add that the syntax of simile, being nonappositional, involves less incongruity and, therefore, more stability. (*Rhetorica* 1410b,15)

The judgment that a statement is metaphorical or ascriptive should be viewed as one of those judgments of gradience similar to that experienced when we put our hand in warm water from a tap and wait for it to become hot. Rather than search for sharp demarcations which ascribe to necessary conditions, we must endeavor to understand a continuum. The process must start with our understanding of individual words. The preference rules we use in making judgments about word meaning are also in effect with regard to larger syntactic units. We have seen that judgments about word meaning can occur only in the context of a broader syntactic unit. Thus, what pushes us from one point on the continuum toward another point must be embedded in the very nature of our decoding of the individual words in their relationship to the larger relational structures of a statement. These judgments are not linear in nature; judgments regarding the meanings of indiviual terms are constantly in flux as we integrate more and more of the discrete linguistic units and other relevant conditions that contribute to the meaning of a statement. We constantly adjust our framing of each constituent of a statement, seeking specific meanings at the micro level (words) and overall coherence at the macro level (the full statement in context). Were we to try to map out this process, our best tool might be a multidimensional diagram—similar to one plotting three dimensions in space and one in time—which would allow for simultaneous (or near-simultaneous) computations as well as sequential ones. At some point, we say that we either can or cannot understand a given statement—that is, we do or do not attain a degree of confidence in our assessment of its semantic stability.

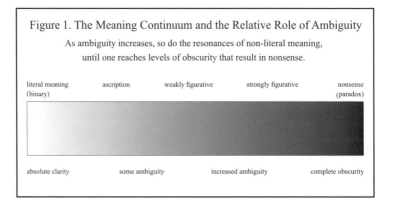

Figure 1. The Meaning Continuum and the Relative Role of Ambiguity

As ambiguity increases, so do the resonances of non-literal meaning,
until one reaches levels of obscurity that result in nonsense.

| literal meaning (binary) | ascription | weakly figurative | strongly figurative | nonsense (paradox) |

| absolute clarity | some ambiguity | increased ambiguity | complete obscurity |

Aristotle found the role of incongruity to be central to all metaphorical statements. His discussion of metaphor in the *Rhetorica*
(1410b,28) takes place in the context of considering the different functions of "antithesis" in statements. The conceptual sequence is described as "antithesis, metaphor, and actuality." Regarding the aesthetic appeal of metaphor, Aristotle states that it is actually the
antithetical form and character of a statement that appeals to us.
Many scholars since Aristotle have devised terminologies and approaches to the role of tension in metaphorical statements.[23] Ricoeur,
summarizing Beardsley, describes it as follows: "Incompatibility is a
conflict between designations at the primary level of meaning, which
forces the reader to extract from the complete context of connotations the secondary meanings capable of making a 'meaningful self-
contradictory attribution' from a self-contradictory statement" (1977,
95). Were we to take "All the world's a stage" literally, we would be
struck by the anomaly. In decoding the anomaly, we think to ourselves: "What do you mean? The world is *not* a stage!" In this case,
the incongruity is apparent to the interpreter of the phrase, perhaps
by virtue of the great disparity between the images of "world" and
"stage." Consequently, the literal meaning is abandoned and a
metaphorical meaning is sought.

I do not mean to oversimplify the problem of establishing incongruity. Ricoeur provides a comprehensive summary of the scholarship on the question, and I see no reason to rehearse that here.[24]
As I am placing metaphor on a continuum, incongruity is simply
derived from the ease or lack of ease with which a subject can accept the identity conveyed in a predicational statement. The cognitive process naturally suffers a certain amount of indeterminacy, and

---

[23] Ricoeur (1977, 18) uses the word "paradox" to describe the semantic tension. The incongruity takes place between the two halves of the predicative statement, what Lakoff and Turner call the "source domain" and the "target domain."
See Black 1962 on "misapprehension", Beardsley (1958, 139) on "self-contradictory attribution"; Traugott and Pratt (1980, 207ff.) speak of anomaly. Jean Cohen
(1966, 106ff.) writes about the process of seeking to validate the identity of a
predicational phrase despite the logical tension caused by the underlying incongruity. Cohen argues that metaphor emerges out of our attempts to connect the
two objects of the predicational clause, despite their lack of identity. There may be
slight differences in the connotations of these various terms. I am not invested in
the superiority of one set of terms over another set, but for the sake of clarity I
shall stick to using "incongruity" and now and again "anomaly" as indicative of
the tension in predicational phrases that cause one to seek metaphorical meaning.

[24] See Ricouer 1977, 5ff.; also Kittay 1987, 64ff.

in doing that, we can assume a computational process which allows ambiguity to be "measured." If we hear someone say, "My wife is a woman," we do not sense any deviance in what we might call "expected" meaning with regard to the predication. However, if we hear someone say, "My wife is a washing machine," we find ourselves computing the variety of typicality conditions acceptable for "wife" and then cross-referencing the typicality conditions acceptable for "washing machine." The fact that the typicality conditions for both of these concepts are now "strained" when they are juxtaposed indicates incongruence. Where one goes with that incongruence—that is, how one decodes the metaphor—will depend upon the way one assesses the variety of conditions determined to be relevant to the decoding process.[25]

Incongruence, which derives basically from our failure to find within the expected domain of typicality conditions acceptable meaning, is itself gradient.[26] There are instances when incongruity

---

[25] Notice that is it unclear whether the metaphor means to communicate something about the man's attitude toward his wife, or something about his wife's activities independent of his attitudes, and so forth. We should also note that the phrase "my wife is a woman" may be using its terms with irony (another form of nonliteral speech). "Woman" could simply be a term identifying gender (and hence the phrase would be literal); but the term could also have innuendos that move beyond the literal connotation of "female." Consider the tongue-in-cheek idiom that was in circulation a short time ago, "Real men don't eat quiche." The phrase, "My husband is a *man*," in the sense of "a *real* man" (whatever that is supposed to mean), certainly does not intend to identify the gender of the man in some literal sense. This particular meaning could be intended with regard to a woman as well. Moreover, if the context of such a statement were same-sex marriages, the intention might indeed be irony or opposition: "Well, as for me, *my* wife is a woman!" Most of the phrases we confront in Scriptures are relatively simple. Extended metaphors or allegories appear mostly in the literary prophets and concern social circumstances rather than divine imagery (with notable exceptions, such as the groom-bride imagery in Hosea and Jeremiah).

[26] While I am not offering a full critique of Lakoff and Johnson's discussion of Western Objectivism (1980, chap. 26), it should be understood that my approach here is not that of objectivism, nor that of Lakoff and Johnson. The introduction of "gradience" into a theory of meaning allows us to account for concepts of truth as being both object-based and dependent upon human subjectivity. Lakoff and Johnson argue that the only objectivity we can legitimately speak of is "a kind of objectivity relative to the conceptual system of a culture" (1980, 193). Such a belief system would suggest that there is no correlation between our neurological perceptions and the material world around us, except insofar as culture allows us to conceptualize that material world. Throughout this work, I have endeavored to create a more appropriate approach to meaning; one which is grounded in the realities of life, which I believe are not culture-dependent, and the realities of human interpretive strategies, which are the result of learned behaviors and meta-cultural neurological structures.

is extremely subtle and involves hardly any adjustment in our assessment of typicality conditions. This may be the case when metaphor derives from an overstatement. The following verse from Robert Frost can serve as an example:

Two roads diverged in a wood, and I—
I took the one less traveled by,
And that has made all the difference.[27]

Incongruity is signaled by the phrase *all the difference*. If the poem had read as follows

Two roads diverged in a wood, and I—
I took the one less traveled by,
And that made a difference

a metaphorical effect would be lost. Had Frost written the second rendition of the verse, we might easily have imagined a person walking along in the woods and making a decision about which path to follow. But "all the difference" subtly forces us to take this divergence, this less-traveled path, out of the realm of walks and woods, and to find meaning in it regarding life generally and its significance as an altering factor.

Theorists offer an array of solutions as to how we conceptually go about identifying and interpreting incongruity. Some have suggested that an author uses a literally false or incongruous expression in order to indicate that they mean something else. That is, the falseness triggers a response which causes the reader/hearer to begin decoding for meaning that is other than literal.[28] To put it in terms of relevance theory: an interpreter starts with the assumptions that an utterance is meant literally, until something causes the interpreter to recognize that the literal meaning is not identical with the speaker's intent (Sperber and Wilson 1986, 234). As such, the metaphor is taken to be a particular kind of speech act, one that involves a clash between the intent of the speaker and the character of an expression.

The traditional insight about literal anomaly is worth preserving. In an earlier study, Ray Jackendoff and I worked out a rough diagnostic for detecting the presence of incongruity in statements (Jack-

---

[27] From "The Road Not Taken," in *Collected Poems of Robert Frost* (New York: Henry Holt, 1939), 131.
[28] See Davidson 1979; Sadock 1979; Searle 1979; Lappin 1981; Fernandez 1974; Kittay 1987.

endoff and Aaron 1991). The diagnostic does nothing other than make overt one's underlying interpretive process, in the simplest terms. To accomplish this, we took the basic slogans that Lakoff and Turner claimed to be metaphors and employed them in conjunction with a more complex statement. Recognizing that shared strategy can affect even what appear to be simple literal statements, I am asking the reader to assume sincerity and simplicity on the part of the writer for the purpose of working this exercise. With that as our context, let us work through these basic claims and then I will reintroduce the issue of shared strategy more cogently.

For the general slogan A RELATIONSHIP IS A JOURNEY, we analyzed the statement "Our relationship is at a dead end"; for the slogan MACHINES ARE PEOPLE we considered the expression "My computer died on me." This is how the diagnostic works:

(a) A RELATIONSHIP IS A JOURNEY
(b) Our relationship is at a dead end.
(c) Of course, relationships are not really journeys—but if they were, you might say ours is at a dead end.

(a) MACHINES ARE PEOPLE
(b) My computer died on me.
(c) Of course, computers are not people—but if they were, you might say mine has died on me.

In each case, the (c) statement constitutes the cognitive procedure for decoding the incongruity. Recognizing that the simple predicational statement of (a) underlies the metaphor of (b), the first part of (c) acknowledges the incongruity of mapping what Lakoff and Turner call the *source* domain onto the *target* domain. The logic is overtly expressed as follows:

> Since relationships *are not* journeys, when "journey ideas" are used regarding relationships, one must be speaking about change in terms of movement in relationships. Ergo: the statement is metaphorical.

> Since machines *are not* people, when "people ideas" are used regarding machines, one must be speaking about some behavior or event in a machine which is like one expected of people. Ergo: the statement is metaphorical.[29]

---

[29] I recognize that "people" need not have been the source domain here, since

To demonstrate the diagnostic further, we employed as an example a sentence that did not contain any incongruity on the surface (again, assuming a basic shared strategy on the part of the interlocutors). The example is based on a personification of animals that is specifically parallel to the personification of machines used above.

(a) ANIMALS ARE PEOPLE
(b) My dog ran down the street.
(c) Of course, animals are not people—but if they were, you might say my dog ran down the street.

Statement (c) strikes one as a nonsequitur. Everyone acknowledges that personification engages metaphors that fall into the domain ANIMALS ARE PEOPLE, but since running is not a uniquely *human* characteristic, any attempt to give this expression a hypothetical reading, as in the "but if" clause in (c), provides us with an absurdity. Consider the following:

> Since dogs *are not* people, when "people ideas" are used regarding dogs, one must be speaking about some behavior or quality of a dog that is like one expected of people, and that is not also characteristic of dogs.

This proves to be a good definition of personification, but what if "running" is substituted for "people ideas." This is now absurd. "Running" is not exclusively a "people idea," but applicable to most creatures with legs. Indeed, running comes originally from a word describing a quality of liquids rather than vertebrates, the essential meaning of which connotes quick movement. To be sure, humans and dogs run differently, but one does not conceptualize "running" in a dog any differently from "running" in a human. Thus the statement "my dog ran down the street" must be literal. One might charge that we have identified the wrong generic underlying metaphor in this instance; but I cannot find another one that results in a different conclusion.

As it turns out, running has several equally primary connotations that make it rather banal to speak of a grounded notion that underlies subsequent metaphors. Consider an automotive engine.

"died" could relate to any living organism. Thus, the (a) statement of this example might simply have read,"machines are living organisms." However, since computers are quite frequently referred to as "thinking" in human terms, I thought this would probably serve as the dominant source for computer metaphors.

(a) MACHINES ARE PEOPLE
(b) My car [engine] is running well today.
(c) Of course, machines are not people—but if they were, you might say that my car is running well today.

The LJTT would have this as a metaphor, albeit a common or generic metaphor. The problem is that in English we do not even have another term for what the engine does when the car is functioning (steadily). Is this an instance of polysemy? Hardly. All of the various usages of "running" (running feet, running water, running for office, etc.) relate in one way or another to movement. None of these usages constitute metaphor.

The Problem of Cultural Context and Mistaken Metaphors

It almost goes without saying that a greater percentage of interpretational failures occur when the subject is an ancient literature. In biblical studies, there may be an unavoidable circularity to the majority of our judgments. If we have 150 phrases that appear to be personifications, how can we go about making decisions for each one independently of the others, all of which should also be in question? Schauber and Spolsky's remarks regarding reader competence and culture are insightful:

> Like any other social institution, the institution of literature is embedded in the larger culture that is its context, and changes in the preference rules for literary genres cannot be independent of changes in the larger culture. Readers' competence in drawing inferences outside literary texts is therefore part of their sensitivity to understanding changes in the purpose or effects of genre, or to what might be called new genres. In theory, the experienced reader has sufficient competence for all the literature he or she reads. In practice, the competence of even experienced readers is limited to a partial set of subsystems, and only readers who are familiar with a particular subsystem can really interpret innovations within it. (1987, 82-83)

Our interpretive competence is ultimately commensurate with our grasp of the culture and language of a work's era of composition, especially aspects of that culture which are external to the literature (body language, colloquial usages, distribution of terms according to class or educational divisions, scientific knowledge, and so forth).

One's cultural and linguistic distance from a work's origin will inevitably contribute to interpretive problems. There will always remain a higher degree of uncertainty (or instability) regarding texts that derive from outside of one's own time and place. The following examples endeavor to illustrate how misjudgments might be made without some necessary pieces of information in place.

Taking Lakoff and Turner's cognitive domain LIFE IS FLUID IN THE BODY; DEATH IS LOSS OF FLUID (1989, 19), let us contrast a biblical phrase with a verse composed by W. H. Auden. The test looks like this:

(a) LIFE IS FLUID IN THE BODY; DEATH IS LOSS OF FLUID
(b) Vaguely life leaks away.[30]
(c) Of course, life is not a fluid—but if it were, then one might say it vaguely leaks away.

(a) LIFE IS FLUID IN THE BODY; DEATH IS LOSS OF FLUID
(b) For the life of a being is in the blood. (Lev 17:11)
(c) Of course, life is not a fluid—but if it were, then one might say it is in the blood.

There are some who might be tempted to read both of these phrases metaphorically; however, given what we know about the belief system of the ancient Israelites, who very literally attributed physical and psychic functions to different organs of the body (strict materialists), the phrase "the life of a being is in the blood" turns out to be quite literal.[31] On the other hand, regarding Auden's verse, (c) proves quite satisfying as an explanation for Auden's image of a slow gradual deterioration and ultimate demise. In the first case, convention, or shared strategy, renders the (c) phrase a reasonable hypothesis, whereas in the second case, the first clause of (c) "of course, life is not a fluid," is false. Again, if one does not understand the

---

[30] From W. H. Auden, "As I Walked Out One Evening," in *Collected Poems*, ed. Edward Mendelson (New York: Random House, 1976), 115. The whole verse is, "In headaches and in worry / Vaguely life leaks away."

[31] Obviously, I am rejecting claims regarding "reification" in parts of the Bible. The burden of proof remains on those who wish to show that ideas started out metaphorical and then underwent "reification," rather than vice versa. Further, I am not claiming that this statement is meant literally everywhere in the Bible. Some strands of literature will use blood in a metaphorical sense, though I believe Leviticus uses it quite literally in these instances.

ancient Hebrew preference rules regarding bodily organs and their functions, even (c) might be interpreted as decoding a metaphor.

A few other examples will show yet other realms of ambiguity. The Hebrew liturgy preserves the following phrase to be recited upon awakening in the morning: "I render thanks to you, Eternal King, who has mercifully returned my soul to within me." There is significant evidence that the writer believed the soul quite literally departed the body during sleep, so that awakening was transformed into a miraculous act of restoration performed by none other than God himself. Conversely, death was considered a form of sleep, differentiated only by its length and quality. Even resurrection in the earliest of Judaic and Christian sources was viewed as awakening from sleep, as the Hebrew liturgy once again bears witness.[32] With these pieces of cultural information in place, we consider the following diagnostic:

(a) DEATH IS SLEEP
(b) Upon awakening, God mercifully returns my soul to within me.
(c) Of course, sleep is not death—but if it were, you could say that in awakening my soul is returned to me by God.

In this case, there is considerable ambiguity. For the contemporary listener, the incongruity of the metaphorical domain SLEEP IS DEATH is altogether self-evident ("sleep is surely not death"). However, what if Almoni, a second-century commoner living in Roman Palestine, believes that each night his soul departs his body? Almoni would then not be willing to acknowledge the first clause of (c) as true. His response might be, "What do you mean 'sleep is not death?' Surely it is—sleep is simply a short death!"[33] The commonly cited expression from Aristophanes' *The Frogs*, "For what is death but an eternal sleep?" proves even more ambiguous. Nothing compels us to read this metaphorically, nor can we marshal an argument that convincingly shows it to be literal.

In such cases, it is not the diagnostic that fails; on the contrary, one of the functions of the diagnostic is to highlight those phrases that demand caution. Put differently: the diagnostic will always work

---

[32] See the second benediction of the *Amidah* prayer: ". . . who keeps faith with those who sleep in the dust."

[33] See Frazer 1963, chapter 18 §2, "Absence and Recall of the Soul," for numerous examples of this literal belief.

if we share the speaker's strategy or if we are adequately informed about the speaker's belief system and cultural context. To put it in the technical terms we established earlier: given shared preference rules, the diagnostic will render a usable solution if enough conditions of relevance can be adequately understood and assessed with regard to their weightings. If we cannot confidently construe the first, negative, part of any (c)-statement, thereby articulating the incongruity overtly, then we cannot proceed with any certainty with regard to a statement's place on the meaning continuum. Let me repeat that the diagnostic only makes overt the very cognitive process we all undergo when making a decision about metaphor. The problems in interpretation occur when that process is muddled by assumptions that prejudice our preferences for some typicality conditions over others, without taking into consideration the stability of our preference rules.

The more we know about both literary and cultural context, the greater the diagnostic's chances of yielding an unambiguous result. Sometimes the decoding of a metaphor takes place within the literary context itself. A marvelous example of an overt decoding of the covert metaphor takes place when Hamlet acknowledges the incongruity of his own ironic comparison of death and sleep. This occurs in his renowned "To be or not to be" soliloquy:

> To die; to sleep—
> No more; and by a sleep to say we end
> The heart-ache, and the thousand natural shocks
> That flesh is heir to; 'tis a consummation
> Devoutly to be wish'd. To die, to sleep—
> To sleep; erchance to dream—ay, there's the rub,
> For in that sleep of death what dreams may come,
> When we have shuffled off this mortal coil,
> Must give pause; there's the respect
> That makes calamity of so long life.[34]

Hamlet himself unravels the question: Is death sleep or is it something different? If it is not sleep, but some end which allows one to take a blissful refuge from the misery that fills one's life, then perhaps it is desired. But what if the notion of death as sleep is not just a metaphor, but somehow true (that is, the comment contains no incongruity)? What if, as in sleep, we maintain some form of con-

---

[34] Shakespeare, *Hamlet*, act 3, scene 1.

sciousness (and conscience) in death? Since sleep brings on dreams, we are left to wonder what visions death-as-sleep might bring upon us. Hamlet plays both sides of the statement, the literal and the metaphorical, and it is his inability to decide which of them captures reality that renders him unable to act. Who would "grunt and sweat under a weary life," he muses,

> But that the dread of something after death,
> The undiscover'd country from whose bourn
> No traveller returns, puzzles the will,
> And makes us rather bear those ills we have,
> Than fly to others that we know not of?
> Thus conscience does make cowards of us all . . . .

Death, rather than being an absolute escape from it all, might only be a permanent sleep. Thus, the suffering of conscience would continue indefinitely, permitting no escape from eternal ruminations. The power of Hamlet's struggle captures for us the very tension we are trying to identify in the nature of metaphor. Hamlet is simply not convinced that there is any incongruity in the proposition SLEEP IS DEATH;[35] and as long as this statement might prove literal—if death will offer no relief from life's "slings and arrows"—he might as well remain "awake."[36]

In summary, five possible outcomes may result from applying the diagnostic model proposed here to a given statement.

1. Incongruity is sensed and a hypothetical reconstruction of the phrase's meaning is sensible (e.g., "All the world's a stage").

2. Incongruity is not sensed, and a hypothetical reconstruction of the phrase's meaning results only in a restatement of the original literal statement (e.g., "The dog runs down the street").

3. Incongruity is sensed, but no hypothetical reconstruction of the phrase's meaning is sensible, hence we have paradox or nonsense (e.g., "Colorless green ideas sleep furiously").[37]

---

[35] Or perhaps in this context, the directionality of the metaphor shifts to DEATH IS SLEEP; but in this case, the directionality is part of the literary play devised so brilliantly by Shakespeare.

[36] See Shakespeare's seventy-third sonnet, where sleep is referred to as death without being explicitly named: "Death's second self that seals up all in rest."

[37] The phrase was coined by Noam Chomsky (cited in Jackendoff 1972, 18) to illustrate that it is possible to have a grammatically sound statement which is altogether meaningless. The whole point is that we perceive the grammaticalness of the phrase, despite the fact that we cannot explain what the phrase means.

4. Incongruity is not sensed, but it should be; a misreading occurs (i.e., a metaphorical statement is read literally).

5. Incongruity is sensed, but it should not be; a misreading occurs (i.e., a literal statement is read metaphorically).

The diagnostic in instance (1) determines that the statement falls on the continuum to the right of literal (see Figure 1). Whether it is ascriptive, or metaphorical, or some other species of figurative language depends on the degree of incongruity sensed. In instance (2) it is determined that the statement is literal. In the third instance, the statement is judged to be nonsense. In the fourth and fifth instances, interpretation is problematic, either because the ambiguity is too great or because the statement under consideration falls outside our linguistic competence.

Summary

This study has thus far considered some examples of how scholars undermine literal meanings of a text, or give preference to a figurative reading, without establishing a method for scrutinizing such judgments. Yet more examples will follow in subsequent chapters. An alternative approach to the standard binary classifications of figurative/literal has been offered, introducing the notion of *conceptual ascription*. This has provided an alternative conceptualization of how appositional phrases were used in various strata of biblical literature. But the introduction of conceptual ascription was just the first step toward a broader reconceptualization of meaning as part of a gradient continuum.

To further elucidate that continuum, a thorough consideration of Jackendoff's preference rule model was explored. Here we endeavored to show that semantic stability is dependent on our assessment (or weighting) of an array of conditions of relevance. Once it is clear that preferences are based on typicality conditions rather than a more rigid (necessary) conditionality, we are better able to handle nuances of meaning and to accommodate ambiguities. By showing how different conditions interact on a gradient scale, we are able to place nuances of meaning on a continuum. With these principles in place, a diagnostic was proposed for measuring relative degrees of incongruence in appositional (predicational) statements. We indicated that this diagnostic assists us in determining whether or not a statement is literal or in some way figurative, specifically, a form of figurative language that functions with incongruity. However, it will frequently indicate that we are unable to make a decision either way (a condition especially common in the context of mystical texts). When we are unable to decide, it is usually because we lack knowledge of enough conditions of relevance to determine whether the statement exhibits the kind of incongruence that would cause us to search for nonliteral meanings. Put differently, *semantic stability* is lacking. Unless we can establish incongruence, we cannot assert the presence of metaphor (or related forms of figurative language).

What, then, are our choices? We could reevaluate our understanding of various conditions of relevance to determine whether we might have been justified in readjusting our weightings to evoke greater semantic stability. We might also search for other conditions that would shed light on our context—that is, seek to base a decision on the strength of the convergence of available conditions. The beauty of the preference-rule model is that unusual meanings can be accommodated by the gradience of our continuum. We may not always be able to establish which conditions are functioning in a given context, but at least we can be sensitive to the fact that statements are embedded in contexts that can alter the conditions of relevance in such a way as to significantly influence meaning.

Since establishing incongruence is so heavily dependent on our assessment of authorial intent, we cannot ignore the significant problems scholars face when deciphering meanings of composite texts. When interpretations are rendered in the absence of so significant a condition of relevance, we should be highly skeptical as to its value.

7.

IDOLATRY: THE MOST CHALLENGING METAPHOR

In the scholarship on biblical thought, no issue pits literalism against metaphor as powerfully as that of idolatry. Ancient sources portray idols as either immensely powerful, because they *literally* bring about divine intercessions, or hopelessly impotent, because they are nothing other than lumps of stone or wood. This is how a binary conceptualization of meaning frames the issue. My goal is to show how the controversy might appear in discourse that operates with gradient meanings.

Until this point in our study, most of the scholarly interpretations considered have forced nonfigurative expressions into the domain of metaphor. Although this is the dominant tendency, scholarly inquiry often works in the reverse direction as well, interpreting figurative idioms literally. When it comes to aniconism, an underlying literalism dominates the conditions of relevance in virtually all scholarly debate. To justify this lopsidedness, scholars wrap the issues of aniconism and monotheism together in one theoretical approach. Nothing is more dependent upon a binary conception of the world than monotheism. There is no question that numerous passages in the Bible itself endeavor to fuse these issues irrevocably together. But we should not so easily hand victory to the final redactors; these passages should be placed in their appropriate historical and ideological context, and interpreted accordingly. Only then can the issues of aniconism and monotheism be treated as they deserve to be: separately.

The complexity of the subject matter will require the development of a number of supporting themes and secondary layers of evidence. Such digressions might cause one to lose sight of the main issues. To guard against that, I will first offer a brief sketch of how my discussion will progress, and then I will indicate my main conclusions in anticipation of the more complete arguments.

As might be expected, idolatry proscriptions figure prominently in the Torah, but frequent echoes of these prohibitions appear in

the prophetic literature as well.[1] While I will indicate briefly some
of the standard approaches to the central issues, we need not tarry
with an extensive history of the scholarship.[2] Moshe Halbertal and
Avishai Margalit were the first scholars to frame the aniconic proscriptions in terms of metaphorical conceptualizations. I will summarize the central thesis of their book *Idolatry* and offer a critique.
The works of a number of scholars who have approached the theoretical issues behind the aniconic proscriptions will be mentioned.[3]
Building on this survey, I will reframe the issue of the aniconic
proscriptions with the gradient model of meaning.

What has been written thus far on the subject of idolatry is based
on an artificial binary conceptualization of what idolatry is about.
In my opinion, this has resulted in certain paradigmatic misreadings
that have dominated the history of interpretation. The problem of
understanding the role of statues in the ancient religious contexts,
and our delight in finding religious tendencies that fundamentally
reject them, derive from our conceptualization of the world of religion as a juxtapositioning of literal and metaphorical meanings.
Ironically, this conforms to the literary plans of those biblical editors who frequently sought to purge texts of those ambiguities natural to figurative imagery.

I will claim that at certain stages in history, statues in the spacial
world were direct parallels to functional and structural ascriptions
in the linguistic world. The treatment of idols in Mesopotamia are
best understood with the concepts of functional and structural ascription in place; that is, neither as simple literalisms nor as full-
fledged metaphors. The object made by human hands, but imbued
with meaning through divine participation, duplicated the presence

---

[1] The standard prohibitions are in Exod 20:4, 34:17; Lev 19:4; Num 33:51f.;
Deut 4:15-20, 5:8, 27:15. Of thematic relevance: Isa 37:19, 40:19-20, 42:17, 44:15f.,
48:5, 60:17; Jer 2:27, 3:9, 10:14, 51:17; Ezek 8:3-5, 20:32; Hos 13:2; 1 Kgs 14:9;
2 Kgs 17:16; 2 Chr 28:2, 34:3. In contrast, Judg 18 and 1 Sam 19, among many
other passages, demonstrate the commonness of idols in Israelite culture.

[2] For broad discussion of this history of scholarship, see Bernhardt 1956; Dietrich
and Loretz 1992; Dohmen 1985. The most comprehensive and most recent treatment of the archaeological evidence from Mesopotamia, Egypt, and Canaan, is
Mettinger 1995. There, too, one can find a brief survey of the scholarship, though
I will treat some authors who are not considered in his study.

[3] I will touch upon the approaches of Umberto Cassuto, Gerhard von Rad,
Yehezkel Kaufmann, A. Leo Oppenheim, Walter Zimmerli, William W. Hallo,
Matitiahu Tsevat, José Faur, Thorkild Jacobsen, Ronald Hendel, Tryggve Mettinger,
and Carl Evans.

of the god in all ways *except ontologically*. The people behaved regarding the statue the way they would behave regarding the god, as if the latter were ontologically present in the temple. This is no different from the psalmist calling God his victor, or the Levitical priest presenting an offering for God's delight. The difference is in the medium, not the conceptualization.[4] All that would otherwise be ascribed to the god was ascribed to the object. Because of the god's real-world intelligence and ability to view what was happening to the object, people thought the god would recognize their actions as directed toward him or her. The gulf between the human realm and the divine realm was bridged by the object, not through metaphor, nor with literal meaning—the idol is *not* the god—but with functional and structural ascription. In this sense, the acts surrounding the idol—its associative rituals—were literal acts and the words were meant literally, but the performer knew to distinguish between ascriptive and ontological presence. This is a different way of thinking about the connotations of predicational statements.

As noted, the binary misreading that has heretofore dominated the approach to this subject is not a modern phenomenon. The shift in the weightings of conditions of relevance find their origins in the biblical world itself, so that by the time we get to the period during which much of Hebrew Bible was written, the preference rules that enabled people to conceive of things according to functional and structural ascription were apparently no longer dominant. For example, in Isaiah 44, the aniconic satire is clearly directed at a literalist's idolatry. The prophet shows no awareness of any other set of preference rules for the world of anthropomorphically representative objects. But ironically, Isaiah's own words indicate that the creator of the idol was fully aware that it was nothing more than a hand-fashioned piece of wood. What is so astounding to the prophet is that this realization did not alter the wood-carver's behavior toward the idol. The fact that Isaiah is able to draw attention to this paradox highlights the clash between the semantics of idols for the idolater and the semantics of physical representation for Isaiah himself. The two people are operating in blatantly distinct speech communities. Unable to recognize that the idolator did not insist on ontological identity, the prophet is left with a literalist's idolatry, one he finds utterly futile.

---

[4] I am specifically speaking of those texts in which ascription is detectable. Obviously, such is not the case in a later document.

This is the end of the story rather than the beginning; and our path to this particular point in history is hardly direct. Our discussion here is essentially a history of how and why a given form of meaning—conceptual ascription—was lost. When it is framed in this way, we understand the proscription of icons as a casualty of long-coming cultural change, one whose roots are the semantics of ancient Israelite religion and culture more broadly.

Some Standard Approaches: Intellectual and Moral Superiority

Many historians have argued that the ancient Israelite religion emerged from the Canaanite cultures of the Levant.[5] Even so, the voices of those who have argued for the separate origins and unique character of Yahwism have continued to hold sway over the study of Israel's aniconism. For Umberto Cassuto, for instance, Torah presents a "new conception" of God, a "completely transcendental view of the Godhead." In "the Torah's view there is an absolute barrier between the Creator and the created, which no creature in the world can transcend." This transcendence is what made icons useless. In real terms, "God cannot be depicted by any material form whatsoever, for every form resembles a natural object, which cannot even remotely accord with the absolute, transcendental character of the God of Israel" (1987, 236f.). Hence, the utter dissimilarity made physical representation useless. Cassuto assumes that any phrase that gave reality to other deities or to unacceptable theological principles could be explained away by appealing to the concept of non-literal language. With respect to "the expression *other gods*," Cassuto writes that in the mind of Scripture this had become "a regular, stereotyped term for the gods of the gentiles, who are no-gods. Every deity apart from the Lord is *another* god" (237). As such, the monotheistic theological revolution is integrally connected to the emergence of Israelite aniconism.

Many scholars, similarly convinced of the theological superiority of monotheism, start from the premise that Israel rejected polytheism and advocated aniconism because of some intellectual and spiritual insight. The prejudice not only causes some to trumpet Yahwism but

---

[5] See Ahlström 1963, Lemche 1985, 1988, 1994; Gottwald 1979, 1985; Finkelstein 1994, among others.

to disparage Canaanite religion in a wholesale fashion so as to annul any notion that the two might be either diachronically or synchronically related. This is precisely Oldenburg's goal when he writes the following in the preface to his often-cited *The Conflict between El and Ba'al in Canaanite Religion*: "The more I studied pre-Israelite religion, the more I was amazed with its utter depravity and wickedness. Indeed there is nothing in it to inspire the sublime faith of Yahweh. His coming is like the rising sun dispelling the darkness of Canaanite superstition" (1969, Preface, xi).[6] In the same camp we find Yehezkiel Kaufmann. Once the Israelite religion was in place, its superiority was never affected by the more primitive fetishes of pagan cults. Kaufmann (1960) maintains that the Israelite religion

> never knew of nor had to sustain a polemic against representations of Yhwh. Intuitively, it rejected representations of God because such images were regarded in paganism as an embodiment of the gods and, as such, objects of a cult. This idea was to Israelite religion the very essence of idolatry; hence from the very outset it rejected without a polemic representations of Yhwh. (237)

The prohibition against image making, according to Kaufmann, derived from the notion that images "were not conceived of as representations of the other gods, but as objects which in themselves belong to the category 'other gods'; they do not symbolize, they *are*, other gods" (237). For Kaufmann, the exclusivity of Israelite monotheism defines idolatry both in terms of the nonreality of other deities and the uselessness of objects representing those non-deities. In Kaufmann's thought, since statues of non-gods are banalities, it only follows that a statue of the only-God is banal.

A similar proclivity for romanticizing the aniconic proscriptions is found in Gerhard Von Rad's two-volume *Old Testament Theology* (1962-65), in which he links aniconism to the antimythological tendencies he finds so prominent in Hebrew Scriptures.

> Myth, just because it is myth, is a way of thinking by means of symbols and images: but Israel fought with all the resolve she could command against the most important thing in all the mythic symbols which her religious environment offered her, namely, their capacity to serve as means of revelation. This awareness of the barrier which men erect between themselves and God by means of images is, however, *Israel's*

---

[6] This is cited and discussed in Cornelius 1994, 264.

greatest achievement. This, and this alone, her insight into idolatry and myth, furnished the key to her loneliness in the company of the religions of the world. (2:340, my emphasis)

Despite this highly idealized depiction of aniconism, Von Rad maintains that "the Old Testament pictures of [Israel's] history suggest that the mass of her population were never conscious of the dependent status of creation, and that it was only a few historians and prophets who fought against the seductions of idolatry or the cults of foreign gods" (341).

This dichotomy between believers and nonbelievers was also argued by A. Leo Oppenheim with regard to Mesopotamian religion: one should not assume identity between the literary evidence and the religion of the average person (1977, 171ff.). Jean Bottéro, among others, disagrees, arguing that there is no reason to assume that the literate classes "were sequestered in their own circles and were entirely isolated from the rest of their contemporaries," producing texts that were elitist and irrelevant to mass religion. He claims that the sanctuaries were public and that religion was open and part of a social continuity that included both high literary documents and common religion (1992, 208).

This is a key issue in the history of religion. On the basis of archaeological evidence, John S. Holladay Jr. has argued for the existence of two parallel strata of religious practice. One he calls "establishment," by which he means those dominant cultic sites that are understood to have been organized around a priestly caste defined on the basis of birthrights and recognized by the monarchy; he calls the other "nonconformist," as they are essentially sects that emerged "from irreconcilable differences over either content of religious thought or form of religious expression" (1987, 267).[7] Holladay cites an abundance of what appear to be household cultic objects (small idols) and ritual objects found at out-of-the-way shrines, which are fundamentally at odds both with those objects found at mainstream sites and with the literary testimonies in Tanakh. Not only do the mainstream sites appear to be, for the most part, aniconic in char-

---

[7] But this depiction of why "nonconformist" groups might exist is too narrowly defined. Holladay himself notes that the priesthood was hereditary. He suggests that "divisions would at first give rise to rival political parties within the same cultus" rather than separatist groups. We should not minimize the importance of issues of power and control in the emergence of separate religious groups (i.e., in contrast to political parties), simply because of the hereditary character of the priesthood.

acter (as most would expect), but they have not preserved for us those symbols, images, and cultic objects that *are* consistently depicted in biblical literature as part and parcel of the official cult. This tension between the literary description of the cult and the archaeological remains makes the scholar uneasy. On the one hand, we might attribute the absence of these objects and artworks described in Tanakh to the fact that few movable artifacts would have remained unplundered through the course of history. In contrast, nonconformist sites would not have had the wealth to produce objects of such significant value, at least not in contrast to what would have been available—and desirable—at official shrines. On the other hand, the dating of the literary evidence that pertains to the Jerusalem Temple could turn out to be a crucial issue. Perhaps the descriptions of cultic sites in both Israel and Judah are themselves anachronistic and therefore at odds with the earlier "hard" evidence found at archaeological sites.

Whatever the solution—Holladay suggests a number of reasonable approaches[8]—there is no doubt that there existed a variety of religious institutions in ancient Israel, some controlled by the official priesthood, and others most likely linked to more popular religious forms of observance. However, while Bottéro's argument for an overall continuity between official and popular religion cannot be maintained, the distinction between an "establishment" religion and a "nonconformist" religion "totally isolated from the life of the official shrines" may also prove too rigid a depiction of history. (Notice its binary character.) Given the evidence from postbiblical literature and histories, there is reason to assume that people moved back and forth between various strata of religious observance, whether they be officially sanctioned by a central authority or the cult practiced among local clans.[9] We also need not attribute "nonconformist" sites solely to political or religious conflict. Even proximity to official sites, when combined with long-standing local traditions of ongoing, local priesthoods, can just as reasonably account for nonofficial religious practice as anything politically or religiously inspired. In any

---

[8] See his Summary Conclusions (280-82) and his long Endnote, both of which grapple with the conflict between the archaeological and literary evidence.

[9] Sara Japhet (1989) preserves a dichotomy between "ruling class and general population," but writes: "the stringent Pentateuchal prophibitions and the stinging condemnation [of idolatry] in prophetic and historiographical literature suggests that the problem plagued both ruling class and general population" (203).

event, the main point of differentiation always lay with who controlled ritual. With time, differentiation would also be manifest in the actual cultic behaviors and perhaps even beliefs, but these factors would appear to have been subordinate to questions of personnel. That, at least, is the conclusion we shall draw from the literary evidence, which invariably associates countercultural behaviors with specific individuals or groups of individuals. Our goal here, then, is to excavate the literature. While we shall be assisted greatly by archaeological evidence, it will serve only as a secondary factor in our understanding of what the biblical authors were trying to say about the use of images and icons.

W. Zimmerli has argued that a main motivation for the abolition of idols was that the physical objects would somehow infringe upon Yahweh's freedom (1959, 246). Zimmerli creates a highly abstract notion of a deity who is a god of history rather than the gods of nature who dominated the beliefs in other ancient Near Eastern cultures. This distinction moved the Israelites toward aniconism as a way to differentiate their deity from those of other religions. The relevance of magic and the use of icons in magical contexts also serves Zimmerli's thesis. Unfortunately, his position is founded on idealized notions of both the Israelite religion and other contemporary beliefs. James Barr has shown that the Mesopotamian gods were as historically active as Yahweh (1991, 65ff.). Ronald Hendel (1988, 368ff.), summarizing other arguments against Zimmerli's position, notes that the distinction between Israel and Mesopotamia in the realm of magic is equally dubious.

William Hallo (1983) shows surprise at any suggestion that Israelites might have used icons for Yahweh-related rituals:

> Not only is biblical legislation explicitly aniconic and anti-iconic, but even the non-legal descriptions of the divine attributes in the biblical texts are so thoroughly and deliberately aphysical that it would be impossible to translate them into representational, artistic terms. Excavations in Israel have yielded thousands of icons and cultic figurines, but to suggest that even a single one of them represents the God of Israel is to operate in the realm of pure hypothesis. (1)

The logic of Hallo's position is strained by its anachronistic assumptions. There are no detailed descriptions of deities in *any* of the classic Mesopotamian texts—the field of Hallo's expertise—and yet Mesopotamian cultures, from early Sumeria through late Ugarit, had no shortage of reliefs, figurines, amulets and statues monumental and otherwise.[10] Leaving aside the issue of periodization, there is no reason to expect one to have turned to Torah for instructions with regard to God's appearance. Hallo considers the portrait of God in Hebrew Scriptures as "deliberately aphysical," thereby judging all of the anthropomorphic depictions, which he acknowledges to be the common mode of description, as "innocent of theological implications."[11] But this is a distortion of the evidence. The portrait of God— as it might be—is not deliberately aphysical by any stretch of the imagination. Indeed, a survey of Scriptures will indicated passages mentioning virtually every limb of the body.[12]

Despite its problems, Hallo's article on this subject raises a number of questions regarding Mesopotamian practices that frequently escape the attention of students of this field. Not all depictions of gods in Mesopotamia were anthropomorphic. Frequently a god-symbol is even placed alongside an anthropomorphic figure that is thought to represent the very same deity. Some have suggested that was to enable viewers to distinguish the god from the statue, though such a notion is purely speculative. Others believe the symbol was necessary because none of the statues had facial features that would allow them to be recognized.[13] In an illiterate society, the symbolism thus served the practical purpose of differentiation. What is more important is that the use of abstract symbols suggests a certain kind of sophistication in the Mesopotamian use of imagery. We shall return to this when considering the question of whether an idol is actually the god itself.

The positions discussed thus far start with the premise that

---

[10] See Hallo's discussion on when the earliest positive identification of a god-statue (which Hallo distinguishes from "cult statues") can be made (5ff.). Many have argued that anthropomorphic imagery did not actually enter Mesopotamian rites prior to the second millennium; see Hallo 1983, 11, Curtis 1990, and Mettinger 1995, chapter 2. Providing a contrary position, see Cornelius 1994 (esp.chap.4) on the locations and ubiquity of Reshef and Baal throughout the Mediterranean down to the Hellenistic Period.

[11] Hallo accomplishes this move by appealing to the Targumim—another anachronism (1983, 2).

[12] Some have even argued that Yahweh was originally described as a sexual being, though admittedly, the redactional process largely neutralized all aspects of gender with sexual overtones. Despite some questionable readings, see Eilberg-Schwartz 1994; see also Olyan 1988.

[13] See Mettinger 1995, chap. 2; also Cornelius (1994, Introduction, and passim), who repeatedly treats the question of symbolism along-side reliefs.

aniconism is fundamentally a theological discovery, derived from one or another intellectual realization. Matitiah Tsevat also argues for a philosophical foundation, linking the issue to the Israelite understanding of the nature of language. Tsevat finds the prohibition against image making rooted in the ancient Israelite conviction that language is the unique avenue for contact between God and humanity. While Isaiah taught that God is invisible, he was also said to be knowable, not through an image, but through language:

> Everything that can be thought, felt or willed can be expressed reliably and plainly in language and only in language. . . . This is the uniqueness of language, the first achievement of man, as the Bible says insightfully . . . and biblical religion appropriates it in full. . . . They [God and man] can become partners; in a certain respect speech places them on the same plane. Since, then, the medium of communication of God and man is the audible word and not the visible image, images are proscribed; their very presence may derail or misdirect communication. (1986, 216)

The claim that "everything that can be thought, felt or willed can be expressed reliably and plainly in language and only in language" cannot be defended. The thoughts and emotions evoked by and expressed through the non-language based-arts—music and dance, painting and sculpture, even architecture—cannot be adequately conveyed in language at all. The integral role of music in worship throughout the world derives from the fact that the sounds themselves produce feelings—which are, after all, simply "thoughts" from the perspective of neurochemistry—often far more potent than the semantic value of any spoken phrase. There is simply no basis for pegging aniconism on a notion that religion saw language and images as competitive because of one's superiority over the other. While this may have been the ex post facto conclusion of a culture that made the decision to eliminate idols, it cannot be construed as the motivating factor.

Tsevat further maintains that idols are inadequate because their immutable expressions are such that they cannot adapt their image to the demands of emotions or the context of a living situation. The "rigid features" of the stone or wood representations "are also potentially inimical to monotheism or henotheism because of the need to multiply images that manifest different characteristics corresponding to the variety of human experience" (217). The inadequacy of an idol's expression appears not to have been a hurdle for other ancient cultures. We know that in Mesopotamia statues were dressed very ornately and that attire was changed to fit the demands of whatever festival was being observed. People brought expression and relevance to the appearance of the statue through its accoutrements; the permanence of its facial expression proved irrelevant in their eyes and was even, perhaps, a sign of serenity and stability.[14]

Finally, Tsevat ignores the integral function of sacrifice in accomplishing what words might otherwise have done alone, namely, influence God. To elevate language to an exclusive pedestal of efficacy cannot be justified, especially not in the face of an elaborate slaughtering ritual. I am not arguing that Israel did not ultimately become linguacentric in contrast to other cultures. But its preference for language, and its ultimate (alleged) disdain for images, cannot be explained on the basis of an advantage inherent in the nature of language itself, nor in any ancient theory that language was the unique avenue to divine favor.

The Halbertal-Margalit Hypothesis

What is new in Halbertal and Margalit's diachronic study *Idolatry* (1992) is the attempt to frame the question of aniconism in terms of metaphor. The authors follow the conceptualization of representation offered by Charles Sanders Peirce in his 1933 article "Icon, Index, and Symbol" (1960).[15] Peirce's theory suits Halbertal and Margalit quite well, as it sets up a clean and neat dichotomy. As the authors explain in *Idolatry*, the biblical faith proscribed "similarity-based" representations of God, but allowed causal-metonymic representations. A metonym is understood as a representation that stands for something in the way that a symbol represents a person or concept, but where the association is not made on the basis of any physical similarity.[16] Problems arose when Israelites failed to distin-

---

[14] See Oppenheim 1977, 183-198; Lambert 1993.

[15] See also Mettinger (1995, 21-22), who briefly considers the relevance of Pierce's approach to his own study. However, Halbertal and Margalit are not considered in Mettinger's work. No critique of Peirce's basic notions of causal-metonymic representations and conventional representation is offered in *Idolatry*.

[16] Such a concept might, in fact, be relevant for the symbolic representation of deities in Mesopotamian reliefs.

guish between a causal-metonymic representation (such as the ark, altar, cherubim, Temple, etc.) and similarity-based representations. According to Halbertal and Margalit, the acceptance of metonymic representations slowly spilled over onto nonmetonymic objects.

There is merit in the distinction between metonymic and similarity-based representation when it comes to understanding the roles of the ark, altar, cherubim, and Temple. With regard to the philosophical basis for proscribing representational idols, however, the theory is not convincing. We do not have a single instance in the literary record of any Israelite ever attempting to make an *anthropomorphic* (i.e., similarity based) statue of Yahweh.[17] The human-like idols are regularly referred to as "other gods" (see Cassuto's remark, above). When calves or other nonanthropomorphic objects are present, they can be categorized only as causal-metonymic representations.

Despite these problems, Halbertal and Margalit's treatment of the tension between linguistic and nonlinguistic metaphors is framed with the right questions:[18]

> What is the reason for this ban on the representation of God, and why are linguistic representations of God apparently permitted while visual representations are forbidden? If it is permitted to describe God as possessing a hand, why is it forbidden to draw it? What is the difference between a statue of God and a verbal description of him? (10)

The discussion must start here because any given linguistic expression and any given physical object may be interpreted metaphorically or literally. Like Tsevat (though not citing him), the authors suggest that part of the issue relates to the need to enter into dialogue with God. God chose language, not drawings, because of its intrinsic power. The authors see metaphor as the primary tool of the biblical (and, eventually, the postbiblical) authors, who needed to introduce theology by means of a language that derives from the human condition.

---

[17] This is in contrast to the fact that we have found literally thousands of small, anthropomorphic figurines.

[18] They begin with a series of questions that relate to the aniconic nature of ancient Israelite religion and its early postbiblical manifestations, tracing the issue through the Middle Ages and beyond. My consideration of their study will limit itself to the ancient and rabbinic literatures.

> The explanatory power of *metaphor* derives from the familiarity of the realm it is drawn from (the realm of human relations), and in the metaphorical process we attempt to extend our understanding beyond the image to the realm it represents. This is the transition from the primary, or representing, realm to the secondary, or represented realm. The way the Bible explains what is bad about idolatry by using images of flaws in human relationships teaches us that the basis of our understanding of the sin of idolatry is our moral standpoint with respect to what is permitted and what is forbidden in interpersonal relationships. (10)

It is never made clear why metaphor is a necessary vehicle for what could have been said literally. Surely the ethics of human relations can be and regularly are explained in nonfigurative terms. Without an obvious answer, the authors construct a link between the sin of idolatry and what is forbidden in interpersonal relationships, most specifically adultery. But we require something more compelling than the notion that God's choice of Israel and his restriction regarding images are somehow "anchored in interpersonal relationships." None of this is intuitive and none of this is anchored in morality. Moreover, the fact that a morality metaphor is used is ultimately irrelevant to an iconic proscription. As I noted at the outset, one need not use metaphor.

From the adultery metaphor, Halbertal and Margalit move further into their theory of representation. This passage is especially important for our current study, because the authors deal with the problem of distinguishing literal anthropomorphisms from figurative ones. Finally, the whole interpretative enterprise is pinned on the concept of idolatry. I will let the authors present their issues in their own words:

> But one could make the claim that the very act of interpreting anthropomorphic images literally is itself idolatry. Now we have reached the hermeneutic circle, in which the very representation of God in anthropomorphic terms is perceived as part of the problem of idolatry. On the one hand we can grasp what idolatry is only by understanding the metaphors that express opposition to it, but on the other hand the understanding of these metaphors, particularly the question of how literal or metaphorical they are, depends on how we understand idolatry in the Bible. . . .
>
> Here we are confronted with another circle within the first circle. Those who read the anthropomorphic expressions in the relational metaphors nonliterally will nevertheless give a literal reading to other

expressions connected with the question of whether the Bible only prohibits the worship of other gods or denies their existence altogether. Those who forbid the anthropomorphizing of God as idolatry certainly consider any statement that other gods exist to be a form of idolatry. *... The question of which texts to read literally and which to read metaphorically depends on the question of what conception of idolatry the reader holds, a conception which those very texts are supposed to anchor.*

We chose to enter the circle from the standpoint of a literal, anthropomorphic reading of the metaphors, because we see the nonanthropomorphic abstraction as a later product of a philosophical viewpoint that regards the concept of God as an abstract concept, and the distinction between idolatry and monotheism as a difference in the degree of abstractness of the concept of God. According to this viewpoint the main problem of idolatry is not the worship of other gods but the improper and erroneous representation of God himself, including anthropomorphic representations. In our opinion this approach does not reflect the anthropomorphic biblical viewpoint. (35-36, my emphasis)

The claim that the difference between monotheism and idolatry is a matter of abstraction stands on thin air. If an idol is a metaphor it may turn out to be just as abstract in its conceptualization and in the conditions of relevance employed by the framer as any literary metaphor. A distinction should have been made between the question of whether other gods exist and the question of whether one should create idols of Yahweh. Even an absolute monotheism could have used idols without compromising its belief in the singulariy of its deity.[19] Moreover, the question of which *texts* should be read literally and which should be read metaphorically should not be dependent upon one's conception of idolatry. There is simply no necessary connection between conceptualizing an object metaphorically and conceptualizing a literary passage metaphorically. This is not to say that one's attitude toward idols will not be carried over into the way one interprets literature about idols; but that is not the issue central to Halbertal and Margalit's discourse. These central concerns are made more confused when the authors speak of "a literal, anthropomorphic reading of the metaphors." One would think that by definition, if something is literal, it is not metaphorical. Anthropomorphism is either an accurate, literal description of God, or a figurative one; but not both simultaneously. Undoubtedly, a gradi-

---

[19] On this, see Brichto 1983, 42ff.

ent conceptualization of how these idioms are meant would facilitate our understanding of how such depictions were understood and also help us avoid saying that metaphors have literal, anthropomorphic readings.

Diatribes against the worship of other deities' idols need not be related to the prohibition against creating a physical depiction of Yahweh. The Bible is sensitive to this distinction. Consider, for instance, Elijah's refutation of the prophets of Baal in 1 Kings 18. Elijah commences his challenge with the phrase "You invoke your god by name, and I will invoke Yahweh by name." Here we have a battle of names, not a battle of images. In the face of Elijah's victory, the people acknowledge "Yahweh, the [superior] of the gods."[20] The victory is achieved specifically in the context of a cultic rite; the issue is efficacy. Idol worship is altogether absent. As this chapter in Kings presents things, the Baalists could be just as monolatristic and aniconic as the Yahwists. The passage *may* indicate that Elijah was arguing for "pure" monotheism, or it may just show the defeat of a lesser god by the greatest of gods; it is very hard to say. What is clear is that with regard to the cult, Elijah sets out to prove the other deity inferior and impotent in such matters as prayer and sacrifice.[21] But

---

[20] The Hebrew to the end of v.24 reads והיה האלהים אשר יענה באש הוא האלהים which JPS translates "the god who responds with fire, that one is God." Verse 39 יהוה הוא האלהים יהוה הוא האלהים is then translated as "The LORD alone is God, The LORD alone is God!" The translators are somewhat inconsistent, perhaps ignoring the nuances of the determining article. The word "alone" is altogether presumptuous. The "aloneness" of God is indicated in the following verses, though not always without controversy as to its exact meaning: Deut 4:32; 2 Sam 7:22; Isa 26:13, 44:6,8; 45:5, 21; 64:3; Hos 13:4; Ps 18:32; 1 Chr 17:20. The non-Deuteronomistic verses appear to indicate superiority rather than deny the existence of other deities. Consequently, 1 Kgs 18:39 should probably be rendered: "Yahweh, he is *the* supreme deity." See Albright (1994, 171), who maintains that Elohim designates the "totality of the gods, the supreme god," and then adds the dubious note that this concept goes "as far back as the Song of Miriam and other poems from the thirteenth and twelfth centuries B.C." Also see Ahlström 1984.

[21] See Cross (1973, 191f.), who believes the passage is "marked strongly by traits of oral composition, and in their present form are little shared by the Deuteronomistic historian." I take it that by this comment, Cross is trying to date this form of monotheism to a pre-Deuteronomic era. The argument is hardly defensible, and the assessment that this reflects an "oral composition"—again, trying to show its antiquity—is altogether unacceptable. There is no evidence of "oral composition" anywhere in a written text, and there never can be. To assume that a written text has grounding in a social-oral context posits a kind of historicity for which absolutely no proof can be mustered. This is not to say that legends did not circulate orally for some time; but it is to argue that the literary structures of biblical litera-

just as striking is that he uses very corporeal magic to make his point.
The fire from heaven is hardly a miracle of finesse. Any shaman worth
his performance price could have replicated what Elijah performs.[22]

Ultimately, the *origins* of the aniconic proscriptions in Torah have
nothing whatsoever to do with the metaphors of loyalty and covenant that occupy the prophets, or the concern for the devaluation
of God. The prophetic metaphors are later literary developments that
added meaning to premonitions long since transformed, none of
whose origins can be linked to any theological principle. Originally,
aniconism had nothing to do with chosenness or monotheism. A close
scrutiny of the texts will show that various eras interpreted the proscriptions differently; moreover, no consistent theoretical foundation
is discernible. The literary evidence must also be integrated with the
evidence from material remains. While archaeology cannot provide
information about conceptualizations, it can help us verify how
concepts were manifest in material culture.

The claims that dominate the scholarship noted thus far all alert us
to a common chauvinism when it comes to theories of Israel's anti-
idolatry stand: language is superior to artistic representation because
of its intrinsic relationship to thought; aniconism is superior to idolatry because of its ethical standards. Stuart Hampshire, in a discussion of Alberto Giacometti's art, writes of this prejudice as it functions in contemporary artistic and literary theory:

> Why has it often been thought that concentrating on abstract argu-
> ment, remote from ordinary perceptions, is the highest activity of a
> person, the nearest to the divine? Because Aristotle and the Christian
> theologians have told us so, and their fiction has passed into the lan-
> guage we use when we distinguish reason from emotion, or intellect
> from imagination, or science from art. (1995, 46)

These rationalist distinctions do us considerable harm, especially
when it comes to analyzing the pre-rationalist *Weltanschauung* of ancient societies. What one considers intellectually superior should ultimately be irrelevant to any analysis of an ancient culture's preferences. Indeed, the meaning of cultural patterns ultimately has nothing
to do with judgments of superiority; such "realizations" all come post-

---

ture are the results of artistry and conceptual strategies that separate it significantly
from whatever oral traditions were in circulation.

[22] See Exodus 7, where Pharaoh's magicians compete with Moses and Aaron.

factum. As Oppenheim notes, "the aversion to accepting images as genuine and adequate realizations of the divine presence, manifested in a traditional human form . . . has played an important role in the religious development of the Western world" (1977, 183f.). Whether it is specifically the rationalism Hampshire attributes to the influence of Greek thought on the West, or a less rational but more emotional response inherited from biblical rhetoric itself, remains an historical conundrum. But at this point in history, they are inextricably linked. The longstanding practice has been to integrate any remnants of iconographic usage in Scriptures into the dominant Israelite aniconism. This involves an unjustifiable bifurcation between the images conjured by language and the images conveyed in graphic or plastic shapes. For some reason, scholars approach the all-too-abstract world of visual imagery as if it can depict only crude *literal meaning*, while the world of literary imagery is credited with sophisticated metaphorical meaning. Rarely does anyone entertain a parity between representational expressions and linguistic expressions, so as to recognize the possibility that if metaphor dominates language expressions regarding the gods, then metaphor might likewise dominate the representational images of deities. From an objective perspective, there is no real difference between a linguistic depiction of a deity and a graphic one. Objects are just as symbolic and metaphorical as words—in some cultures, perhaps even more so.

We shall return to this very dichotomy later. I will also endeavor at that time to integrate the discussion of semantics as it was presented in the previous chapters, for the meaning of images is as much a question of conditions of relevance as is the meaning of words. My goal is to place the controversy on a gradient scale, thereby accommodating the natural ambiguities in both linguistic and spacial imageries. Ultimately, the question of why Israel chose not to use idols has more to do with making a choice between available metaphors than with anything else. The issue comes down to *why* this particular choice was made.

José Faur understands ancient Israel to have maintained a selective aniconism, in that images of God were excluded by biblical law but other icons were permitted. Indeed, there was in ancient Israel "a legitimate iconolatry." Faur notes that the veil of the Tabernacle and the doors had graven images on them; the sanctuary itself had representational sculptures of cherubim that served as a throne for God.[23] Faur argues that "the distinction between licit and illict iconology is fundamentally arbitrary and is an extension of the Biblical idea of monolatry; . . . certain images were included in the Biblical ritual, others were proscribed" (1978, 1-2).

Faur's distinction between the use of icons regarding God and other forms of iconolatry is important, but I will argue that its origins have nothing to do with monolatry. He rightly argues that in order to understand more fully the meaning of aniconism in Israel, we must start by appreciating the meanings of idols in iconic religions of the ancient Near East more generally. He draws attention to the elaborate mouth-washing rituals whose "purpose of consecration was to transform the image into a living idol by imbuing the image with the spirit of the god" (10).[24] According to Faur, the gods were fully identified with their idols.[25] Whoever had possession of the idol controlled the god. The idols, brought to "life" through the mouth-washing ritual, were able to see, speak, smell, and exercise other senses. The importance of the mouth-washing ritual—fundamentally a form of libation—leads Faur to understand the rejection of the idols, called מסכה, as a rejection of objects whose efficacy had been initiated by means of anointment.[26] The root of מסכה is נסך, meaning "ritual libation." Faur postulates that the term עגל מסכה— a *massekhah*-calf, mentioned in Exodus 32:4 and 8, Deuteronomy 9:12 and 16, and elsewhere—refers to "an image of a calf that was consecrated (through anointment or libation)," and that the polemic in these passages is aimed at the non-Israelite beliefs that objects become alive through ritual ablution (12).

---

[23] There is much debate over the appearance of the cherubim, but the conclusion is less important than the fact that everyone acknowledges that the winged creatures are symbolic representations of different powers and that they are understood to be creatures that flanked divine thrones. There will be further discussion of this below.

[24] Faur provides references to a number or scholarly treatises on these texts in his notes; and see Jacobsen's more recent study (1987) for a detailed description of the ceremony and translations of important passages.

[25] Unfortunately, the question of just *how* the gods were identified with their idols is not altogether certain, though most scholars accept that the identity is quite close and that the objects are treated as if they were the gods. See our discussion below; also Jacobsen 1987; Bottéro 1992, 211f.; Oppenheim 1977, 183ff.; Lambert 1985a, 1985b, and 1993; Mettinger 1995, 22f.

[26] Faur (12) attributes this theory to Benzmozegh, in his commentary אם למקרא (Livormo, 1862), 89a-b.

These details have importance for Faur's thesis because they make relevant the biblical diatribes that satirize idols of wood and stone as blind, deaf, powerless objects. As Faur puts it:

> The Biblical polemics against idolatry were intended to undermine the belief in living idols and in the ritual efficacy of the pagan consecration. . . . [The prophetic polemics] were intended to shake the popular idea of "living idols." Accordingly, the argument advanced by the psalmist, *eyes have they but they see not* (Ps 115:5, 135:16), should be taken literally. Its purpose was to shatter the common notion that idols were capable of sensory perception, movement, and other activities peculiar to living beings. (13)

Almost by accident, Faur touches upon what should be the central issue regarding idolatry: the question of literal versus figurative understanding. But it is exactly this point that causes us the greatest difficulties. Faur uses the term "literally" only in this one sentence. The continuation of his argument veers from this point:

> Illegitimate iconolatry evolved from the notion that ritual consecration had the intrinsic power to induce the spirit of the gods to dwell in the image and thus identify itself with it. Among the Israelites, too, there was a strong popular belief that this ritual had the power to produce the same effect with God. (13)

The Tabernacle, the ark and the cherubim-throne were all used as objects by which the presence of God was manipulated. It is true, Faur says, that the ark is *not* God in the manner that an idol is a god, but there is much in common in terms of both ritual and function. Faur interprets Jeremiah 16:20, "Can a man make gods for himself? No-gods are they!" as alluding to "the widespread belief that it is possible to fashion a 'living idol.' Disbelief in the operative power of consecration reduces all image worship to the worship of 'wood and stone'" (14). Thus, at best, what we have is a selective condemnation of the foreign acts of consecration, for Israel still required its own ablution rituals for objects and humans alike.

Faur does emphasize for us the distinction between legitimate and illegitimate icons, thereby providing an insight that does not occupy most scholarship on the issue. His theoretical approach—which we have only briefly summarized—ultimately hangs on the question, What did an idol mean to an idolator? A full appreciation of Israel's aniconism will emerge only if we understand exactly what it is that was rejected. Unfortunately, conclusions cannot be drawn from the aniconic literature itself, since depictions of idoatry most often conform to literary tropes and stereotypes. To gain some insight into this question, let us consider in greater depth the mouth-washing ritual referenced by Faur.

Thorkild Jacobsen has considered the ritual in some detail (1987). As part of the water-consecration of an idol in Mesopotamia, there were elaborate rituals that distanced the human artisans from the product of their handiwork. Jacobsen explains:

> The officiating priest then pretends to cut off the goldsmith's hand with a knife of tamarisk wood (the red wool symbolizes the blood), and the goldsmith swears an oath, saying: "The god Gushkinbanda, Ea of the goldsmiths, verily made it. I did not make it!" Then the carpenter who fashioned the wooden core of the statue has the same done to him and swears that Nin-ildu, Ea of the carpenters, made it, not he. The meaning of what is here done is of course clear: The fact that the statue is the work of human hands is ritually denied and thus magically made non-existent, nullified. (23-24)

Jacobsen considers the idol-rites "a foreshadowing of and a stage in a divine presence, a theophany. Here the god can be found, can be approached. If he becomes angry and denies his presence to a community, he lets the cult statue of him be lost or transferred elsewhere." The basic evidence, according to Jacobsen, is contradictory: "the god *is* and at the same time *is not* the cult statue" (18). Jacobsen turns this apparent paradox into a statement of Mesopotamian philosophy:

> The contradiction of *is* and *is not* in the matter of the cult statue is so flagrant and cuts so deep that there must seem to be little hope of resolving it unless one goes to the most basic levels of understanding and attempts to gain clarity about the very fundamentals of ancient thought, about what exactly "being" and "nonbeing" meant to the ancients. (18)

Jacobsen arrives at a resolution of the contradiction by seeing the relationship between the god and the statue as

> a purely mystic unity, the statue mystically becoming what it represents, the god, without, however, in any way limiting the god, who remains transcendent. In so 'becoming,' the statue ceases to be mere earthly wood, precious metals and stones, ceases to be the work of human hands. It becomes transubstantiated, a divine being, the god it represents. (23)

The "mystical, transcendent" aspects of Jacobsen's understanding makes the whole world of Mesopotamian idolatry a kind of metaphor incarnate. There are numerous problems with this approach. First of all, the "contradiction" Jacobsen sensed is a contradiction only if the equivalence between the statue and the god is understood literally. Should this understanding be the case? Consider Jacobsen's description of the expurgation of brick-demons from a newly built house.

> When a man had built himself a new house he went through an elaborate ritual to expel "the brick-god" from it. An image was made of the god, it was placed in a little boat with provisions, and the boat was set adrift on the river with farewell wishes to see the god along. The concept of "brick" for which the brick-god stood was that of the separate, loose brick, and that separateness had to be removed from the house, in which the bricks were to shed their separate identity and become part of the solid wall. (19)

Is this ritual a manifestation of a literal belief in its proposed efficacy, or is the whole act symbolic? The rites of Leviticus 16, where Aaron somehow passes the sins of the community onto the head of a goat and, like the brick-bearing boat, sends it away, cannot possibly be differentiated from the Mesopotamian rite either in its intended efficacy or in the degree of literalness overtly manifest in the text. The Mesopotamians used ablutions to make their idols functional; the Israelites used oil anointings and water ablutions to validate an altar and other objects. The priests gained powers of intercession by wiping blood on their right ears, right thumbs, and right big toes, dripped blood in front of a curtain, dashed it against the side and horns of an altar, and donned special garb (Lev 1-8). The ark, the altar, the *ephod*, the engraved lazuli stones (Exod 28:9), the *ḥośen* of justice with its mounted stones, the *urim* and *tummim*, all of these objects had power in some *literal* sense. Surely they are part of a continuum, and any sudden break in that continuum begs explanation.

From detailed literary descriptions we know that the idols of Mesopotamia were fed, dressed, talked to, taken on trips, just the way one would treat a king.[27] How does one deal with the elaborate ritual of denial, whereby artisans went through symbolic acts of severing the hands and testifying by oath that the statue before

---

[27] See Jer 10:9, "their clothing is blue and purple" (indicative of royalty).

them was not a product of their handiwork? If the ritual is to be
understood literally, then we are positing a rite in which the person
who actually creates a wooden object swears an oath that he did not
fashion it and then fully believes that he did not. Perhaps this is a
form of ascription, where the powers of the artisan were themselves
transferred (temporarily) from a god. We must also compare this to
the function of the *ephod,* for there is fundamentally the same structure here, albeit without the denial ritual. A priest believes that an
object, fashioned by human hands, can imbue him with decision-
making powers derived from the divine. Thus, despite the lack of a
denial ritual, we still come down to the problem of trying to understand why humans believed that objects they fashioned influenced
or served as conduits to gods.

Scholars such as Faur have focused on the differences in detail
and, to a certain extent, rightly so. I am trying to show here that
the details in the character of the objects must be scrutinized more
at the level of function than appearance. I believe Jacobsen only
obscures the matter by introducing an approach that borders on nineteenth-century idealism. The language and actions of the Mesopotamians are fundamentally metaphorical, according to Jacobsen.
His reason for reaching this conclusion is quite simple: if they are
not metaphors, then they are nothing but paradoxes. A solution to
the conundrum Jacobsen senses can be found in the principles of
functional and conceptual ascription. We are freed from paradox
when we recognize that statements of equivalence can be statements
that relate to *parts* of beings (in this case, their structures or functions) without conveying ontological identity. By breaking the binary conceptualization of categories, we help liberate ideas from conflicts the ancients never sensed, but that modern scholars have
imposed.

Ronald Hendel (1988) transfers the issue from a dominantly theological concern into one that derives from certain social and political tensions in ancient Israel. Though I believe he pins the origins
of aniconism too specifically on certain historical events, his change
of focus proves instructive. Hendel sees the emergence of kingship
imagery as the crux of the problem.

> To put it briefly, the iconography of the cherub throne implies two
> interconnected images: the image of the god and the image of the king.
> In early Israel there existed a strong bias against the institution of

kingship. Once the image of the king was rejected, the image of the god, which was essentially a mirror image of the king, was also rejected. Since there was no place in the early Israelite universe for a king, the divine image that symbolized the authority of the king was prohibited. In short, the motive for the aniconic tradition in early Israel was the bias against kingship and its iconography. (378)

The Israelites' rejection of the kingship models of other cultures (Egypt, for instance, related to its kings as gods) also altered the corollary principles, Hendel believes. The anti-kingship bias set the precedent for

> an important shift in the structure of religion and society in the formative period of early Israel [that would follow]. . . . The prohibition of the image of Yahweh was a reflection, on the level of religious iconography, of the early Israelite bias against the institution and the ideology of kingship. . . . The shift in the structure of the society was accompanied by a shift in the concept of God, of which the aniconic tradition was one manifestation. (381)

I believe Hendel has identified what should be required of any theory of aniconic origins, namely, that we must seek its motivation in a social rather than a purely philosophical movement.[28] However, I do not believe the kingship imagery is the key. Hendel argues that the anti-kingship sentiment was dominant in the era of the tribal league, and gave way only because of Philistine expansion during the mid-eleventh century. He then notes that "later voices, such as the prophet Hosea, continued to recall the anti-kingship sentiments of early Israel" (379).[29] The process proposed by Hendel is what strikes me as far-fetched. A fundamental problem with the theory is, quite simply, the question of who would have instituted so radical a cultic change.

All things related to ritual and cult are fundamentally conservative and slow to change. Hendel's theory requires that some group sat down at some point during the tenth century and decided that a king was needed after all. Aniconism would have been instituted as a kind of conceptual limitation on human kingship. There is not

---

[28] Mettinger (1995, 195) expresses this most directly, stating that aniconism is an "inherited convention of religious expression which only later formed the basis for theological reflection."

[29] Citing Hos 8:4, "They have made kings (הם המליכו ולא ממני), but not with my sanction; they have made officers, but not of my choice. Of their silver and gold, they have made themselves images, to their own undoing" (JPS).

a single document in existence from a truly antimonarchic period; indeed, the whole movement was easily ascribed to an era of tribalism by a late author particularly because no authentic voice survived. There were many reasons to perpetuate the fiction of antimonarchism on the basis of some theological ideal, but that ideal is only conceptually possible in a postmonarchic world.[30] Those who ultimately found a monarchy inappropriate—the post-exilic priesthood—sought to justify Israel's new form of existence on the basis of an old justification: "You see, originally we were not meant to have a king!"

I agree with Hendel that a shift in the structure of society may have motivated a reconceptualization of God in a formal sense, but this shift would have been long in coming and, ultimately, far removed from the anti-kingship images of tribal constituents. Hosea's oblique reference to unsanctioned kings that draws Hendel's attention cannot reliably be interpreted as a reference to a bygone era of antimonarchism. Rather, the critique, if intelligible at all, should be taken as referring to those kings who ascended the throne after bloodbaths or other coups, subsequently perpetrated antireligious acts, and then brought upon themselves the wrath of prophetic indignation. One of Hosea's concerns is the fact that these kings and their officers—all unsanctioned—make idols. If anything, this indicates that the kings' notion of what a king is and what god is had not changed at all.

Finally, Hendel does not endeavor to explain why kingship imagery would be so altered in graphic form, but not in the parallel literary format. As Brettler (1989) shows in great depth, the "God is King" expressions are ubiquitous and highly anthropomorphic. In fact, they are so burdened with human imagery that Brettler is inclined to pronounce them all metaphorical. However, to argue that we must differentiate the king from the god by banishing certain icons, even while maintaining graphic anthropomorphic idioms in our language, is simply not compelling. Again, the bifurcation of language and physical representation does not allow for a cogent explanation of Israel's aniconism.

---

[30] See Brettler 1995, 91-111.

Competing Images and Social Forces

Tryggve Mettinger has turned to the question of aniconism a number of times in print.[31] In his most recent monograph on these issues, *No Graven Image?* (1995), Mettinger draws three important conclusions:

> First, Israelite aniconism is as old as Israel itself and not a late inno-
> vation. The express prohibition of images is just the logical conclu-
> sion of a very long development.

> Second, Israelite aniconism as such is not the result of theological
> reflection. Instead, it must be seen as an inherited convention of re-
> ligious expression which only later formed the basis for theological
> reflection. Various attempts . . . to explain aniconism as deriving from
> specific Israelite beliefs are to be considered disproven.

> Third, this *de facto* aniconism does not constitute one of Israel's *differ-
> entia specifica*. Here our investigation has made a contribution to the
> issue of the distinctiveness of Israel, and even a negative conclusion
> may be a significant result. (145)

I am in agreement with each of these points. Mettinger's thorough
consideration of the archaeological evidence skillfully builds his
arguments. While the purview of this study (1995) includes the artifactual evidence almost exclusively, extensive discussions of literary passages appears in his earlier works. These include "The Veto
on Images and the Aniconic God in Ancient Israel" (1979), in which
Mettinger draws close attention to the inner-biblical contradictions
regarding iconism. For example, in the Decalogue, Moses proscribes
images of "anything that is in the heaven above or the earth beneath"
(Exod 20:4), but in Numbers 21:4-9 we are told that Moses set up
a bronze serpent on a pole.[32] Similarly, Mettinger relates that the
Golden Calf story is "made up of a neutral or even positive account
of how the people made a bull image in the wilderness," which was
only later branded as a violation (1979, 17-18). In the same vein is
Gideon's *ephod* in Judges 8:27; the creator is unaware of its questionable nature.

---

[31] See especially Mettinger 1979 and 1995, but also 1982a, 1982b, 1988, and
1990.
[32] See 2 Kings 18:4, on Hezekiah's abolition of this apparently longstanding,
institutional use of the "Nehushtan." See my comments in the following chapter
on this passage.

Mettinger prefers to see Jeroboam's cultic bulls (1 Kgs 12:28-31) as an example of the assimilation of older El and Yʜᴡʜ imagery rather than as Baal syncretism. Ultimately, this historical incident was disparaged by the biblical writers because it went against the dominant forces of the cultic oligarchy that would eventually come into power. Mettinger views aniconism as the result of *competing* images. The north had the bull image, the south had the empty cherub throne in the Jerusalem Temple. Eventually, even the ark-theology gave way to the "spreading iconoclastic tendencies associated with Hosea and the Deuteronomistic movement" (1979, 22). Mettinger here follows Gerhard von Rad's discussion of how the ark's "traditional character of a numinous symbol for God's presence . . . via a process of rationalization was reduced to a mere container for the tablets of the Law (Deut 10:1-5; 1 Kgs 8:9)."[33] Ark theology itself is fundamentally aniconic, according to Mettinger. "The official Jerusalem cult was imageless in the sense that it lacked a direct symbol for Jʜᴡʜ. The cherub throne with the ark can not be regarded as such a symbol" (22).

When would a dogma concerning icons, as expressed repeatedly in Torah, have come into being? Mettinger holds that it was the Deuteronomists who turned against created symbols in general, not only those that were representational but even the more "'formless' cultic objects such as the originally legitimate *maṣṣeboth*" (22).[34] Prior to that, Hosea worked out the first broad rejection of graphic images. The Deuteronomists would make it part of law, but Hosea, and perhaps prophets before him, anticipated the official expression of aniconism in their iconoclastic declarations. Aniconism would become a positive expression of distinctiveness, as well as an internal prohibition against the worship of other gods.[35] A corollary to aniconism would be the prohibition against misuse of the divine name in magical contexts. The aniconic tendency in Israel was, according to Mettinger, quite ancient, but the particular expressions that survived in our texts are Deuteronomic.

I believe the broad strokes of Mettinger's picture provides a fundamentally accurate understanding of the evolution of aniconism. Independently, I came to the same conclusions that (1) aniconism

---

[33] See Von Rad 1962-65, 1:109ff.

[34] See also Mettinger 1995 on these issues, as well as Dohmen 1985.

[35] Mettinger does not go with this thinking in 1995, where he refutes the notion that distinctiveness was an issue.

was originally an issue of competing symbols,[36] and (2) the expressions of aniconism as we have them in Torah are to be stratified, with the majority deriving from (the very late) Deuteronomic and post-exilic models.[37] Regarding the details, I have some concerns, and I shall endeavor interpretations of some literary evidence that has been broadly overlooked. Mettinger's desire to pin the origins of the controversy on a feud between the northern bull imagery and the southern ark-theology images does not stand up to scrutiny. The problem with this thesis is that the aniconic proscriptions are universal, such that the cherubim (among other graphics on the ark and its accoutrements) should have been as offensive as that of the northern bulls. Indeed, if the cherubim resembled what many scholars take to be the prototype—a creature with a human head, lion's body, eagle's wings, and bovine hindquarters—it is hardly possible to distinguish the two in terms of their relative representationality. Mettinger, recognizing this weak link in his theory, suggests that the cherubim were hidden in the Holy of Holies and therefore protected against

> the false interpretations inevitable in a degenerate popular cult. Its very form—a cherub throne with the ark—did not invite the same Baalistic misunderstandings as a bull image; for the bull was not only El's, but also Baal's animal. Moreover, we may suppose that the notion of a throne in Jerusalem was for a long period sufficiently alive to guarantee that the cultic symbol as such was not confused with the unseen deity who sat above it. (22)

Some problems derive from this description. Mettinger introduces the notion that the bull image was more dangerous because of its similarity to other cultural statuaries, especially those of Baalism. If the "false interpretations" of a "popular cult" did indeed contribute to the rejection of the bull, then we do not need the argument regarding competing icons at all. Instead one could say, simply, that images close to those of foreign worship practices were too problematic to be permitted. In other words, either the conflict is one of syncretism or it is one of competing icons, but Mettinger has somewhat merged the two. We might also point out that winged creatures (cherubs) are just as prominent as bulls in foreign cultic imagery.

---

[36] Faur also established this as central, though he took it in a different direction.

[37] On the relationship of Deuteronomy to the development of other parts of the Pentateuchal literature, see Nelson 1981; Levenson 1975; Levinson 1997.

Mettinger's argument thus provides two distinct motivations: the anti-Baalization of Yahweh and the south's attempt to suppress northern competing cultic sites. While ultimately it may be that these two issues were important at *some* point in history—as I believe the textual evidence of Hosea suggests—they do not provide a cogent analysis of why either struggle would manifest itself as aniconism.

The weakness here is in part connected to my second concern, and that is the character of the literary evidence. The declaration in Hosea (8:6) that the Samarian calf is not a god was, according to Mettinger, "directed against just such a confusion of the pedestal animal and the deity" (23).[38] We previously pondered the question of whether the ancients considered the statues to be the actual gods or some form of intermediary. Despite the ambiguities that still remain, I believe there is much evidence indicating that the ancient Mesopotamians related to the statue of a deity by means of conceptual ascription, without ontological identity. The simple fact that the Mesopotamians had no problem producing, in different locales, numerous versions of a single god should demonstrate that ontological identity was never an issue. Moreover, we know that in battle, as well as in other contexts, symbols on banners were used to evoke the *functions* of the deity, despite the absence of the primary image.[39] This, of course, is in great contrast to the Israelites, who (at least according to the literary evidence) permitted the production of only one ark, one set of cherubim, and so forth; when they were not present, we are told, battles were lost.[40] Although the cultic statue was not identical to the god, it received the physical and ritual treatment that would be accorded a god who actually appeared in a room with a human. When it came to the temples, Bottéro concluded, "it really seems that people were convinced that the gods lived there, with a real but mysterious presence in their cult statues" (1992, 212). In contrast, Mettinger writes that "at least in later periods, [Babylonian] religion did not consist of crude image worship; the statue was conceived of as the abode of an extension of the person of the god, who otherwise lived in heaven or in hell." I am suggesting that

---

[38] This is Halbertal and Margalit's notion of confusing metonymic with more direct forms of representation; see above, pp.135ff.

[39] See Mettinger 1995, 38ff.

[40] For a discussion of Numbers 14 and Deuteronomy 1 regarding the Battle at Hormah, see below chapter 8; on Deuteronomy 1, see also Weinfeld 1981 (Introduction and ad loc.).

the "realness" alluded to by Bottéro is not mysterious but hopeful in terms of both function and efficacy. Taking up on Mettinger's notion of "extension," I seek to clarify this religious phenomenon by reconceptualizing it as functional ascription.

Carl D. Evans (1995) focuses on the question of whether Yahweh-aniconism is a retrojection from a later period upon an earlier, more limited, set of prohibitions. He suggests that aniconism may be the result of a long struggle over the use of certain images, rather than a revolutionary theology. "The origins of aniconic tradition in ancient Israel," argues Evans, "can be found in the complex of social forces that produced an exclusive Yahwism in the late monarchic period" following the destruction of Israel (200). Thus, for Evans, aniconism is part of the program of differentiation that caused certain transformations in Israelite thought.[41]

> Exod. 34:11-16, for example, warns against making a covenant with "the inhabitants of the land"—identified here as Amorites, Canaanites, Hittites, Perizzites, Hivites and Jebusites[42]—lest their ways become a snare to the worshipers of Yahweh. Instead, observant Yahwists are instructed to destroy the native altars, מצבות and אשרים. The rationale for such action is that no other god besides the jealous Yahweh is to be worshiped (v.14). The clear implication is that the cult objects that are to be destroyed are used to worship other gods (cf. vv.16-17), *despite the evidence* that in various circles מצבות and אשרים were acceptable features of the Yahwistic cult. Thus, the differentiation process sought to define "Yahwism" in narrow and exclusive terms. The native altars, מצבות and אשרים were rejected as "non-Yahwistic," even though other Yahweh worshippers included these features in their form of "Yahwism." (200-201, my emphasis)

I believe Evans is very close to striking at the root of this whole issue, but he does not fully exploit the nuances of the evidence he brings to the reader. The *evidence* is that in various circles, *maṣṣevot* and *asherim* were acceptable features in the Yahwistic cult. This is not a battle of differentiation with an external adversary; this is a battle between

---

[41] Evans here adopts the term "differentiation" in the sense that it was used by Mark Smith (1990a); note the similarity to Mettinger 1995, as quoted above, p. 149.

[42] We should keep in mind that the list of occupying nations is itself an anachronistic trope enabling a biblical author to make his contemporary concerns with intermarriage stem from the Sinai era. See Fishbane 1985, 115ff. Changes in the list occur when the most threatening local population needed to be included, but archaic entries are also preserved so as to give it antiquity, and hence, the air of authenticity.

Yahwists—those whom we would come to know as the P-Yahwists—
against those who would no longer reign as authoritative priestly
Yahwists. I hope to show this more fully in the next chapter. Like
Mettinger, Evans recognizes the origins of aniconic proscriptions as
social, not theological:

> Rather than positing a "stream" of thinking that influenced the de-
> velopment of iconoclastic royal policies, it is more plausible to posit
> that aniconic thinking was developed to justify policies that called for
> the elimination of images. Aniconism, in other words, had its origins
> in the social rather than the theological realm. (35)

From the positions noted by Faur, Hendel, Mettinger, and Evans,
we can draw some basic conclusions. The main points include
Mettinger's conclusions that Israelite aniconism was neither a late
development, nor the result of theological reflection, nor a distinctive characteristic of ancient Israel; and the realization that aniconism
was motivated not by abstract theological principles but by social
and/or political struggles over the control of certain types of images.
Underlying all of these concerns is the question of how icons
functioned in the ancient world: whether they needed to be physically similar to the gods or could be abstract representations. The
other side of the question is this: for what purposes did the literary
remnants of the various biblical periods utilize the connotations of
idols? If we place the origins of aniconism in social developments,
then we must recognize that those developments do not dictate the
rhetorical applications of their imagery.

According to much literary evidence, at various stages the Israelites conceived of their deity in the most anthropomorphic of terms.
No bull, ark, pillar, *ephod*, *maṣṣevah* or *maskit*, even remotely resembles the imagery of the divine repeatedly related in the extant documents. Thus, to think that metonymic iconism was somehow transformed into literal idol worship must assume that the "image" was
mistaken for the God. Any discussion of the origins of Israelite
aniconism must recognize that during the periods when iconism
flourished, God was not viewed as either ontologically identical to
or similar to the objects created. And yet, as I have argued above,
the early literary remnants also convey the notion that the deity did
actually dwell in the ark and later the Temple of Jerusalem. Thus,
just what Hosea meant when he said of the calf of Samaria, "it is
not god" (8:6), leaves us pondering the whole understanding of the

prophets regarding images and objects. Would any Israelite have thought that a statue of a bull *was* Yahweh or any other god, even as he accepted that Yahweh was somehow present in the Temple? It all comes down to *who controls what*. Israelite iconography is selective because its aniconism is only relative.

On these conclusions, I now wish to build.

8.

ANICONISM AS A NARROWING OF THE
CONDITIONS OF RELEVANCE

What did idols mean to the idolater? Were they literally gods, meta-phors for the gods, or some other form of reification? As noted earlier, Thorkild Jacobsen has argued that no one confused icons with the actual deity despite the elaborate washing, feeding, and transport-ing rituals. Similarly, Marjo Korpel (1990, 87) has argued that the literary depictions of the gods and idols presented in biblical and Canaanite literature must be understood metaphorically. Were this otherwise, we would be left with what Korpel considers "childish" primitivisms.[1] Let us explore the implications of this thesis against the backdrop of the biblical materials.

According to the Books of Kings, twelve kings among the mon-archs of Judah alone allowed for the practice of idolatry during their reigns.[2] But numerous others in both Israel and Judah either toler-ated the "foreign" cultic practices introduced by their predecessors or now and again participated in it themselves. When we read the books of Kings and Chronicles, we come to recognize that idolatry became a literary motif in the assessment of a king's historical im-pact.[3] "It is responsible for military defeats, the death of kings, and, ultimately, the destruction of the Temple" (Japhet 1989, 215). As we might expect from a motif, its use need not reflect an historical

---

[1] This unfortunate evaluation of idolatry surfaces at numerous points in Korpel's study. Indeed, Korpel sees all descriptions of the gods as metaphorical, so that when she is forced to acknowledge what appears to be a break in the metaphorical imagery, she demurs that "it must have been difficult to escape from the impression that the myth wanted to describe the world of the gods as an existing reality comparable to that experienced by man" (632); in other words, the authors used literal speech every once in a while to reassure the audience that they were talking about real beings—not just mythic ones.

[2] They are Solomon (1 Kgs 11:6), Rehoboam (14:22), Jehoram (2 Kgs 8:18), Ahaziah (8:27), Manasseh (21:2), Amon (21:20), Johazhaz (23:32), Jehoiakim (23:37), Jehoiachin (24:9), and Zedekiah (24:19) and by implication Ahaz (2 Kgs 16:2) and Abijah (1 Kgs 15:3).

[3] See Japhet 1989, 203-16.

reality.[4] Some kings who are depicted as having supported idol worship during their reigns may still receive only approbations; others, deemed a failure in one way or another—perhaps even in ways unrelated to the cult—may be condemned as idol worshipers simply to convey the most intense execration possible. As far as literary structures go, we might see the idolatry motif regarding the monarchs as parallel to the apostasy motif repeatedly visited during the Wilderness narratives in the Pentateuch.[5] As Jeffrey Tigay puts it, "the sweeping Biblical indictments, in sum, are based more on theological axioms than historica data" (1987, 179).[6]

When we combine the impressions we gain from the historiographic writings (including Torah) with those of the prophetic literature,

---

[4] Sara Japhet suggests that despite the fact that the Chronicler's Judaism was "unaffected by pagan worship," the idolatry motif "retains a high degree of vitality" in his writings (1989, 215) However, Japhet argues further that "although the actual phenomenon [of idolatry] had disappeared, Israelite awareness of its dangers had not. It is this awareness that we find in Chronicles." It is unclear to me how Japhet can be so confident that paganism was not a viable alternative to Judaism during the Chronicler's era and that his Judaism was "unaffected by pagan worship." Indeed, the argument is presented in this manner despite the fact that we have no way of assessing the character of cultural syncretism or the threat of assimilation during the period from 450-250, a period to which we can date with confidence very few sources. Remarkably, this very wisdom is articulated by Japhet in her Epilogue where she notes, with regard to the "spiritual and social reality of the Chronicler's time," that "we know very little of this reality and are therefore in danger of arguing in circles when we attempt to ascertain the relationship between the book and the period in which it was written" (507).

[5] See Coats (1968) whose survey also notes how the wilderness era is depicted in the prophetic literature.

[6] Tigay argues that by "combining the evidence of the inscriptions and the more circumstantial statements of the Biblical writers [we learn that] there existed some superficial, fetishistic polytheism and a limited amount of more profound polytheism in Israel, but neither can be quantified" (179). Despite Tigay's thorough treatment of the evidence, there remain many questions about the character of the evidence. The material is highly selective (mostly building inscriptions from the eighth century) and based on a shaky assumption, namely, that just as other ancient Near Eastern cultures used divine names in personal names, we should expect to find a substantial number of Israelites named for many of the gods they are said to have worshipped. My concern is that the focus of multi-god worship defines too narrowly the issue of syncretism. Tigay writes: "a unilatry which ignores the gods of other *nations* can be classified as monolatry. But a unilatry that ignores phenomena on which *all* nations depend looks like monotheism" (178, emphasis original). This is true if we emphasize the *-latry* stem of monolatry or unilatry, in which worship is the focus. But belief in the existence of other deities among the populace and worship of a single deity by the official cult need not be manifest in some social tension, except, perhaps, the very social tension that constitutes the prophetic critique of society.

the biblical materials prove enigmatic. On the one hand, the literary motif must have had some basis in a cultural reality or else it would always have seemed irrelevant. On the other hand, if it became a standard trope used to condemn those who failed to follow the Yahwist's political and religious plan, we might expect there to be stereotypical characterizations that were not grounded in the realities of a given historical moment. As such, we should not be surprised to find within Tanakh a number of passages whose links to real idol worship are tendentious. Our aim is to not be swayed by them.

Matitiahu Tsevat commences his article on the prohibition against divine images by drawing attention to how the textual evidence suggests that idols were, indeed, mistaken for gods. He cites a number of biblical passages that plainly state that "images are powerless and, by implication, worthless, the proof being that they cannot use their limbs and other apparent resources of their bodies" (1986, 211).[7] Isaiah 44:15, for instance, appears satirical of the one who "makes a god of [wood] and worships it, fashions an idol and bows down to it!" The criticism would appear to be that the fashioned object can hardly be of any significance, never mind a god, since man himself made it. But within this very chapter (44:9) we read: "All of the idol makers are altogether purposeless; and their fineries are functionless; *and their own testimony is that [the objects] neither see nor understand,* such that they should be ashamed." According to Isaiah, the makers of the idols are themselves *aware* that the objects have no powers of perception.

As John L. McKenzie notes, chapter 44's polemic does not make sense in terms of any ancient Near Eastern practice known to us (1968, 68). That is, McKenzie accepts the notion that no one confused idols for gods; consequently, he must explain why the Isaiah polemic woul set out to criticize a nonbelief. Tsevat poses the question as follows: does anyone doubt that "the difference between a picture and the object it pictures was clear to people of the Ancient Near East as it is to us of the modern civilization of the West?" (1986, 212). Let us extend the concern to icons based on nonsimilarity. I will argue, with McKensie, that the presence of an idol "was not dissimilar to the Israelite ark of the covenant, which was also the symbol and seat of the presence of Yahweh in Israel" (McKenzie

---

[7] Tsevat cites Deut 4:28; Jer 10:5; Hab 2:18; Ps 115:5-7, 135:16-18.

1986, 68).[8] Basically, we seek to understand whether it is legitimate
to differentiate the use of the ark from the use of an idol. But such
an investigation makes sense only with an understanding of what both
idols and the ark meant to their respective communities. Only with
a clear sense of their functions can we begin to discuss whether belief
in the powers of idols was literal or metaphorical and how such beliefs
were manifest in Israelite attitudes toward icon worship.

This is not easily accomplished. The biblical material, even very
late writings, preserve a variety of confusions regarding the meaning of idols. Sometimes these confusions are not endemic to the texts
but the result of our misunderstanding key terms. Consider the
passage in 1 Chronicles 16 which shadows Psalm 96:4-5. First I will
provide the Hebrew, and then Sara Japhet's (1993) translation:

כי גדול יהוה ומהלל מאד
ונורא הוא על־כל־אלהים
כי כל אלהי העמים אלילים
ויהוה שמים עשה

> For great is the LORD, and greatly to be praised
>> and he is to be held in awe above all gods.
> For all the gods of the peoples are idols;
>> but the LORD made the heavens. (1 Chr 16:25-26)

The meaning of verse 26 as given in this translation makes very little
sense following the meaning provided for verse 25. How, on the one
hand, can you say that Yahweh is to be held in awe above all gods
and then say that the gods are nothing other than idols? If the other
gods are nothing but idols, then they are not gods at all. So the
preferable argument should be like that of Deutero-Isaiah: "I am
Yahweh, there is none else; beside me, there is no god" (Isa 45:5).
The confusion may stem from a mistranslation of the word אלילים,
which occurs a mere twenty times in Scriptures. The term is rendered "idols" quite consistently by the major translations.[9] In many

---

[8] McKenzie's position is also articulated in Faur 1978 and Mettinger 1995.

[9] See JPS; the Revised Standard Version, and the New RSV, and, as noted,
Japhet to 1 Chr 16:25. However, see Dahood 1968-70, vol. 2, to Psalm 96:5, where
he translates, "where all the gods of the peoples are but rags." To justify this, Dahood
writes that אלילים is "usually translated 'naught' or 'idols,' Heb. 'elilim, which is
still lacking an etymology, may find one in Ugar. all, a type of garment whose sense
comes through from its pairing with lbš, 'clothes, garment.' This etymology is of a
piece with Albright's possible explanation of biblical terapim, a type of idol and object
of reverence as literally denoting 'old rags,' since Canaanite trp is now known to
have meant 'to wear out.'"

of these contexts, the translation "idols" makes no sense, and a preferable rendering would be "gods" or in some contexts "minor gods." Consider how 1 Chr 16:25-6 would read with this in mind:

> For great is Yahweh, exceedingly praiseworthy,
>> he is awesome beyond all the gods.
> For all of the gods of the nations are but [minor] deities
>> while Yahweh has made heavens.

Similarly, consider the usage of אליל in Isaiah 10:10-11:

כאשר מצאה ידי לממלכת האליל
ופסיליהם מירושלם ומשמרון
הלא כאשר עשיתי לשמרון ולאליליה
כן אעשה לירושלם ולעצביה

> Just as my hand overcame the kingdoms of the [minor] god[s]
>> whose statues exceed those of Jerusalem and Samaria;
> Just as I have done to Samaria and her gods,
>> shall I not also do to Jerusalem and to her icons?[10]

Even the oft-rehearsed Leviticus 26:1 makes more sense with this understanding of אלילים: "Do not establish for yourselves deities [אלילם], nor erect statues and icons [פסל ומצבה] for yourselves, nor should you put *maskit* stones in your land which you would worship; but I am Yahweh, your God."[11] The word אליל has no intrinsic relationship to iconolatry, and the idiom אלילי כספו ואלילי זהב (Isa 31:7) should not be rendered "idols of silver, idols of gold," but rather, "gods of silver, gods of gold," just as we render אלהי מסכה as "molten gods" rather than "molten idols" (cf. Exod 34:17; Lev 19:4).[12] As one moves through the literature using the term אליל it is apparent that sometimes the intent is quite specifically the minor deities of whom statuaries were frequently made, while other times the word may stand for the idols themselves. This is surely consistent with the

---

[10] In each verse the first colon has אליל for gods, while the second colon focuses on the iconic representations of those gods (פסל, עצב).

[11] Here the verse begins with אליל for gods, lists the iconic representations and then ends with *the* god for Israel, Yahweh.

[12] The Hebrew אליל is parallel to the Akkadian *ililu*, a term for a god of highest rank, which itself is a derivative from *enlil*. See *The Assyrian Dictionary* (Chicago: Oriental Institute, 1960), 7:85. The term eventually became a generic reference for gods, not unlike the transformation witnessed in the originally formal name Ishtar, which became *ishtaru* as a general term for female deities.

polysemous use of other terms for gods, such אלים, אל, אלהים all of
which can mean real gods, the God, judges (in the case of אלהים),
or even representations of gods (usually in conjunction with other
terms). By recognizing how integral the question of god-belief is to
our understanding of idol imagery we are able to establish more sensible conditions of relevance when translating. Thus, if the textual
environment suggests monolatry rather than monotheism—as is the
case in 1 Chronicles, Isaiah 10, and many other passages using אליל
in the context of idol proscriptions—we should avoid forcing the vocabulary into certain stereotypical renderings. In the process, we also
gain access to the function of idols as they were understood in biblical materials.

But if we may go back for a moment to the verse in 1 Chronicles
16 that motivated this digression: I chose that passage over its parallel in Psalm 96 quite specifically because it is used in the context
of an ark-related ritual. This passage in Chronicles retells the story
of how David brought the ark to its final resting place, Jerusalem.
Although we cannot determine whether these verses already existed as a free standing anthologized psalm prior to being included in
this chapter of Chronicles, what is clear is that the redactor had many
options when it came to depicting the character of this ceremony.
The fact that these particular verses were chosen, so laden with
monolatristic idioms, should inform us as to the redactor's understanding of the ark processional's meaning. That is, by situating the
ark in Jerusalem, one is demonstrating the superiority of Yahweh
over the other deities. If this reading is correct, we have a window
into the prominence of monolatry late in Israelite history. In any
event, the passage testifies to the limited influence of the Deuteronomic worldview on the post-exilic priesthood.

Whatever their function, there can be little doubt that there is a
long history of icon use in ancient Israel. The archaeological evidence is such that it is very difficult to distinguish household idols
that were in the homes of Canaanites from those that were found
in Israelite abodes. But the ubiquity of such objects suggests that they
were commonly found in the homes of both religious communities.[13]
The ambiguity in the area of material culture can be resolved with
use of the literary evidence. Earlier we drew attention to the serpent

---

[13] See Greenberg 1962 on the use of these effigies for safety during travel. See
also Cornelius 1994 (122 and elsewhere) for a discussion of "protective private
amulets" that appear to have been "carried on strings."

first attributed to Moses (Num 21:9) and apparently not removed from the cultic rituals until Hezekiah's reign (2 Kings 18:4).[14] I am not terribly concerned with whether this text represents an accurate dating for the demise of the Mosaic serpent. What is of importance is that the redactors willingly suffered the continued existence of this icon in the Temple from Moses' time (as it is understood in these passages) down to the end of the eighth century. Whether they realized it or not, they gave testimony to the creation of an icon by Moses and (ostensibly) its continued use for many centuries thereafter. Let me make clear that I am not arguing that this icon actually dates back to Moses' time (if there is such a thing). What is important here is that the mythology that justifies the use of this icon associated its origins with the Exodus narrative. Why and how this came to be is an issue we cannot go into here. Whatever the true origins of the serpent in the sanctuary, what remains clear is that the biblical historian did not hesitate to leave the reader with the impression that it derived from Moses himself and lasted well into the eighth century.

Similarly, Deuteronomy (27:15) indicates the ongoing secretive use of sculptured and molten images (פסל ומסכה). Here again, it is the lateness of this proscription that should lead us to assume a prolonged cultic involvement with such artifacts.[15] If we can take Ezekiel at his word, these devotional objects apparently occupied a special section of a dwelling, as indicated by the reference to בחדרי משכיתו ("in the rooms of his idol," 8:12). Some texts suggest that the public, inscribed stelae (אבנים . . . ושדת אותם בשיד) that stood next to the stone altar, were authorized and employed as integral symbolizations of covenant.[16] The fact that Deuteronomy 27 promotes the use of *these* stelae rather than the tablets in the ark may demonstrate that the shift toward centralization altered the character of the tablet-icon from a portable object to a set of permanently standing markers.[17] The

---

[14] Hezekiah is thought to have ruled for almost 30 years beginning in 715.

[15] I would not rule out the possibility that these references are themselves allegorical expressions about some other highly scrutinized aspect of society. For the time being, I treat these expressions as indicative of a polemic focused upon some real historical circumstance rather than a straw man.

[16] See Deut 27:2, 4. As Faur (1978) suggests, the difference between a common מסכה and the אבנים in this Deuteronomy passage may have something to do with anointing. However, the text is awkward because of its redundancy, where vv. 2-3a are repeated in 3b-4. See also Hos 3:4 and my discussion of it below.

[17] In Deut 27, it would appear that the stones of the unhewn altar also have "every word of this Teaching" inscribed upon them.

ark and the stelae present the greatest challenge to our notion of a purely aniconic religion. A greater appreciation of Israelite aniconism can only occur when these objects, along with related accoutrements, have been appropriately contextualized. Our goal is to understand the development of such icons diachronically, without attempting to harmonize conflicting data.[18]

The Ark Mythology

Let us start, then, with the ark quite specifically. There have been a great many attempts to make sense of the ark narratives. It is incumbent upon any historian to distinguish stages in the development of the mythology about the ark. Frequently this development is divided into three eras: the pre-monarchic period, the era of the ark's repose in the Jerusalem Temple, and post-exilic times.[19] Early on, scholars began to question whether during the early stages of its development, the ark was even a "box" at all, as the later priestly documents define it.[20] Suggestions as to its form ranged from a throne to a tent to a container, not for the Decalogue, but rather cultic stones that represent the proto-mythology of the later Decalogue tradition (Morgenstern 1942-44). The Hebrew ארון is rather enigmatic. The root is used in no other Hebrew words. Etymological surveys do not prove terribly helpful as the term in both Akkadian and Ugaritic connotes either a simple box or sarcophagus. As described in Exodus 25, the ark is ostensibly a container in which the "pact" is deposited.[21] However, it is also quite specifically the place where God meets Moses, and from where he pronounces edicts for the Israelites to follow. The flanking cherubim, whose wings shield the cover of the ark, are standard symbols for royal thrones.[22]

---

[18] I take this as an important mandate, recognizing that it is in contrast to the common approach to writing Hebrew Bible theologies. I seek to show the evolution of a concept and will treat what some call anomalies as indicative of stages in that evolution. For a contrasting perspective, see the survey in Hasel 1991; also Korpel 1990, 620-22.

[19] This is basically Morgenstern's approach (1942-4, 155).

[20] For the scholarly discussion of this issue from the nineteenth century, including dissertations, see Morgenstern 1942-44 and Kaufmann 1937-56, 2:349; for more recent scholarship, see Haran's summary and bibliographic listings (1985, 246-47).

[21] "Pact" (עדות) is the term in Exodus 25, but elsewhere this is identified as the Decalogue.

[22] Sarna (1986, 212) interprets the presence of these winged creatures as in-

Menahem Haran acknowledges the utter confusion of the texts, but believes the solution lies in separating the two distinct symbols involved in this controversy: the ark, which is a container of holy objects, and the throne, which is symbolized in the ark's cover, the *kapporet*, thereby keeping the ark from having to literally serve as the seat of God. Haran, who generally approaches the text with a lack of skepticism regarding historical veracity, justifies this separation of the objects on the basis of a description of the Solomonic temple in 1 Kings 6:23-36 and 8:1-9. The D writer speaks of the ark while ignoring the cherubim altogether (Deut 10:1-5), therefore leading Haran to believe that the roles of the two devices were altogether distinct—although he never distinguishes stages in the development of these objects (1985 246-59).

Some scholars have suggested that the ark was actually a kind of dwelling place, parallel to the boxes used in other ancient Near Eastern cultures to house their idols, especially during transport (Morgenstern 1942-44, 154). In his extensive commentary on the book of Numbers, Jacob Milgrom (1990) focuses on the role of the ark in Israelite theology, particularly with regard to this question of dwelling. Milgrom asks, Is the ark "the permanent residence of the Lord, or is His association with it temporary, unpredictable, and symbolic?" (1990, 374).[23] His initial answer runs as follows: "The preponderant view of the texts indicates that the latter is the case: For the Lord to manifest Himself or to speak from the ark, He arranges to 'meet' with Moses or 'appears'—His *kavod* is visible—to Israel (e.g., 14:10; 16:19; 17:7; 20:6)" (374).[24] At first, Milgrom's

---

dicative of "God's mobility or, as we should say, His omnipresence, an attribute that, as we have seen, is also emphasized in the Tabernacle in other ways." Sarna never entertains a nonfigurative meaning for any of the objects that dominate the Israelite cult, specifically because a literal meaning could not be harmonized with "the otherwise characteristcally strict rejection of pictorial representations and of the plastic arts in Israel" (211). On the cherubim, see Albright 1938; Haran 1959 and 1985, chap. 13; Morgenstern 1942-43; and sources cited below.

[23] The question itself suffers from logical tensions. Permanent is the opposite of temporary, but an "unpredictable" association does not conflict specifically with either of these terms. The abode could be "symbolic" regardless of our conclusion concerning the temporal issue. In plain language, Milgrom meant to ask, Does God really live at the ark? If the answer is yes, then we might further question whether it is meant as a permanent association or a temporary one. If the answer is no, then we might conclude that the ark as a "residence" is altogether symbolic. Even if we answered affirmatively, we might still investigate the symbolic connotations of the ark.

[24] It would take us too far afield to consider each of the examples cited by

evidence is derived exclusively from the Book of Numbers, but then he expands his discussion on the ark to Tanakh more generally. He notes that there is evidence contrary to this "preponderant view," evidence suggesting that the ark is actually a dwelling place. He cites 2 Kings 19:14-15, regarding Hezekiah's entreaty before God, and David's dancing before the ark in 2 Samuel 6. Regarding this "contrary" evidence, Milgrom writes:

> These verses, however, *are not to be taken literally*. Sacrifices are always said to be offered "before the Lord" without implying that He is physically present in the sanctuary. Indeed, that the cherubim are winged means that the divine seat is *in reality* a chariot: His dominion is the world and only when He wishes to manifest Himself to Israel does He condense His Presence upon the ark-cherubim inside the Holy of Holies. (374-57, my emphasis)[25]

Since the evidence from the few verses cited contradicts the thesis regarding God's symbolic presence at the ark, Milgrom instructs his reader that the verses in question *must not be taken literally*. The example Milgrom calls upon—the idiom "before the Lord"—is employed as an instance of when the literal interpretation of a phrase is unacceptable. But no evidence is mustered to show why "before the Lord" does not very specifically imply that God *is* physically present in the sanctuary (cf. Exod 33:1-11). Milgrom's conviction fits in with his overall approach to the question of whether the ark is a true domicile or a symbol. "Israel's religion . . . was imageless from the outset . . . and regarded the ark not as a representation of the Deity but only as His footstool" (374).[26] The issue of images unnecessarily complicates the matter. Whether or not Israelites accepted images has nothing to do with their conceptualization of a divine

---

Milgrom, but they do *not* all support his argument. Num 16:19 relates to the confrontation between Moses and Korah; it takes place at the Tent of Meeting, but the word "ark" is nowhere near to be found. The same is the case with 17:7. Surely there is a difference between the Tabernacle and the ark itself; only the latter has the cherubim which are God's accompanists. There is also an ambiguity in Milgrom's expression "the preponderant view of the texts indicates . . ."; does he mean to speak of most texts in Scripture, or the view of those reading the texts?

[25] By "in reality" I take Milgrom to mean "literally."

[26] Milgrom does not offer the reader a discussion of whether the need for or use of a "footstool" implies that God has a foot. On the notion that the ark is the footstool, see Japhet (1989, 77-79) who argues that in most contexts, the Temple itself is God's footstool. The concept that the ark is the footstool, claims Japhet, is an "innovation" of the Chronicler (1 Chr 28:2).

abode. Even a god invisible to human eyes might still dwell in an ark.

Numerous texts suggest that a very different interpretation may be the accurate one. Consider the often-discussed passage in 1 Kings 8:

> But will God really dwell on earth [in the Temple]?[27] Even the heavens to their uttermost reaches cannot contain You, how much less this House that I have built! Yet turn, O Lord my God, to the prayer and supplication of your servant, and hear the cry and prayer which Your servant offers before You this day. May your eyes be open day and night toward this House, toward the place of which You have said, "My name shall abide there"; may You heed the prayers which Your servant will offer toward this place. (vv. 27-29)

The theologians behind this passage were clearly combating the theology that placed God very literally—physically—in the Temple. They have substituted prayer for the previously dominant role of sacrifice; actual, physical presence has given way to an "abiding name." As Jon D. Levenson notes, the authors of Solomon's speech reiterate repeatedly that God's true dwelling place is the heavens (see vv. 27, 32, 34, 36, 39, 43, 45, 49). So vigorous a diatribe against a *literal belief* in a divine (terrestrial) domicile indicates that many quite simply held that belief. The theological norm against which the writers of this Kings passage were writing, was the belief that God dwelled in the ark. Levenson also argues that this insertion is contemporaneous with Isaiah 66, or "distinctly Exilic" (1981, 159). Minimally, we must acknowledge that this polemic, penned not before the end of the sixth century, indicates that a literal belief in God's physical sojourn at the Temple (= ark) was prominent enough to evoke this diatribe. Since there is no evidence suggesting that the Deuteronomist was ideologically victorious on this issue, we have no reason to believe that Israelites did not continue to maintain belief in the literalness of God's earthly dwelling, as associated first with the ark and then with the Temple.[28]

---

[27] I have added the words "in the Temple" because that is the overall context of this text; that is, it is not just a question of whether God will dwell on earth, but more specifically, will he dwell in the edifice Solomon has just created? I take the ark to be an imaginary construct that developed into temple imagery.

[28] See Levenson 1975 and 1981 on the bifurcation of the Deuteronomic writer into Dtr 1 and Dtr 2, where for Levenson Dtr 1 is pre-exilic and Dtr 2 is exilic. The point is that an exilic community might have the most interest in the nonliteral

G. W. Ahlström argues that the ark narratives in the books of
Samuel and Kings are literary fictions composed to "tell how the
god of a small people worshiping at Shiloh rose to the position of a
supreme deity, one whose power reached outside Israel and Judah
proper"(1984, 148).[29] Tryggve Mettinger (1979) uses the material
somewhat differently. He envisions the ark as part of the religious
struggle for centralization; it was the ark versus other (northern) cultic
images. As such, the powers of the ark had to have been conceived
of *literally* until well after it was demythologized by the Deuteronomists.

The winners in history usually get the last say, and the composite
nature of the ark-related passages reflects that reality. Preponderant views are bluntly diachronic, often merging generations of transformations in a single narrative, while providing little insight into
the nuances of developing beliefs. Periodically, vestiges from earlier
eras do manage to survive. For instance, in Numbers 14:39-45 we
learn that the Israelites embarked on a battle not sanctioned by God:
"Yet defiantly they marched toward the crest of the hill country,
though neither the Lord's Ark of the Covenant nor Moses stirred
from the camp" (v. 44).[30] God is quite literally present wherever the
ark is situated; consequently, defeat results when the ark is absent.
One might call upon the Ark Song as evidence, but here again, it
all comes down to whether it is literal or figurative.

> During the journey of the ark, Moses would say:
>   Rise up Yahweh; may your enemies be scattered;
>   May your foes flee from before you.
> And when [God / the ark?] was [again] resting,[31] [Moses] would say:
>   Return Yahweh, Who is Israel's myriads of thousands. (Num 10:35-
>   36)[32]

---

nature of a divine abode, since a literal connotation would imply distancing from
the deity. See also Nelson 1981.

[29] On the fictitious nature of the ark imagery, see also Morgenstern 1942-44.
In contrast to this position, see Miller and Roberts 1977, discussed above. See also
Seow (1989), who discusses at length the mythology of the imagery, but roots it in
the actual ascension of David to Jerusalem.

[30] The name used for the ark here, ארון ברית יהוה appears only in this verse
and in Numbers 10:33, preceding the Ark Song.

[31] The meaning of Hebrew ובנחה is altogether uncertain.

[32] I have given the common translation here, though אלפי may be pointed אַלֻּפֵי,
which might indicate "leaders" in the sense of military groups.

On the basis of this poem it is clear to Milgrom that the ark is not God's permanent residence:

> The song is *only* a prayer. . . . Moses petitions the Lord to arise from His throne and attack the enemy and then to return to His throne on the ark-cherubim after the battle is over. There is no assurance that He will do either.
>
> Thus *even in the oldest sources,* the ark does not guarantee that the God of Israel is with Israel in all of its endeavors. Because of its special sanctity, its hallowed tradition, and, above all, the belief that the Lord ordained the ark as the place where He will make His will and Presence manifest, the assurance that the ark is within the Tabernacle during peace and is visibly present with the army during war suffices to give Israel courage and hope that when she turns to God He will answer. (1990, 375, my emphasis)

The questions of whether God will act and whether he is present at the ark are not inextricably connected. Milgrom has made broad assumptions about the truth value of biblical statements, ignoring, in this case, the implications of other contrasting texts. By seeing the Ark Song as "only a prayer," he determines that it cannot be literal speech. But the evidence pushes us to the opposite conclusion. We have just noted the battle at Hormah as it is described in Numbers 14. The absence of the ark is indicative of God's absence and the resulting "defeat was due to Yahweh's absence" (Campbell 1975, 149).[33] Deuteronomy 1:41-45 recounts the same incident at Hormah, without any mention of the ark. This is fitting, given the Deuteronomist's ideological proclivity to disparage belief in the potency of priestly cultic artifacts and the theological notions of physicality associated with them.[34] Were you to ask a Deuteronomist whether God dwells in the ark, you would expect a negative answer and the theologizing we met in 1 Kings 8; the same question posed to a member of the priestly caste (non-Deuteronomic in ideology) would receive an affirmative answer. As for the Ark Song, which precedes the description of the Hormah incident in Numbers 14, nothing

---

[33] See Campbell (1975) also on the 1 Samuel 4-6 ark narratives: it is "beyond doubt that the defeat is to be attributed to the absence of the ark, the absence indeed of Yahweh from the battlefield" (150), but in a note on the same page, he backs off the theological implications of 4:7.

[34] See Weinfeld (1972, 208; 1981, 39f.), who provides this and other examples demonstrating theological shifts manifest in textual reinterpretations. And see Miller and Roberts 1977 and Seow 1989. Note that the ark in Deuteronomy is made by Moses himself (10:5), taking the task away from the priestly caste who performs the construction in Exodus 25.

compels us toward a figurative interpretation; on the other hand, the evidence supporting a literal understanding *is* compelling.[35] According to Sara Japhet, the Chronicler understood the presence of the ark as indicative of "the king's presence . . . and there is no doubt that He sits upon His throne. With the footstool there, divine presence is real, not merely metaphorical" (1989, 78-9). Just how the ark and Temple relate conceptually in this late literature remains difficult to decipher; nonetheless, the literalness of the ark's association with the divine presence cannot be disputed.[36]

The Ark as Icon

As noted, some scholars have drawn attention to the possibility that the ארון (*'aron*) did not start out as a tablet-holding container, but as some form of cultic icon. Thus, we are seeking to establish the conceptual evolution of the object. Julian Morgenstern's "conjecture is that הארון was a proper name, the specific designation of one particular object of outstanding significance among a large number or class of similar objects, viz., clan or tribal tent-sanctuaries" (1942-44, I, 264).[37] There is much to recommend this approach to the terminology.[38] Morgenstern's contention that ארון actually started out as a kind of tent is difficult to evaluate, as is his belief that the ארון originally contained two large stelae. Morgenstern argues that with time "the ארון in the *debir* came to be regarded as the throne of Yahweh." Moreover, "the two sacred stones, the ancient betyls, within the ארון were transformed, in tradition, into the two tablets of the decalogue" (259-60). The ark of the Priestly Code, and perhaps even in some pre-exilic traditions, had this twofold function.

The Deuteronomic historians forcefully link the tablets and ark in their retelling of the Golden Calf story (Deut 9-10). Surely the way they construed the narrative became the lasting and most dominant image in subsequent period's of Jewish history. There, Moses

---

[35] A full consideration of these issues should take note of Psalm 132, often interpreted as liturgy for an ark ritual. See Seow 1989, chap. 3, for a fine discussion of the relevant scholarship and a strong reading of the text.

[36] See Japhet's fine treatment of this material in the Chronicles literature, 1989, chap.4, "God's Presence in the World."

[37] See also Von Rad 1962-65, 1:234ff.

[38] See Morgenstern 1942-44 (Part II (1944), §7, p.1ff.), where he sees אפוד as the general umbrella term for cultic objects, of which ארון is but one.

is credited with making the ark himself (10:3)—apparently, prior to reaching the camp[39]—and we are told in his voice, "I deposited the tablets in the ark that I had made" (10:5, JPS). Just when this narrative would have been written is difficult to establish, but we clearly have here the final stage of the ark's purpose and symbolic meaning. Morgenstern argues that this stage could only have developed after a period of time during which the ark would have been sequestered within the Temple, long invisible to the general public. Only then could the transformation take place that allowed the generic stelae container—or icon—to become the holder of the tablets given by God to Moses at Sinai/Horeb. With all memory of the original forms and purposes gone, the box with the now-mythological Decalogue could be (literarily) transposed back to the wilderness experience, with no physical remnant visible to evoke questions.

My sense is that Morgenstern's basic notion is correct, that the ark mythology underwent radical transformations over time. I wish to introduce a few additional pieces of evidence regarding the ark that, to my knowledge, have not been adequately integrated into the scholarship on the ark's role. The evidence suggests that the original designation אָרוֹן served a ritualistic function, either because of the stelae, or simply on its own. In its earliest stages of development it paralleled the function of an idol, or indeed, was an idol. This function is hinted at in a few biblical phrases. It was then transformed in the Deuteronomic strata, only to be remythologized with some dependence upon more ancient materials by the post-exilic priesthood, which would explain why we have such a difference between the priestly conception of the ark's construction (Ex 25) and the Deuteronomic conception (Deut 10).

When writing about the tablets of stone as the Decalogue, scholars frequently point out that it was customary to deposit important documents (especially treaties) "before the god" or "at the feet" of the deity in a temple.[40] For some, the Decalogue represents the treaty which bound together a new nation where none had previously

---

[39] Constrast this with Exod 25:10-22, which describes the creation of the ark not only as a joint project, but as a project that is subsequent to Moses' mountain experience.

[40] On the placement of documents at the feet of or before the deity see Mendenhall 1954 on treaty practices. For an overview, Calderone 1966; McCarthy 1963, 1965; Childs 1974, chap. 17, also provides a fine sampling of the bibliography both pro and con this position.

existed.[41] Frequently cited as relevant is a treaty between the Hittite king Suppiluliumas and Kurtiwzaz, king of Mitanni, which begins with this statement:

> A duplicate of this tablet has been deposited before the Sun-goddess of Arinna, because the Sun-goddess of Arinna regulates kingship and queenship. In the Mitanni land (a duplicate) has been deposited before Tessub, the lord of the *kurinnu* of Kahat.[42]

As the continuation of the document makes clear, the function of this act was to engage the deity in enforcing the treaty: "the gods of the contracting parties" would "serve as witnesses" if the stipulations were transgressed. A similar function was ascribed to the Decalogue tablets in a later stage of the Deuteronomic mythology: "Take this book of Teaching and place it beside the ark of the Covenant of the Lord your God, and let it remain there as a witness against you" (Deut 31:26).[43]

In Levitical passages relating to the ark in Exodus (25:16, 21) there is an awkward expression that has not caught the attention of commentators. Here is the Hebrew, followed by the JPS translation.

ונתת אל הארן את העדת אשר אתן

> And deposit in the ark [the tablets of] the Pact which I will give you. (v.16)

ונתת את הכפרת על הארן מלמעלה ואל הארן תתן את העדת אשר אתן אליך

> Place the cover on top of the ark, after depositing inside the ark the Pact that I will give you.[44] (v. 21)

The verb נתן appears more than 2,000 times in the Masoretic Text, and while it is possible that I missed it, I was unable to find a single instance besides these particular Exodus verses in which the prepo-

---

[41] See Mendenhall 1973, 21.

[42] This is probably a mid-fourteenth century B.C.E. document; see Pritchard 1969, 205.

[43] Compare the awkward מצד ארון ("beside the ark")–perhaps מצד is in place of לפני as an attempt to soften the aspect of personification in its function–with 1 Sam 6:8, which has תשימו בארגז מצדו ("place it in the *argaz* at its side"). Morgenstern (1942-44, 251f.) speculates that the *argaz* is a permanent fixture of the ark. However, the "side" may constitute a place of safekeeping, as in Exod 16:32f. In contrast, see 1 Sam 10:25, where Samuel places the rules of kingship, which he wrote in a *sefer* and placed before Yahweh (וינח לפני יהוה).

[44] The passage is paralleled in Exodus 40:20.

sition אל (or ל) is thought to convey the sense that something was being placed *inside* an object.[45] The standard preposition ב is used invariably for this task. In fact, the verb נתן is used only in these particular Exodus passages with regard to deposition "in" the ark. In Deuteronomy the expression is ושמתם בארון and ואשם את הלחת אשר עשיתי בארון (10:2, 5); in 1 Kings 8:9 the verb is הניח, also with the preposition ב.[46] Needless to say, the verb נתן was well known to the Deuteronomist. Might there be a reason he opted to employ different language in this instance? The standard translations ignore the parallelism in the verb-prepositional phrases which relate quite clearly that God gives the testimony *to* Moses and that Moses then gives it to the 'aron.

In his study of the identity and function of *El/Baal Berith* (1996), Theodore J. Lewis has shed light on the relationship between Israelite and Canaanite imagery and iconography used in convenantal contexts. The dating of this material makes it considerably more relevant to the elucidation of the Decalogue than the more ancient Hittite treaties discussed in most scholarship. In a Neo-Assyrian text brought by Lewis (407), we find the following declaration as part of the covenant language between Ashur and King Esarhaddon:[47]

> For Aššur, the lord of the gods, am I.
> This is the *šulmu* which is before the [divine] statue.
> This tablet of the *adê*-treaty of Aššur . . .
> They pour out fine oil.
> They make sacrifices.
> They burn incense.
> Before the king they read [it].[48]

Lewis emphasizes the concept that the tablet represents the oath or

---

[45] See, for instance, Cassuto's commentary (Hebrew edition (1951) ad loc.), which draws attention to the phrase but comments as follows: ונתת אל הארון, אל תוך הארון ("[the words ונתת אל הארון mean 'you should place it] *into* the ark'"). His rendering receives no justification at all. Knohl (1995), who cites these two verses six times, comments on the first-person character of the verbs, and then extensively on the word עדות, but never draws attention to the awkward prepositional phrase. See, however, Lev 8:8, ויתן אל החשן, which JPS renders, "put *into* the breastplate."

[46] The syntax, however, is more complex: אין בארון רק שני לחות האבנים אשר הנח שם משה בחרב.

[47] Esarhaddon ruled from 680-669 B.C.E.

[48] The text is known as Tablet K2401 (NAP 3.3) from the library of Ashurbanipal. The phrase of most importance to this discussion is as follows: *annu šulmu ša ina pān ṣalme tuppi adê anniu ša d Aššur*. The number of cognates with Hebrew indicates the closeness of the biblical idioms and conceptualization of this material.

agreement—in Ugaritic, *adê*—which is clearly parallel to the Hebrew
הָעֵדוּת.[49] He reports that a number of scholars reading this passage
have concluded "that the reference to the *šulmu* which is placed before
the gods and the statue (presumably of Ashur) . . . refers to 'some
sort of ceremonial' linked to a covenant between the deity Assur and
King Esarhaddon" (407). What is clear is that the *šulmu* and the divine
statue are distinct.

Considering Exodus 25, we notice that just as the Neo-Assyrian
text has the *šulmu* resent before the statue (pān ṣalme = לִפְנֵי הַצֶּלֶם),
so does the biblical text have the agreement given *to* (rather than
placed *in*) the *'aron*. Let us consider the possibility that originally, the
'aron was nothing other than an icon for God, an idol, and that what
underlies the description in these verses of Exodus 25 was a ceremony that in structure and function was parallel to that mentioned
in Tablet K2401.[50] With this in mind, perhaps the Exodus verses
might best be rendered:

> You [Moses] will give to the *'aron* the Agreement/Testimonies I [God]
> shall give to you. (v. 16)

> You will place the curtain up over the *'aron;* then give to the *'aron* the
> Agreement/Testimonies which I shall give to you. (v. 21)[51]

The scene described is that of a document transference designed to
mirror in a public ritual the giving of a covenant by God to Moses
for the people. God gives the document (stele) to Moses and then
Moses gives the agreement or testimony (עֵדוּת) to God's own effigy,
the very object Yahweh himself designated and designed.[52] The func-

---

[49] See also Stephen A. Kaufman (1974, 33, 152) on the root of this term and
its usage in Akkadian and Old Aramaic, as well as on the possible Canaanite origins. See also Brinkman (1990) on the prominence of this term in other Mesopotamian
cultures.

[50] The idol need not be anthropomorphic in shape, or even suggestive of a
human form. As we shall discuss below, the Nabateans employed idols in the shape
of a modest obelisk (what we would today recognize as similar to a standard tomb-
stone); until late in Nabatean history, no images were carved into this stone.

[51] And similarly Exod 40:20.

[52] This, of course, is the natural conclusion in Exodus 25; however, the anachronistic description of the wilderness object cannot be assumed of an earlier period. The point is that the author wants the reader to believe that the object looks
as it does because God required it as such: indeed, "the later redaction of the
instructions emphasized that every detail of the design was made by explicit command of God" (Childs 1974, 540), but Childs draws no attention to the awkward-
ness of the idioms discussed here. See Korpel 1990, §3.4.2 on habitation imagery

tion of witness, not articulated in Exodus 25, did ironically get preserved in the Deuteronomy 31:8 passage noted above. The fact that the ritual reverses the direction of the transference (and hence, was literally designed to mirror God's actions) may symbolize the people's acceptance of the statutes. In contrast, the mythology pursued by the priestly writer is focused on the function of the ark as a meeting place. This adumbrates the exclusive function of the דביר where the ark will eventually be deposited: a place to which only the priests have access.[53] As Morgenstern and others have suggested, the notion that the 'aron must be a box into which something is *deposited* derives from the later transformation of the 'aron icon in conjunction with the transformation of the earlier roles of the stelae. Based on the archaic language in Exodus 25, we see that the Yahweh 'aron and the Ashur statue served the same purpose. In support of this interpretation, let us add a few pieces of additional, albeit circumstantial, evidence.

Like the divine effigies carried into battle in various Mesopotamian cultures, the 'aron had an important role during the era of conquest described in the Book of Joshua.[54] We are reminded of its theurgic powers when the 'aron splits the Jordan River.[55] Priests are described as carrying it before the entire nation. The 1 Samuel 4-7 ark narratives and Psalm 132 are understood to represent ceremonies devised to celebrate the return of an exiled ark to its original seat of power.[56] Both Miller and Roberts (1977) and Seow (1989) present texts to demonstrate how the function of the ark in Israelite culture was parallel to the function of city deities in Mesopotamia, especially in the context of military confrontations.

The 'aron is eventually portrayed as a container, but this form is not evident in Joshua. If it had been a container in the Joshua traditions, what would it have held? The Book of Joshua shows no cognizance of a Decalogue or of a pact or testimony written on tablets. Indeed, when Joshua crosses the Jordan, he erects a stele upon which he records the covenant the Israelites established with their God at the moment of passing into the "promised" land. "Joshua

---

in Ugaritic and biblical literature, and especially §3.4.2.2, though with caution.

[53] See 1 Kgs 8 and 2 Chr 5:7.

[54] See Miller and Roberts 1977; Seow 1989, 56ff.

[55] Josh 3:3, 6, 13; 4:5, 7, 11, 18; 8:33.

[56] Or, alternatively, to celebrate the ark's initial arrival at a newly designated site. See Campbell 1975; Miller and Roberts 1977; Seow 1989.

recorded all this in a Book of Teaching of God [[מ]אלהי תורת ספר] and he took a great stone and erected it there under the oak tree as a holy shrine of Yahweh" (24:26). The salient absence of any previously inscribed stone is remarkable. This is not just an argument from silence (based on the notion that the God-inscribed Ten Commandments are not mentioned); this argument derives from the fact that this passage offers an exclusive alternative to the Decalogue imagery. Had the "tablets" been extant (in the minds of the writers), the newly erected stone would have been not only redundant but a radical departure from the treaty established between Yahweh and Moses.[57] As it turns out, the 'aron is not mentioned at all in Joshua 24, as it appears to be irrelevant to the establishment of this newly articulated covenant.[58]

There may be some relevance to the fact that Samuel's initial epiphany takes place "in the Palace[59] of Yahweh where the 'aron of God is" (1 Sam 3:3). The importance of effigies for divine communication in other religions is well attested, for the icon's most basic function was to serve as a conduit (Jacobsen 1987, 23ff.).[60] In 1 Sam

---

[57] Alternatively, the Joshua author could be rejecting and replacing the Decalogue imagery with the covenant of this chapter, thereby seeking to displace the icon of Jerusalem—the ark and its tablets. As such, the passage becomes a polemic against the southern dynasty and its symbolic seat of power.

[58] Concern with the ark in Joshua occurs in chapters 3, 4, and 6. There one finds the following idioms, all variants on one another: כל אדון יהוה ארון, הארון. הארץ, ארון ברית יהוה אלהיכם, ארון הברית. In one verse, 4:15, we read ארון העדות, which is so uncharacteristic of the verbiage in these chapters that it must constitute a late, tendentious emendation. By the time we get to the Chronicler, the terms no longer appear to have ideological significance. See Japhet 1989, 96-100.

[59] Or perhaps more simply, "house" or "shrine"; בהיכל יהוה אשר שם ארון אלהים. See Haran 1988, 17; Kaufman (1974, 27) indicates the ubiquitous use of the term among northwest Semitic languages. See also Korpel 1990, 282, 372, 377.

[60] Unfortunately, the terminology used regarding the 'aron is inconsistent in 1 Samuel 4-5. Many scholars address this issue; see, for instance, Campbell 1979; Ahlström 1984. Verse 4 includes a rather tendentious emendation linked to a quasi-liturgical refrain (cf. Ps 99:1): first we have וישאו משם את ארון ברית יהוה צבאות ישב הכרבים, and then ושם שני בני עלי עם ארון ברית האלהים חפני ופינחס. See, for instance, Haran (1985, 247), who judges this and 2 Sam 6:2 to be glosses. To render the verse in a meaningful way, JPS transposes the order of the verses' sections, perhaps sensing that the present structure could not be original. The first awkward phrase of 1 Sam 4, "the 'aron of the Covenant of Yahweh Tzevaot, sitting [upon?] the Cherubim," is echoed in 2 Sam 6:2. That verse actually has a double emendation; first אשר נקרא שם שם יהוה (apparently a dittography), and then יהוה צבאות ישב הכרבים עליו. The lack of a preposition both here and in Psalm 99 makes a clear translation of ישב הכרבים difficult, but supposedly, this imagery is

4:7 the arrival of the *'aron* in the Israelite camp indicates the literal arrival of God, as the Philistines themselves declare.[61] Here too we have no indication that the *'aron* contains anything. The capture of the ark indicates the absence of God in Israel.[62] The Philistines know just what to do with the *'aron*: "they brought it [אֲרוֹן הָאֱלֹהִים] to the House of Dagon; and they set it up right by Dagon" (5:2) Although no other culture of the ancient Near East used a simple *box* as its symbol for its gods, the Philistines plainly knew to situate their prize booty parallel to their own god-icon. From an Israelite perspective, Ahlström (1984) argues, the juxtapositioning of the two deities ultimately results in the defeat of Dagon.[63] Altogether absent from this narrative is any mention of the loss of those all-so-precious tablets, inscribed by God's hand, delivered to Moses, and supposedly deposited *within* the *'aron*.

How might we summarize the development of the אֲרוֹן? During the earliest stages, the term may have stood for a divine effigy. It is possible that this structure included some form of stelae (as Morgenstern suggests) or that it developed distinctly but simultaneously in parallel traditions in multiple tribal units. I am inclined to believe that originally the stelae had no relevance to the ark's function as an icon for tribal gods. As there formed the tribal confederacies that eventually came to be Israel, covenant documents (including legal statutes) became increasingly important, especially as they involved various renderings of the land-victory motif. Hence, it was altogether appropriate that such a document be deposited by the divine effigy, as was done in other cultures of the ancient Near East.[64] By the time

---

fitting for the throne-connotation of the Cherubin and ark as a unit. On the reworking of this material in 1 Chr 13, see Fishbane 1985, 392f. Most scholars recognize that 2 Sam 6 and 1 Sam 4-6 are independent narratives. For a summary of this evidence, see Miller and Roberts 1977, 9-16, and also their conclusions; and McCarter 1984, 173-84.

[61] See Campbell (1975, 150 n.1), who argues that "it would be unwise to deduce the theological convictions of the narrator from the utterances he puts in the mouth of the uncircumcised," a comment characteristic of those seeking to avoid the obvious conclusion that in some strata of the literature God's presence was inextricably linked to the whereabouts of the ark.

[62] See 1 Sam 4:22, גָּלָה כָבוֹד מִיִּשְׂרָאֵל, where *kavod* is either a euphemism for God or a literal term for God's physical presece.

[63] On the importance of confiscating a people's icons, see Cogan 1974, chap.2; Hallo 1983, 13. The capture of an idol clearly meant for the defeated people the absence of its deity.

[64] See Mendenhall 1987, 343f. for parallels with ANE regarding land acquisition and divine dispensation. Greenberg (1995, 283) writes that the "storing the

a Decalogue mythology emerged, both a portable (double) stele, delivered by Moses and a container for that stele were grounded in Israelite literature. The current structuring of the Decalogue narratives themselves must be seen as late, considering the multiple versions and conflicting depictions. We may also speculate that counter-mythologies struggled for survival until the very end. Thus, with an insistent authoritative voice, the author of 1 Kings 8 writes: "There was nothing inside the *'aron* but the two tablets of stone which Moses placed [הִנִּחַ] there at Horeb, which Yahweh established with the Israelites upon their Exodus from Egypt" (v. 9). The writer includes neither the בְּרִית (covenant) nor עֵדוּת (testimony) terminology, though these terms frequently accompany the *'aron* in other passages. In this final stage of development, nothing of the throne motif appears operative. With the ascendancy of Jerusalem to the status of God's earthly abode, the *'aron* lost all vestiges of its primeval iconic connotations.[65]

Our original concern here was with the literal or figurative character of ark-related images. We end up seeing not only that ark-dwelling would have been literal for some sources, but that the *'aron* itself may have been other than a simple box for holding stone tablets. As with each of these problems in interpretation, every source must to be scrutinized individually; conclusions can pertain only to clusters of sources that can be identified as sharing a temporal and/or ideological base. Contradictions should not be judged "nonliteral" simply because they cannot be integrated into some greater theological scheme. But more important, the decision as to whether a text is literal or figurative cannot be made on the basis of whether it fits in with what the author believes or what a mere preponderance of verses conveys. The Ark Song, with the *'aron* as the central idol-icon, is either grossly literal (God, get out there and fight for us!) or highly symbolic. The historian may wish to show that it started as the former and ended up as the latter (as is certainly the case when the verses are recited in the modern synagogue during a Torah

---

tablets inside the Ark is parallel to the ancient Egyptian custom of depositing important documents beneath statues of the gods as evidence of the solemn commitment of the owners of the documents in the presence of the gods (a custom that supports the view that the 'tablets of the Pact' testify to the covenant)." Unfortunately, he gives no indication of a source and I have been unable to substantiate such an Egyptian custom.

[65] See Fishbane 1985, 422.

service). None of these issues are easily resolved; but ignoring them does nothing to bring us closer to an accurate description of ancient Israelite beliefs.

Other Icons: Stelae and the Tablets Mythology

Any discussion regarding the Decalogue mythology and the function of the ark must be placed in the greater context of ancient Canaanite stelae. The prominence of stelae (or betyls) in Hebrew Bible has been the focus of numerous studies.[66] Stelae have been found throughout Palestine, from early Bronze Age sites right down to the Hellenistic period.[67] In Tanakh they may have positive or negative connotations, depending upon the era and who created them. A stele may be identified simply as an erect stone (אבן) or a *maṣṣebah* (מצבה derived from the root נצב, which connotes "standing"). Frequently discussed are the markers set up by Jacob at Beth-el and as a sign of covenant with Laban (Gen 28:18, 22; 31:13, 45-52; 35:14f.). We noted above that the commemoration of the covenant between God and Israel in Joshua 24 shows no cognizance of a Mosaic stele tradition. Joshua erects a large stone by the oak at the shrine of Shechem to serve as a witness for the covenant voluntarily accepted by the people. The stone, it is said, *hears* all the words that Yahweh speaks to the Israelites. Moreover, it is designed to act as an active witness against them, should they break faith with their God.[68] Scholars regularly dismiss this imagery as mere metaphor; and yet, when the same thing is said of a non-Israelite image—such as the Hittite god-icon that hears the testimony of a wronged party, or the statue of Ashur that witnesses a deposition—we are told that the image is either an example of philosophical paradox or a literal primitivism.

Equally curious are the twelve stones erected at Gilgal by Joshua

---

[66] See M. Avi-Yonah's entry under *Avnei Zikharon* in the *Biblical Encyclopaedia* (Hebrew) vol. 1 (Jerusalem, 1950) cols. 50-56; also M. Broshi, *Maṣṣebah* in the *Biblical Encyclopaedia* (Hebrew) vol.5 (Jerusalem, 1968) cols. 221-25; Graesser 1972; Avner 1990. An extensive listing of works, including a number of dissertations written at European universities (to which I was unable to gain access), is included in Mettinger 1995, 34 n.37; also see 168-90. Other references follow.

[67] See Patrich 1990, 175ff.

[68] Josh 24:27 is in the second person, but the Hebrew makes clear that the stone is the actual witness. Compare Deut 31:8, noted above.

upon the splitting and crossing of the Jordan River (Josh 3-4). The
language here is heavily stylized, employing symbolic expressions
(perhaps already stereotypical) of both covenant scenes and the
commemortion of the Exodus from Egypt. For instance, the waters
of the Jordan were "split" (נכרתו מימי הירדן), where the key verb כרת
is used to indicate the breaking of the water. We might have expected,
however, the verb בקע, on the basis of the narrative in Exodus 14,
where we read of Moses' miraculous splitting of the Red Sea.[69]
Moreover, the episode is framed by the notion that the twelve stones
were to function as a sign (אות) for future generations to remember
(לזכרון) the miracle.. The vocabulary here directly reflects the motifs of Exodus 13:8f., where the celebration of the Exodus from Egypt
is described and justified. Most salient for our purposes is that the
'aron is the "hero" of the Jordan River crossing. The content of the
'aron—if there were any—goes unmentioned.[70]

In the aftermath of the Golden Calf episode, Moses is ordered to
carve two stelae of stone like the first ones (פסל לך שני לחת אבנים
כראשנים). Strangely enough, in the first revelation at Sinai (Exodus
20), no stelae are mentioned. The first mention occurs awkwardly
in Exodus 24:12, which is undoubtedly an alternative Sinaitic epiphany scene, displaced in the editing process by the Exodus 19-20 narrative. Of course, this narrative is not without its own problems.
Moses writes down all that Yahweh commands in 24:4; but later,
God gives Moses "the stone tablets with the teachings and the commandments" (24:12).[71] There is no Decalogue here. The association
of the Decalogue with the Sinaitic revelation is obviously what caused
the transformation of the text; however, the complexities of Exodus
24 are so great that we cannot fully reconstruct what the relationship between the originally conceived covenant and the eventual
tablets might have been at this stage in the narrative's development.
To set the stage for the Golden Calf narrative, Exodus 31:18 pulls
all of the loose ends together: "When He [Yahweh] finished speak-

---

[69] See Exod 14:16, 21; 4:7. The Joshua episode (described in Josh 3-4) has the
only use of the verb נכרת with regard to water: 3:13, 16; 4:7.

[70] We noted above Deuteronomy 27:1-8, which in some respects, adumbrates
Joshua's crossing at Gilgal. However, there are salient differences. The plastered
stones—as well as the unhewn stones of the altar (v.8)—all have inscribed upon
them the words of the Teaching (תורה). This is not the case in the Joshua narrative.

[71] This particular verse speaks of a future action, whose completion is only
understood via implicature.

ing with Him on Mount Sinai, he gave to Moses two stone tablets of the testimony [שְׁנֵי לֻחֹת הָעֵדֻת], stone tablets inscribed by the finger of God" [לֻחֹת אֶבֶן כְּתֻבִים]." The redundancy serves the purpose of apposition: the two stone tablets are equivalent to the "testimony" or pact עֵדוּת, but by this is meant specifically the stones that God inscribed by hand. The content of the "testimony" is left in abeyance, and for good reason. The resolution of the Golden Calf story in Exodus 34 does not shadow the Sinaitic/Horeb Decalogues as they are related in Exodus 20 and Deuteronomy 5. Nonetheless, the stelae motif obviously becomes the dominant image.

Exodus 31:18 (adumbrating 34:1) depicts God himself as the one who incised the surfaces of the two stones. Only the *shape* of the object was created by a human being—Moses hewed the stone—while its importance in the cultic context was acquired by virtue of the fact that the deity himself did the inscribing. The relationship between this aspect of the human and divine participation surely parallels the oaths of the artisans that made room in the Mesopotamian cult for divine participation in the conversion of an idol from a mere statue to an efficacious cultic object. The two tablets are used to smash the calf image, an image we know was frequently used in early Israelite cultic sites.[72] What we have is one iconic figure replacing another: but there is a difference between the two. Anyone can make a calf-idol and anyone can have such an icon in their possession. But there can be only one set of divinely inscribed tablets and they can be in the possession of only one person or one group, in one place at a time. If power is in the object, then power is uniquely conveyed to whoever is in control of it.

The numerous stelae found in ancient Canaan (at Israelite and non-Israelite sites), in the Punic regions, and among peoples of Arabia (Edomites, Moabites, Idumeans, and later Nabateans), are fundamentally bare of graphic images. While inscriptions (especially at Nabatean sites) suggest that the stelae were made for or in honor of gods, the lack of documentary evidence makes their exact function impossible to determine. Joseph Patrich has argued that by the time we get to (for the most part, postbiblical) Nabatean remains, we can increasingly assume a cultic purpose for the stelae as idols.[73] Individuals made stelae of various sizes—some large, some portable, some

---

[72] See Evans 1995, 208ff., with particular attention to 1 Kgs 12:30, et al.

[73] See Patrich 1990, 95-96, and Mettinger's 1995 review of the material in the context of other ancient Near Eastern sites.

no bigger than a matchbox—which carried inscriptions identifying
their makers explicitly. There are stelae for numerous gods, sometimes presented in clusters, and stelae that stand alone. Only one
class of stones actually has any graphic markings, and they are often referred to as the eye-stelae. In a very simplistic manner, the Nabateans fashioned two eyes and a simple straight nose; only at the
Temple of the Winged Lions at Petra has a more ornate representation been found, though here, too, realism is not the fashioner's
intent. At Hazor, one stele has hands stretched upward, though it is
in a grouping of stelae with no graphic symbolizations whatsoever.[74]

The archeological evidence has moved many scholars to argue that
the western Arabian religions were against the anthropomorphic
depiction of their deities. Patrich concludes: "We can see that the
Nabatean worship of gods whose form was the stele was neither
unique nor esoteric; a local tradition had existed among western
Semites in the region in deep antiquity" (1990, 183). Patrich maintains that the Nabatean "abstract perception of their gods and dis-
regard for figurative art were innate, growing out of a particular
theological doctrine. The principles of that doctrine have not been
preserved, but we can deduce its existence—and to a lesser degree,
its nature—on the basis of certain archaeological discoveries" (19).
I cannot agree with Patrich on this last point, as I believe it moves
beyond the evidence. Nothing in the artifactual remains discloses
theological principles; and no theological principle is "innate." Use
of an unadorned stone for worship may have become the standard
during a period of nomadic economy when engraved or ornate
depictions were simply impractical.[75] But nothing indicates an abstract perception of the gods. As is the case with numerous biblical
practices, the nonfigurative images may have remained and been
reinterpreted, perpetuated as some link to the past or on the basis
of some mandate from earlier ages. We simply do not know. Indeed,
it remains a mystery why anyone would decide to place a hewn stone
before him or herself, for the purposes of worship or any other

---

[74] See Mazar 1990, 254, for a photograph of the "shrine in Area C, including
basalt stelae, statue of a seated male, relief of a crouching lion and offering table."

[75] In other words, like the Jacob story of Genesis 25, it may be that these stones
were erected by nomadic-type peoples as they moved from one place to another.
As such, they may have managed only to shape the stone and erect it before they
would pass on to another locale. For other reflections on nomadic-desert origins
of stones, see Avner 1984, 119f.

magical ritual. There is no logically compelling reason to associate a stone with a deity or with an act of magic.

Be this as it may, Patrich's discussion, built on the work of Dalman, Kammerer, and Avi-Yonah before him, is of importance because it dispels the notion that idolatry must be paired with anthropomorphic depictions or literal identifications. The blank stone, whether it represents the deity, a god's place of sojourn, or some other conduit between humans and gods, can only be *nonliteral* or serve in an intermediary *function*—that is, it can only be a metonymic rather than a similarity-based representation—unless one is ready to argue that the gods looked like blank stones or lived in solid tablets. The archaeological evidence, then, should lead us to the following conclusions:

1. The use of these monuments does not in itself indicate an abstract, nonanthropomorphic conception of the deity.

2. The question of how a religion uses or limits the use of stelae and graphic depictions must ultimately be seen as independent of whether that religion is monotheistic, monolatristic, or polytheistic.

3. If the non-Israelite peoples who used blank stones did have a prohibition against figurative representations of gods—which does appear to be the case, given the rare exceptions—then it must be maintained that the prohibition is unrelated to the use of idols in cultic contexts.

One other aspect of the evidence requires additional comment. The Nabateans signed their stelae in such a manner as to indicate an awareness of the craftsman's role as creator of an object. An object was always created for a certain deity or cluster of deities, but there could be no secret about who fashioned the stone. Indeed, the nature of the inscriptions makes clear that the creator wished to draw attention to himself. For the Nabatean, it was important that a deity know the creator of the stone so that it would be clear with whom the deity should associate the particular stone, even when the person was not before it. With this manner in mind, Isaiah's satire in chapter 44 is difficult to grasp; for in this case, not only does the creator understand that he fashioned the shape of a stone that otherwise remains blank, but his goal is to draw attention to that fact. The diatribes in the biblical literature relate only to the anthropo-

morphic statues, as Faur has noted, thereby bypassing the entire issue of idolatry in nonanthropomoprhic contexts. Deutero-Isaiah's
argument is anachronistic; it had a function that was independent
of the wide variety of icon uses that were prevalent before him, and
maybe even in his own day.

Excavating a Long-Buried Metaphor

As noted, some scholars have suggested that the reason God was not
physically represented in the cluster of Near Eastern cultures just
discussed derives from an abstract notion of God, one that included
the concept that the deity was invisible.[76] Evidence in support of this
thesis is flimsy; indeed, there are passages in Tanakh that explicitly
indicate God can be seen by humans.[77] The fact that detailed descriptions of God's appearance are absent has been taken by some
to indicate that an abstract notion of deity is prevalent in Scriptures.
The fact is that the Bible contains no descriptions of goats, rams,
bulls, or horses; the physical attributes of even the central biblical
characters are never conveyed. The most we can assume is that
appearance was not especially important to the Israelite narrators
in general and that, in particular, they did not spend time describing what was either well known or unessential. The fact that God
goes undescribed must be placed in the context that except for ritual objects, basically *everything* goes undescribed. That God is no
exception is not an incidental oversight on the part of the biblical
writers, or a theologically charged omission; it is actually a consistent mark of much biblical writing.

The prohibition against graphically representing God is not a
blanket rejection of icons. It is, however, a limiting factor. While
neighboring peoples may have used blank tablets to represent their
deity, the Israelites were limited to only those stelae that were sanctioned by the central religious authorities. It may be that eventually
all such obelisks lost prominence. But there can be no doubt as to
their original importance and efficacy in the Israelite cult. When

---

[76] Mettinger is among the few to emphasize the contrary: "I do not take it for
granted that an aniconic divine symbol should imply a more spiritual notion of
deity than an iconic one" (1995, 20).

[77] For example, Gen 32:31; Exod 24:9, 33:7, 33:17ff.; Num 12:8, 14:14; Ps
17:15; Ezek 1, 9:3f.

Hosea summarizes the destroyed institutions of Israel, he includes, alongside the king, altar sacrifice, ephod, *maṣṣebah* and *terafim*.[78] While pietistic commentators read the syntax as juxtaposing a permitted thing with a proscribed thing, such interpretations are not convincing. Hosea was identifying those icons that were sanctioned and functioned in his very day. The obelisk and the terafim were still in vogue.

The issue was apparently who *controlled* which icons. Simple blank obelisk-like idols were the property of whoever made them. If each and every individual could create his or her own domestic idol, then the centralization of religious authority would be impossible. By limiting the use of stelae to those inscribed by the hand of God (or his chosen servants) and housed on the grounds of a central shrine in the designated receptical, the religious authority was able to harness the cultic practices of the religion. Perhaps more important, they were able to undermine the power of those who were not part of the centralized oligarchy. This required the transformation of many icons from antiquity, including the ark itself. Sometimes the transformations were subtle, employing staple images already available but waiting to be applied in novel ways. As noted, Sara Japhet (1989, 75ff.) has suggested that this is how the ark came to be understood as the divine footstool, an image not originally associated with this particular ritual object. Such a function not only helps specify its appropriate location in the singular Temple of Jerusalem, but it also limits its function and consequently, the relevance of replicating it. The ark is just one example of how icons were transformed to conform with the ever-evolving religious ideology.

Over time, the diversity of the *prescribed* iconography increased beyond the simple stelae, undoubtedly based on cultic precedents. We have already discussed the ark. To it must be added the tabernacle, *urim* and *tummim*, special garb, and the *ephod*.[79] The institutionalization of these artifacts should be seen as part of a program of substitution rather than elimination. The status of the God-mandated icons would be transposed back into the exclusive control of the Aaronides of the Torah.[80] The Aaronide literary fiction is yet

---

[78] Hos 3:4, "For the Israelites will sit for many years without king, without prince, without altar, without *maṣṣebah*, without ephod and terafim." The Masoretic Text reads זבח, but as suggested in the JPS translation, perhaps מזבח was intended as parallel to מצבה. On *terafim* see Greenberg 1995.

[79] See Morgenstern 1942-44, Part II, §7.

[80] Whether there were actually Aaronides at some point in the past cannot be

one other strategy in the transformation of ancient iconic practices.
What resulted was a struggle between the official cultic symbols within
the rituals of the authorized priesthood and the unauthorized icons
of unofficial practitioners. By demoting common idols and elevat-
ing priestly artifacts which remain one-of-a-kind, the strategy was
to eliminate the competing religion of the countryside. Priestly icons
were invariably already part of the popular religious culture. In the
process of privileging them, their uses as well as their meanings were
regularly transformed. Whether this strategy proved successful is
another matter. At least with regard to the annals of history we must
admit that it did; the competition leaves us no literature until we
get to the Hellenistic period and the Dead Sea Scrolls.[81] Thus, while
I agree with Mettinger's (1979) portrayal of Israel's aniconism as
rooted in competing icons, I am not attaching it to a specific historical event, and I am nuancing the evolutionary nature of this poli-
cy. While the bull's prominence in Baalism may have figured into a
late diatribe against northern worship practices, bovine imagery was
ultimately no more "dangerous" in the context of popular religion
than a cherub or stele, even when the latter was left blank. In short,
the fight against such images is a fight over the exclusion of certain
objects that had long been accepted as relevant to religious rites.
Moreover, the struggle is rooted in the politics of religion almost
always in the guise of theology.

The Golden Calf story testifies to this struggle over images. Putting aside the problematic details in the text of Exodus 32:1-24, which,
as Mettinger notes, remains neutral on the connotation of the calf,
the conclusion of the story makes quite clear that the legend was
restructured in order to empower the Levitical caste. After the Levites have slain those among their fellow Israelites who partook in the
non-Mosaic rite, Exodus reads:

> Moses stood up in the gate of the camp and said, "Whoever is for the
> LORD, come here!" And all the Levites rallied to him. He said to them,
> "Thus says the LORD, the God of Israel: Each of you put sword on

---

determined. It may be that the Aaronides symbolize the ancestors of whichever
priestly clan was in control when the documents are redacted, whether or not there
was any genetic link between the redactors and some ancient priestly caste.

[81] Patrich (1990, 183f.) notes that the law forbidding the erection of pillars in
the Temple Scroll (51:19-21; 52:1-3) was interpreted by Y. Yadin not merely as a
reiteration of the biblical injunction, but rather as a law relevant to the Hellenistic
era, which saw the continuation of this practice in local shrines.

thigh, go back and forth from gate to gate throughout the camp, and slay brother, neighbor, and kin." The Levites did as Moses had bidden; and some three thousand of the people fell that day. And Moses said, "Dedicate yourselves[82] to the LORD this day—for each of you has been against son and brother—that He may bestow a blessing upon you today." (32:26-9, JPS)

It is doubtful that these verses factored in the original story. The Levitical slaughter makes no sense preceding Moses' comment (32:30): "You have been guilty of a great sin, yet I will now go up to the LORD, perhaps I may win forgiveness for your sin." Presumably, the Levites slaughtered all those who were guilty. If we bypass the Levitical episode, the story makes much more sense. The plague brought upon the people in 32:35 serves as divine retribution, something altogether unnecessary if the Levites had already executed the perpetrators. The author wishes to make clear that those who aligned themselves with Moses and executed the calf worshipers are also those who received the blessing.[83]

One of the great curiosities of the story's history relates to the fact that Aaron comes out of this entire episode free of guilt.[84] This is the case only because of the Levitical restructuring of the story. While the original version had Aaron as the artisan responsible for fashioning the icon,[85] the rewritten version absolves Aaron of this role:

They said to me, "Make us a god to lead us; for that man Moses, who brought us from the land of Egypt—we do not know what has happened to him." So I said to them, Whoever has gold, take it off! They gave it to me and I hurled it into the fire and out came this calf! (Exod 32:23-24)[86]

---

[82] The Hebrew reads מלאו ידכם, literally, "fill your (pl.) hand," an idiom whose exact meaning has been lost. JPS uses "dedicate yourselves," which is probably close; but the general notion would appear to be the mandate for taking the office of priesthood.

[83] See Weinfeld (1981, 413), who picks up on Ibn Ezra's comment to Exod 32:20 that the Levites differentiated the sinners on the basis of an ordeal.

[84] See Aberbach and Smolar 1967 for a study of this passage's relationship to 1 Kings 12.

[85] Exod 32:3-5. Some scholars have suggested that the nonjudgmental character of this part of the story suggests a northern venue, where a precedent was set for the use of the calf in shrines.

[86] One cannot help but wonder to what the ancient mind would have attributed this altogether miraculous event. Surely it can be nothing other than a literal image.

The priestly emendation has the calf emerge spontaneously on its own; Aaron is cast as a bystander. Nonetheless, he was in control of neither the newly formed icon nor the people; Scripture instructs that as soon as the calf appeared "the people were out of control" (32:25).[87] The main point is that at the onset of the debacle, Aaron *lost control* of the icon and the people, whereas at the conclusion of the story, the Levites *gain control* (as well as God's exclusive blessing) by killing those who brought about the mayhem.[88] It should be kept in mind that the calf was not an idol (i.e., statue) anthropomorphically depicting Yahweh. As noted, no story in Scripture implies the creation of a similarity-based idol of Yhwh. The art of the ancient Near East makes clear that a calf or bull served as a pedestal for the deity and was not a representational image of the deity itself (Weinfeld 1981, 292). Thus, what we have in the Golden Calf story is the creation of an alternative icon for cultic purposes that was to be employed in the absence of their heretofore primary intermediary, Moses.[89] It is the application of a *nonsanctioned* alternative that the author wishes to castigate.

Immediately after the Golden Calf episode there follows a description of how everyone donates something to the task of creating cultic icons and ritual objects, including the tabernacle, the ark, the table for offerings of bread, the altar of incense, the altar of burnt offerings, and finally, the service vestments for officiating in the sanctu-

---

[87] The second part of Exod 32:25-26 is very problematic. The close proximity of the two subclauses makes the second one suspect. I would speculate that the Ur-version probably read: וירא משה את העם כי פרע הוא ויעמד [משה] בשער המחנה ("Moses saw that the people were out of control. . . . [He] stood at the gate of the camp.") The phrase I have deleted provides a subtle wordplay on the unintelligible root פרע, but also includes a *hapax legomenon* which is impossible to decipher: כי פרעה אהרן לשמצה בקמיהם. The verse has generally been rendered, "since Aaron had let them get out of control—so that they were a menace to any who might oppose them" (JPS). This rendering is altogether conjectural; there is no way to understand either the individual words or even the syntax with certainty.

[88] Contrast the retelling of this story in Deut 9:20-22, which attempts to reintroduce the guilt of Aaron, perhaps in line with the Deuteronomic desire to caste aspersions on the strong Aaronide priesthood. See Weinfeld (1981, 411), who notes that this is an independent unit, which appears in the Samaritan Pentateuch as part of Exod 32 and in Qumran Exod 32 (4Q *paleoEx* m).

[89] This follows Brichto (1983, 43), who argues that the bull image is devised "to replace the missing human intermediary, Moses. The characterization of this image [is] as 'a god' . . . clearly representing the Power which brought Israel up from Egypt." However, Brichto draws numerous conclusions with which I disagree, and commits some historical errors, such as when he argues that "religious iconoclasm is a phenomenon attested only for biblical religion in antiquity" (42).

ary. In contrast to the Golden Calf story, where Aaron calls for the donations that are ultimately used in creating a nonsanctioned icon, this context suggests complete acquiescence to a divine mandate. Surely we must see this gift giving as parallel to those made to Aaron for the formation of the calf. Regarding the new use for the donated materials, Moses announces that God has

> singled out by name Bezalel, son of Uri son of Hur, of the tribe of Judah. He has endowed him with a divine spirit of skill, ability, and knowledge in every kind of craft and has inspired him to make designs for work in gold, silver, and copper, to cut stones for setting and to carve wood—to work in every kind of designer's craft—and to give directions. (Exod 35:30-34)[90]

The narrative of the inspired artifacts ends with the investiture of the priesthood (Exod 40:12-15). That the issue is control over the sacrificial icons becomes blatant when we learn that Aaron's sons are anointed as "an everlasting priesthood throughout the ages." The priests rule by means of this highly specialized, non-duplicatable set of empowered icons. Replication is not only forbidden, it is impossible. Only the man imbued with the divine spirit may create the icon, and once it is made, no one has access to the inner domain of the Tabernacle except the priests. Duplicate *urim* or *tummim* (Exodus 28) would simply be forgeries. While a statue is just a random icon, the new priestly artifacts are part and parcel of the priestly power. To maintain the power associated with their uniqueness, the priesthood commences a program that will rob all other icon makers of their market.[91]

In this regard, the central importance of the tetragrammaton should be seen as parallel to the iconic proscriptions.[92] It has been

---

[90] It is tempting to compare this endowment with the divine spirit to the rituals in Mesopotamian context that had the artisan denying creation of his artifact. However, too many crucial conditions of relevance are absent, making a comparison overly dependent upon speculation.

[91] The text does not allow us to establish who he particular parties to these struggles may have been. See M. Cohen 1965 on the conflicts between the early Shilonite priesthood and the rise of the religion of the split monarchy. I am not as inclined to accept the historical record of the biblical narratives as Cohen is.

[92] On this point, I concur with Mettinger. Also see Halbertal and Margalit (1992, 148-52) for their discussion of the tetragrammaton. See also Japhet (1989, 20-23), who argues that the pronunciation of the tetragrammaton was long forgotten by the time we reach the Chronicler at the end of the fourth century B.C.E. Moreover, since *adonay* became the standard euphemism, there was no use of the actual word

pointed out that the principal gods of other cultures all had multiple names and that the Israelite God himself was referred to by means of an expanded nomenclature in the earliest strata of biblical literature.[93] The slow but sure elimination of most divine appellations in favor of the tetragrammaton should be seen as part of the same centralizing strategy that sought the elimination of privately producible images; shrines under the control of one centralized priesthood necessitated one uniform divine name. It is not surprising that ultimately, along with its fight against anthropomorphism, the Deuteronomic program would substitute the *dwelling of the name* for the literal sojourn of God himself in the Temple. Thus, the emphasis on *the* name in this stratum of literature might be seen as a continuation of the original program of monopolization pursued by the priesthood. Only now, in a more secularized context, the highly controlled divine appellatives would have the same function as limited access to icons.

Ultimately, the oligarchy solidified its power base by having exclusive control over both the *linguistic* and the *physical* images that assured access to God. The ideology of chosenness, the metaphors of loyalty, all are developed as ex post facto embellishments on earlier symbols in a new harness. One might try to trace the evolution of this centralization of symbols from the earliest priestly literature, through the somewhat transformed concerns of monarchists into the Deuteronomic worldview (which uses the caste system differently), into the final rebuilding era of the end of the fifth century and down into the fourth century, when the priestly caste reemerged as central.[94] As Morton Smith has suggested, this final period of composition is what allowed the cult of the wilderness to become the forerunner of the priestly administration. Smith recognizes the ark and tent narratives as deriving from the exilic and post-exilic priestly writers, who had precisely the goal of precedent-setting in mind.

אדני, which was similarly expunged from more ancient manuscripts as time passed and replaced with the tetragrammaton.

[93] See Von Rad 1962-65, 1:184f.; Mettinger 1988; Smith 1990a.

[94] Interestingly enough, the final stage is virtually devoid of any aniconic literature. Both Ezra and Nehemiah are primarily concerned with the segregation of the populace; therefore we read of their concern over intermarriage (Neh 10:31, 13:23ff.; Ezra 9:12f.; 10), sabbath observance (Neh 13:19ff.) and the restitution of the Levitical cult, especially as an administrative arm for revenue collections (Neh 10:33f.; 11). Nehemiah does, in passing, mention the Golden Calf debacle (9:18), but otherwise, icons are not detailed as part of the Israelite failure to observe the Divine Teaching.

After cult and purity laws comes the sacred tradition, conceived as a collection of precedents for ritual rules. One development deserves special notice. Earlier stor[ies] referred to a tent which housed the ark and (another tent?) where Moses went to talk with Yahweh. The P tradition made this tent the archetype of the Jerusalem temple, and accordingly retrojected, into the wilderness of national legend, not only the equipment, services, ordination ceremonies, and administrative disputes of the fourth century, but also their own notions of what would have been fitting in the past, their dreams of what should be in the future, and their visions of what existed in the eternal present of the heavenly world. The resultant tangle is notorious. (1971, 76)

The control of icons was still a central concern of post-exilic priests; the Golden Calf story is just one in a series of narratives that allow them to insert their priorities into the history of Israelite religion.

The Deuteronomists, proponents of a theology at odds with the earlier priestly caste (and later to be rejected when priestly authority reasserted itself with the exile), employed the centralization aspect in order to control ideological underpinnings, but undermine the cultic practices by replacing many of the objects of sacrificial magic with less cultic institutions. The diatribes against idolatry in this corpus, so very out of touch with what real idol worship was, undoubtedly derive from the readaptation of old themes in an era that no longer knew the meaning of how idols functioned outside the narrow cultic confines. The idolater became emblematic of the syncretist who threatened the transformations the deuteronomist sought in the traditional religion. Literal anthropomorphic idolatry was about as relevant to the Deuteronomist as Moses' tablets on Mount Sinai were to Joshua as he was about to enter the promised land (Joshua 24). Idolatry became the pivot point for a struggle over who controlled meaning and how. The harmless metaphors were sacrificed for a sinister literalism.

Conclusion

The pre-Deuteronomic Torah does not clearly articulate what makes idols bad. It could not have, for two reasons: because the Torah virtually never explains anything theologically, and because icons were not indiscriminately considered bad. The lack of graphic depictions of Yahweh is neither distinct to Israel nor the result of some theological discovery. Nor is there anything whatsoever qualitatively different between a blank stone used in ritual contexts and an ornately carved block of wood depicting the assumed physical form of a deity. How various groups came to determine which acts were efficacious and which objects would assist them in contacting the gods, remains an absolute mystery. Sacrifices, gems, altars, *urim* and *tummim*, *teraphim*, cherubim, tabernacles and temples, blood drops on fingers and ears, ordeals with water, ablutions, and the broken necks of heifers: these are all equally parts of cultic behaviors that have no more efficacy in the real world than an idol made of stone, precious metals, or wood. Indeed, Israel perpetuated sacrifices and an array of cultic behaviors that could not possibly have been interpreted—objectively—as superior to idol worship. The confusion over the history of aniconism in Israel (Smith's notorious tangle) stems from a confusion over a misunderstood domain of thinking—conceptual ascription. Without an understanding of this middle ground, some scholars have metaphorized, others literalized, ideas which are not natural to either category of language usage. The final redactors themselves were no longer cognizant of this way to approach the meaning of objects and acts. Deutero-Isaiah is overcome by the literalism of it all, and since then, scholars have looked for the intellectual superiority of the Israelite theology. It probably all comes down to politics and control, while judgments of superiority amount to nothing more than chauvinism.

9.

CONCLUSION: THE STRUGGLE AGAINST AMBIGUITY

Many interpretive conundrums derive from our attempts to harmonize those sources that understood the world as a graded continuum with those texts that sought the clarity of binaries. In certain eras, gods differed from humans—and from one another—not in absolute terms, but in degrees. In a particular literary strata, Yahweh sees the turpitudes of his fellow deities and proclaims, "I had thought of you as gods, creatures of the uppermost [realm], but now you shall die as mortals" (Ps 82:6). It should be clear that this is a gradient distinction (albeit with a rather irreversible point of differentiation—death). It may not always be possible to establish whether the preference rules employed are those of a binary or a gradient world view. Take, for instance, the word עליון as just used in Psalm 82, in contrast to עליון in Psalm 78:56 (וינסו וימרו את אלהים עליון ועדותיו לא שמרו).[1] In Psalm 78 there are not enough conditions of relevance available to determine whether the meaning is gradient or binary, and in this case it may not even matter. That is to say, the exact meaning of עליון may not require any greater definition in order to establish a high level of semantic stability in the sentence overall. In contrast, is there any doubt that the writers of Exodus 15 were asking quite literally, "Who is like you among the gods?" (v.11), knowing very well that their concept of incomparability would only be understandable in terms of a continuum of divine beings? Exodus 15:11 might

---

[1] "Yet they defiantly tested God Most High, and did not observe his decrees" (JPS). The grammatical form is problematic. If עליון is a place name, it would make this a genitive and we would expect the construct form, אלהי עליון, as is the case with other formal names, אלהי אברהם, etc., or as we see with other constructs using this term, e.g., Ps 46:5 קדש משכני עליון. There is evidence for adjectival meanings with the determining article, e.g., Neh 3:25, 2 Chr 27:3. More difficult are idioms such as לשמך עליון in Ps 92:2. Scholars have speculated that אל עליון (Gen 14:18ff. and Ps 78:35) is derived from ancient Canaanite appellations, so that this is actually a dual name. See Cross 1973, 50-52, though nothing is terribly conclusive.

in turn constitute a semantic unit in and of itself, and therefore serve
as a condition of relevance for the establishment of semantic stability in some other context. But we must be able to show that the other
context shares authors, or, more generally, worldviews, lest our judgments be capricious. We know that the ambiguity of Exodus 15:11
did not sit well with later monotheistic generations who strove for
greater clarity; hence, the theological confusion in the composite text.

Monotheism should be depicted as an early step toward a binary-
dominated conceptualization of meaning. The unambiguous
declaration that "before me no god was formed, and after me none
shall exist" (Isa 43:10) is not only a statement about divine uniqueness, it is equally a statement about *meaning*. The singularity of the
creator dictates the singularity of meaning.[3] The juxtapositioning of
Yahweh with the now *non*-existent gods seen in idols would never
have occurred to the earlier writers, and apparently not to many
monolatristic thinkers in the post-exilic era. Thus, contained within
these texts is the confrontation of two conceptualizations of meaning: one graded, the other binary.

Our goal, then, is to be ever-vigilant as to whether definitions
should follow the preference rules of a gradient or a binary worldview. The same statement can mean radically different things depending on the operative conditions of relevance and their weightings.
While a gradient-dominated worldview can (and does) accommodate
many binaries, the opposite is not the case; a binary-dominated worldview does not adroitly handle gradience.[4] Our sensitivity to the

---

[3] This concept was central to Nietzsche's critique of religion, and he sought to
reverse the process; with the death of the only God comes the meaningless of
existence—or, as he expressed it in *The Gay Science*: "Der Gesamtcharakter der Welt
ist . . . in alle Ewigkeit Chaos." ("The full character of the world is. . . in all eter-
nity chaos") (Nietzsche 1981, 2:389, §109). Alexander Nehamas (1985) sums it up
as follows: "The 'death of God,' both as hero and as author, allows Nietzsche to
deny that the world is subject to a single overarching interpretation, corresponding to God's role or intention" (91). Placing the emphasis on morality rather than
interpretation is Berkowitz (1995, 3 and elsewhere). See also Schacht 1983, 123ff.
The theme also dominates much of John Caputo's study, *Against Ethics* (1993, esp.
chap.3). I am arguing that the original move toward binary conceptualizations in
theological matters was caused by the desire for uniformity of interpretations. Not
that the result was ever achieved, but authority was certainly more easily exercised in the institutions of monotheists than in those of pagans. Contrast the Israelite authority base in the priesthood with that of various pagan cults; for the role
of the latter as functionaries rather than oligarchs, see Zaidman and Pantel 1992,
49f.
[4] Except for artificial systems, purely gradient or a purely binary concep-

character of meaning is dependent upon our success in establishing the functioning preference rules in a given literary stratum. Only with a broad grasp of conditions of relevance and their relative weightings, can we enhance our confidence in the appropriateness of our interpretive strategies. Whether we as interpreters conclude that a given stratum is dominated by binaries or by gradience is at the core of our interpretive strategy, and its effects are far-reaching.

The model for gradient judgments not only determines the placement of a certain statement on a particular continuum of meaning, it also helps us establish whether meaning is too ambiguous to be clearly articulated. When we consider the Hebrew Bible,we find that the meaning of virtually all of the great cultic institutions is beyond our ken. Exactly how sacrifice was *understood* is impossible to reconstruct (leaving aside the difficult gap that may exist between the documents we have and the beliefs of the average Israelite in the countryside, whose "ideas" may not be preserved in any literary document). In the case of cultic rituals, we do have some descriptive texts, but these descriptions do not shed light on how the ancients thought the rituals actually brought about what they were supposed to accomplish.[5] Many scholars have pointed out just how selective Hebrew Bible is when it comes to an entire array of social, religious, and cultic institutions we know existed in all ancient societies: magic goes almost unmentioned in the Hebrew Bible; no laws of marriage are recorded; a clear explanation of how Jubilee years actually functioned is missing; almost no discussion of what happens to the individual after life appears, and so forth. However, our ignorance of those very aspects of life that would provide us with essential knowledge of a great array of cultural and semantic conditions of relevance, is rarely highlighted in the scholarship. In fact, the absence of such conditions of relevance might make a truly stable reconstruction of the culture's belief system impossible.[6] Indeed, it

---

tualizations of meaning do not take place under natural circumstances; hence the hyphenated terms "gradient-dominated" and "binary-dominated." However, I have not consistently used this terminology, simply because of the clumsiness of the compound term. It is consistently implied, however. See Eckstein 1991 for a discussion of this notion but with his own terminology.

[5] Needless to say, there is a massive body of literature on the "meaning" of sacrifice. See, for instance, Eliade 1958, 360ff.; Jensen 1966; Burkert 1983; Zaidman and Pantel 1992.

[6] Compare this, for instance, to writing about the theology of the Talmud, which provides immense detail and constant bases for evaluating conditions of relevance (not to mention a healthy dose of ambiguity).

would be a worthwhile exercise to circumscribe those very conditions that we know *must* have functioned in biblical society, but for which the Tanakh has left us no evidence. If we understand the act of interpretation as derived from our ability to preference discrete conditions, we are left much more humble when standing before the task of writing a history of the development of biblical religion. It is one thing to have conditions but not be able to establish weightings; it is another thing to be handed only a very short list of conditions, knowing that all sorts of other relevancies are absent.

The argument of this study has taken place on two planes. One relates to the biblical text; the other relates to the contemporary proclivity of many scholars to analyze the world according to standardized, linear models of logic and semantics. Perhaps my treatment of the textual evidence and interpretations will be questioned and alternative approaches offered. Such alternatives may derive from different weightings of conditions of relevance, if not from an overall rejection of my world of discourse. As to the contribution this study has endeavored to make, I do not consider the particulars of my textual interpretations as important as my attempt to establish solid footings for gradient interpretive strategies. The model for gradient judgments is designed to sensitize our approach to the complexities and numerous ambiguities of biblical literatures.

Religion is fundamentally about meaning: first, how it is ascertained, and then, who controls it. There can be no doubt that power is most easily maintained when definitions and authority are rigidly defined. Ambiguity may be perceived, especially by those with an interest in power, as a menace to society. Unfortunately, the proposed alternative—binary-dominated thinking—results in just as many problems as a world awash in gradience. These comments apply equally to the history of religion and to the institutions of contemporary scholarship.

Two very strong challenges to the institutionalization of meaning are contained in Tanakh. They are the books of Job and Qohelet (Ecclesiastes). Job satirizes the establishment's choke hold on the people's interpretation of nature. In the very first chapter it portrays two discrete wills in the universe—God's and Satan's; and while the latter may be subordinate to the former, we are directly informed as to why there is so much chaos in the universe. The conclusion of the story is given to us at the very beginning. Job is absolutely blameless; there is really nothing else to be debated, but only the audience is privy to this fact. The interlocutors are forced to argue ad nausem the very theology the Deuteronomist held as divinely conveyed. In Job, not only is the narrator omniscient, so is the audience. We know that Eliphaz, Bildad, and Zophar are ignorant, and that Job's insistence on innocence is grounded in truth. No other book in the Bible takes this approach to meaning. It is just one more part of the satire.

Central to the author's argument is the use of paradox—one that arises from the confrontation of Job's worldview and that of his interlocutors.[7] We noted earlier how paradox violates all preference rules, making meaning impossible to ascertain. The speech by God in chapters 38-39 places before the reader a number of impossible-to-understand facts of nature. Water falls into the sea and upon uninhabited spaces on the earth, where no human being can benefit (38:26).[8] The ostrich has wings with which it cannot fly, and bears its eggs on the ground where they are likely to be destroyed before hatching (39:13-18). There is neither rhyme nor reason to the structure of nature, which is a way of saying that there is no *meaning*. Things are ambiguous at best, despite the Deuteronomist's claims to the contrary. The Book of Job uses as its final trump card not the powers of intellect and intuition but the voice of the deity, in all of its mocking glory. Here the divine voice behind the Deuteronomic worldview is pitted against the divine voice behind the anti-Deuteronomic perspective. It is the latter that is victorious, at least as far as the author of the Book of Job is concerned. Most important is the fact that Job undermines his adversaries by showing how their conception of the world does not match the "creator's intent"; and "creator's intent" translates into "meaning." The conditions of relevance are all misconstrued by Job's interlocutors. For Job, the Deuteronomic monopoly on meaning is proven to be a sham.

Except for one large insertion,[9] the Book of Job has clear *authorial intent*, and that intent is magnificently articulated. Did the au-

---

[7] On the distinction of the Book of Job, the character Job, and the author behind the character, see Michael V. Fox (1977), who applies the same distinctions to Qohelet.

[8] See how this verse and others like it factor into Tsevat 1981.

[9] The Elihu narrative is commonly recognized as a later accretion, filling chapters 32-37. This is not to say that there are no other textual problems; there are many. See Tsevat 1981, whose general approach to Job I accept.

thor of Job read the Book of Deuteronomy as we now have it? There
is no evidence supporting such a claim, yet obviously he was aware
of its theological tenets in great detail.[10] Given the clarity of thought,
the Deuteronomic worldview was not read by the author of Job in
the form of a composite text with priestly overtones. Remarkably,
there is no *political* interest; there is just an antitheology.

Qohelet represents a similarly homogeneous ideological statement.[11] However, in contrast to the strategic choices of Job, here
the divine voice is altogether absent. Understanding is derived from
what is obvious and accessible to everyone, regardless of one's station in life. In Qohelet there is no revelation, there are no intermediary interpreters, just the individual and his or her destiny. Monop-
olies on meaning are overridden on the basis of simple observations.
Authorial intent is blatantly present and (mostly) uniform.[12] Qohelet, too, is entangled in a world of ambiguity. He concentrates on
the fact that one does not know what, if anything, will influence the
future. The ambiguity which derives from our limited understanding of the world's purpose is accepted and used to undermine all
attempts at bypassing its implications. The work argues that one has
no choice but to fabricate meaning out of thin air. Or, to put it in
more theoretical terms: all theology which posits a "meaning" to the
universe is nothing other than reader's meaning.

Together, the books of Qohelet and Job represent powerful po-
lemics against binary theologies, or perhaps more generally, against
the notion that one should have confidence in a specific interpretive strategy. It is certainly a curious fact that the strongest and most
clearly sustained arguments in all of Tanakh are those whose goals
were to show the flaws in the establishment's principles of meaning.
Both of these works argue that despite our greatest efforts, most life
decisions and most interpretations of life events involve high degrees
of ambiguity in the sense that their meaning, their purpose, remains
unknown. We could frame this principle in a manner parallel to

---

[10] This is not to overlook the fact that Job is the most difficult book in Scriptures when it comes to our philological grasp of its vocabulary and idioms.

[11] Obviously, not without some accretions and complexities accrued during the
transmission process. See Fox 1977 on the frame-narrative units, and especially
the last pages, on his conceptualization of the relationship between the "Qohelet
persona" and the author.

[12] The most obvious insertion is the epilogue (12:9ff.), which represents someone's
attempt to controvert the message of the entire work in a few sparse verses. See
Fox 1977, 96ff.

Jackendoff's discussion of fuzziness in semantics: ambiguity should not be treated as a defect; nor is a religion or a theory of meaning that countenances it defective. Rather, ambiguity is an inescapable characteristic of the human creation of meaning, and any attempt to define it out of the pursuit of meaning is only evasion.

One generation's solutions to the unknown become another generation's source of uncertainty, just as one generation's literalisms became another's metaphors. The tolerance for uncertainty constantly shifts with an era's preferences. There is no progression from concrete to abstract, literal to metaphorical, plurality of meaning to singularity of meaning. All of these are natural by-products of the human struggle to make sense. When researching the development of a given religion, we can distinguish the mystic from the straightforward pietist just as much on the basis of their semantic theory as by the outward structures of their beliefs and practices. These theories may never be articulated, but they are always operative. Thus, as we seek to decipher the distinct approaches to meaning that are at the foundations of religious texts and practices, we need to be forever cognizant not only of how ideologies understand the creation of meaning, but also, how they cope with the inevitable ambiguities.

BIBLIOGRAPHY OF WORKS CITED

Aaron, David H. 1999 (forthcoming). Judaism's Holy Language. In *Approaches to Ancient Judaism* 16, edited by Jacob Neusner. Atlanta: Scholars Press.

Aberbach, M., and L. Smolar. 1967. Aaron, Jeroboam, and the Golden Calves. *Journal of Biblical Literature* 86:129-40.

Ahlström, Gösta. W. 1963. *Aspects of Syncretism of Israelite Religion.* Lund: Gleerup.

———— 1984. The Travels of the Ark: A Religio-Political Composition. *Journal of Near Eastern Studies* 43:141-49.

———— 1986. *Who Were the Israelites?* Winona Lake, Ind.: Eisenbrauns.

Albright, William Foxwell. 1938. What were the Cherubim? *Biblical Archaeology* 1:1-3.

———— 1994. *Yahweh and the Gods of Canaan. A Historical Analysis of Two Contrasting Faiths.* Winona Lake, IN: Eisenbrauns. Reprint of the Jordan Lectures, The School of Oriental and African Studies, University of London, 1965.

Austin, J. L. 1975. *How to Do Things with Words.* Cambridge: Harvard University Press.

Avner, U. 1990. "Mazzebot sites in the Negev and Sinai and their significance." In *Biblical Archaeology Today*, edited by A. Biran and J. Aviram. Jerusalem.

Bal, Mieke. 1993. Metaphors He Lives By. *Semeia* 61:186-207.

Banks, Robert J. 1994. *God the Worker: Journeys into the Mind, Heart, and Imagination of God.* New York: Judson Press.

Barr, James. 1960. Theophany and Anthropomorphism in the Old Testament. In *Supplements to Vetus Testamentum*. 7:1-38. Leiden: Brill.

———— 1983. *Holy Scriptures: Canon, Authority, Criticism.* Philadelphia: Westminster Press.

———— 1987. *Comparative Philology and the Text of the Old Testament.* Revised. Winona Lake, Ind: Eisenbrauns.

———— 1991. *The Semantics of Biblical Language.* 1961. Reprint. Philadelphia: SCM Press; London: Trinity Press International.

Barsalou, Lawrence W. 1992. Frames, Concepts, and Conceptual Fields. In *Frames, Fields, and Contrasts*, edited by Adrienne Lehrer and Eva Feder Kittay. Hillsdale, N.J.: Lawrence Erlbaum Associates.

Barstad, H. 1993. No Prophets? Recent Developments in Biblical Prophetic Research and Ancient Near Eastern Prophecy. *Journal for the Study of the Old Testament* 57:39-60.

Barthes, Roland. 1989. *The Rustle of Language.* Translated by Richard Howard. Berkeley: University of California Press.

Beardsley, Monroe C. 1958. *Aesthetics: Problems in the Philosophy of Criticism.* New York: Harcourt, Brace Co.

Berkowitz, Peter. 1995. *Nietzsche: The Ethics of an Immoralist.* Cambridge: Harvard University Press.

Bernhardt, Karl Heintz. 1956. *Gott und Bild: Ein Beitrag Zur Begründung und Deutung des Bilderverbotes im Alten Testament.* Theologische Arbeiten, 2. Berlin: Evangelische Verlanganstalt.

Black, Max. 1948. The Semantic Definition of Truth. *Analysis* 8:49-63.

———— 1962. *Models and Metaphors: Studies in Language and Philosophy*. Ithaca: Cornell University Press.

———— 1972-73. Meaning and Intention: An Examination of Grice's Views. *New Literary History* 4:257-79.

———— 1979a. How Metaphor Works: A Reply to Donald Davidson. *Critical Inquiry* 6:131-43.

———— 1979b. More about Metaphor. In *Metaphor and Thought*, edited by Andrew Ortony. Cambridge: Cambridge University Press.

Bottéro, Jean. 1992. *Mesopotamia: Writing, Reasoning, and the Gods*. Translated by Zainab Bahrani and Marc Van De Meiroop. Chicago: University of Chicago Press.

Boyarin, Daniel. 1990. *Intertextuality and the Reading of Midrash*. Bloomington: Indiana University Press.

Brenneman, James E. 1997. *Canons in Conflict: Negotiating Texts in True and False Prophecy*. Oxford: Oxford University Press.

Brettler, Marc Zvi. 1989. *God is King: Understanding an Israelite Metaphor*. Journal for the Study of the Old Testament, Supplement Series, 76. Sheffield: Sheffield Academic Press..

———— 1993. Images of YHWH the Warrior in Psalms. *Semeia* 61:135-65.

———— 1995. *The Creation of History in Ancient Israel*. London: Routledge.

Brichto, Herbert Chanan. 1983. The Worship of the Golden Calf: A Literary Analysis of a Fable on Idolatry. *Hebrew Union College Annual* 54:1-44.

Brinkman, John. 1990. Political Covenants, Treaties, and Loyalty Oaths in Babylonia and between Assyria and Babylonia. In *Il Tratatti nel mondo antico forma ideologia funzione*, edited by Luciano Canfora, Mario Liverani, and Carlo Zaccagnini. Rome: "L'Erma" de Bretschneider.

Brueggemann, Walter. 1997. *Theology of the Old Testament: Testimony, Dispute, Advocacy*. Minneapolis: Fortress Press.

Burkert, Walter. 1983. *Homo Necans: The Anthropology of Ancient Greek Sacrificial Ritual and Myth*. Translated by Peter Bing. Berkeley: University of California Press.

Caird, G. B. 1980. *The Language and Imagery of the Bible*. Philadelphia: Westminster Press.

Calderone, Philip J. 1966. *Dynastic Oracle and Suzerainty Treaty: 2 Samuel 7, 8-16*. Manila: Loyola House of Studies.

Campbell, Antony F. 1975. *The Ark Narrative, 1 Sam 4-6, 2 Sam 6: A Form-Critical and Tradito-Historical Study*. SBL Dissertation Series, 16. Cambridge, Mass.: Society of Biblical Literature, dist. by Scholars Press.

———— 1979. Yahweh and the Ark: A Case Study in Narrative. *Journal of Biblical Literature* 98:31-43.

Caputo, John D. 1993. *Against Ethics. Contributions to a Poetics of Obligation with Constant Reference to Deconstruction*. Bloomington, Ind.: Indiana University Press.

Cassuto, Umberto. 1951. פירוש על ספר שמות. Jerusalem: Magnes.

———— 1987. *A Commentary on the Book of Exodus*. Translated by Israel Abrahams. Jerusalem: Magnes Press.

Childs, Brevard S. 1974. *The Book of Exodus: A Critical, Theological Commentary*. Philadelphia: Westminster Press.

———— 1985. *Old Testament Theology in a Canonical Context*. Philadelphia: Fortress Press.

Chomsky, Noam. 1975. *Reflections on Language*. New York: Pantheon Books.

Coats, George W. 1968. *Rebellion in the Wilderness. The Murmuring Motif in the Wilderness Traditions of the Old Testament*. Nashville: Abingdon Press.

Cogan, M. 1974. *Imperialism and Religion: Assyria, Judah, and Israel in the Eighth and Seventh Centuries B.C.E.* SBL Monograph Series, 19. Missoula, Mont.: Society of Biblical Literature, dist. by Scholars Press.

Cohen, Jean. 1966. *Structure de langage poétique*. Paris: Flammarion.

Cohen, Mark. 1981. *Sumerian Hymnology: The Eršemma*. Hebrew Union College Annual, Supplement 2. Cincinnati: Hebrew Union College Press.

Cohen, Martin A. 1965. The Role of the Shilonite Priesthood in the United Monarchy of Ancient Israel. *Hebrew Union College Annual* 36:59-98.

Coogan, Michael David. 1987. Canaanite Origins and Lineage: Reflections on the Religion of Ancient Israel. In *Ancient Israelite Religion: Essays in Honor of Frank Moore Cross*. Edited by Patrick D. Miller, Jr., Paul D. Hanson, and S. Dean McBride. Philadelphia: Fortress Press.

Cooper, Alan and B. Goldstein. 1990. The Festivals of Israel and Judah and the Literary History of the Pentateuch. *Journal of the American Oriental Society* 110:22-28.

Cornelius, Isak. 1994. *The Iconography of the Canaanite Gods Reshef and Ba'al: Late Bronze and Iron Age Periods (c.1500–1000)*. Fribourg: University Press Fribourg Switzerland; Göttingen: Vandenhoeck and Ruprecht.

Cotterell, Peter, and Max Turner. 1989. *Linguistics and Biblical Interpretation*. London: SPCK.

Cross, Frank Moore. 1973. *Canaanite Myth and Hebrew Epic: Essays in the History of the Religion of Israel*. Cambridge: Harvard University Press.

Cross, Frank Moore and David Noel Freedman, eds. 1975. *Studies in Ancient Yahwistic Poetry. SBL Dissertation Series 21. Missoula, Mont.: Scholars Press, for Society of Biblical Literature*.

Culler, Jonathan. 1975. *Structuralist Poetics: Structuralism, Linguistics, and the Study of Literature*. Ithaca: Cornell University Press.

———— 1982. *On Deconstruction: Theory and Criticism after Structuralism*. Ithaca: Cornell University Press.

———— 1997. *Literary Theory: A Very Short Introduction*. Oxford: Oxford University Press.

Curtis, E. M. 1990. Images in Mesopotamia and the Bible: A Comparative Study. In *The Bible in the Light of Cuneiform Literature*, edited by William W. Hallo, Bruce William Jones and Gerald H. Mattingly. Scripture in Context, 3. Lewiston, New York: E. Melien Press.

Dahood, Mitchell. 1968-70. *Psalms*. 3 vols. The Anchor Bible 16-18. Garden City, N.Y.: Doubleday.

Dalferth, I. U. 1988. *Theology and Philosophy*. Oxford and New York: Basil Blackwell.

Dalley, Stephanie, trans. 1989. *Myths from Mesopotamia: Creation, the Flood, Gilgamesh and Others*. Oxford and New York: Oxford University Press.

Davidson, Donald. 1979. What Metaphors Mean. In *On Metaphor*, edited by Sheldon Sacks. Chicago: University of Chicago Press.

Davies, Philip R. 1992. *In Search of 'Ancient Israel.'* Sheffield: Sheffield Academic Press..

———— 1998. *Scribes and Schools. The Canonization of the Hebrew Scriptures.* Louisville: Westminster John Knox Press.

Dever, William G. 1983. Material Remains and the Cult in Ancient Israel: An Essay in Archeological Systematics. In *The Word of the Lord Shall Go Forth: Essays in Honor of David Noel Freedman in Celebration of His Sixtieth Birthday*, edited by Carol L. Meyers and M. O'Connor. Winona Lake, Ind.: Eisenbrauns.

———— 1987. The Contribution of Archaeology to the Study of Canaanite and Early Israelite Religion. In *Ancient Israelite Religion: Essays in Honor of Frank Moore Cross*, edited by Patrick D. Miller, Jr., Paul D. Hanson, and S. Dean McBride. Philadelphia: Fortress Press.

———— 1995. "Will the Real Israel Please Stand Up?" Archaeology and Israelite Historiography: Part I; Archaeology and the Religions of Ancient Israel: Part II. *Bulletin of the American Schools of Oriental Research*, 297:61-80, 298:37-58.

Dietrich, Manfred, and Oswald Loretz. 1992. *"Jahwe und seine Aschera": Anthropomorphes Kultbild in Mesopotamien, Ugarit und Israel: Das biblische Bilderverbot.* Ugaritisch-Biblische Literatur, 9. Muenster: Ugarit-Verlag.

Dohmen, Christoph. 1985. *Das Bilderverbot: Seine Entstehung und seine Entwicklung im Alten Testament.* Bonn: Bonner biblische Beiträge.

Eagleton, Terry. 1996. *Literary Theory: An Introduction.* 2d edition. Cambridge, Mass.: Blackwell.

———— 1997. *The Illusions of Postmodernism.* Oxford: Blackwell.

Eckstein, Jerome. 1991. *Metaphysical Drift: Love and Judaism.* New York: Peter Lang.

Eco, Umberto. 1995. *The Search for the Perfect Language.* Translated by James Fentress. Oxford and Combridge, Mass.: Blackwell.

Eilberg-Schwartz, Howard. 1990. *The Savage in Judaism: An Anthropology of Israelite Religion and Ancient Judaism.* Bloomington: Indiana University Press.

———— 1994. *God's Phallus, and other Problems for Man and Monotheism.* Boston: Beacon Press.

Eisfeldt, Otto. 1966. Jahwe Zebaoth. In *Kleine Schriften*, vol. 3 Tübingen: Mohr.

Eliade, Mircea. 1958. *Patterns in Comparative Religion.* Translated by Rosemary Sheed. New York: Sheed and Ward.

Ellis, John M. 1989. *Against Deconstruction.* Princeton: Princeton University Press.

Evans, Carl D. 1995. Cult Images, Royal Policies and the Origins of Aniconism. In *The Pitcher is Broken. Memorial Essays for Gösta W. Ahlström*, edited by Steven W. Holloway and Lowell K. Handy. Journal for the Study of the Old Testament, Supplement Series, 190. Sheffield: Sheffield Academic Press..

Faur, José. 1978. The Biblical Idea of Idolatry. *Jewish Quarterly Review* 69, no.1:1-15.

Fernandez, J. 1974. The Mission of Metaphor in Expressive Culture. *Current Anthropology* 15, no.2:119-33.

Finkelstein, I. 1988. *The Archaeology of the Israelite Settlement.* Jerusalem: Magnes Press.

———— 1994. The Emergence of Israel: A Phase in the Cyclic History of Canaan in the Third and Second Millennia B.C.E. In *From Nomadism to Monarchy: Archaeological and Historical Aspects of Early Israel*, edited by Israel Finkelstein and Nadav Na'aman. Jerusalem: Jerusalem Exploration Society; Washington, D.C.: Biblical Archaeology Society.

Fish, Stanley. 1980. *Is there a Text in This Class?: The Authority of Interpretive Communities.* Cambridge: Harvard University Press.

Fishbane, Michael. 1985. *Biblical Interpretation in Ancient Israel.* Oxford and New York: Oxford University Press.

Foster, Benjamin R., ed. and trans. 1996. *Before the Muses: An Anthology of Akkadian Literature.* 2d ed. 2 vols. Bethesda, Md.: CDL Press.

Fox, Michael V. 1977. Frame-Narrative and Composition in the Book of Qohelet. *Hebrew Union College Annual* 48:83-106.

Frazer, James George. 1963. *The Golden Bough: A Study in Magic and Religion.* Abridgement of the 1922 edition. New York: Macmillan.

Fretheim, Terence E. 1984. *The Suffering of God: An Old Testament Perspective.* Philadelphia: Fortress Press.

Friedman, Richard Elliot. 1995. *The Disappearance of God: A Divine Mystery.* Boston: Little Brown & Co.

Gadamer, Hans Georg. 1988. *Hermeneutics Versus Science? Three German Views: Essays by H.-G. Gadamer, E. K. Specht, W. Stegmüller.* Translated, edited, and introduced by John M. Connolly and Thomas Keutner. Notre Dame, Ind.: University of Notre Dame Press.

Gardner, Howard, with Robin Bechhofer, Dennie Wolf and Ellen Winner. 1978. The Development of Figurative Language. In *Children's Language* edited by Keith Nelson. New York: Gardner Press.

Gardner, Howard, and Ellen Winner. 1979. The Development of Metaphoric Competence: Implications for Humanistic Disciplines. In *On Metaphor*, edited by Sheldon Sacks. Chicago: University of Chicago Press.

Goffman, Erving. 1974. *Frame Analysis: An Essay on the Organization of Experience.* Cambridge: Harvard University Press.

Gottwald, Norman K. 1979. *The Tribes of Yahweh: A Sociology of the Religion of Liberated Israel, 1250-1050 B.C.E.* Maryknoll, N.Y.: Orbis.

———— 1985. *The Hebrew Bible: A Socio-Literary Introduction.* Philadelphia: Fortress Press.

Graesser, Carl F. 1972. Standing Stones in Ancient Palestine. *The Biblical Archaeologist* 35, no.2:34-63.

Greenberg, Moshe. 1969. *Understanding Exodus.* Melton Research Center, Volume II, Part I. New York: Behrman House/Jewish Theological Seminary.

———— 1995. Another Look at Rachel's Theft of the Teraphim. In *Studies in the Bible and Jewish Thought.* Philadelphia and Jerusalem: Jewish Publications Society.

Grice, H. Paul. 1957. Meaning. *Philosophical Review* July.

———— 1961. The Causal Theory of Preception. *Proceedings of the Aristotelian Society*, Supplementary Volume 35: 121-52.

———— 1969. Utterer's Meaning and Intentions. *Philosophical Review*, April.

———— 1971. Utterer's Meaning, Sentence Meaning and Word Meaning. In *The Philosophy of Language*, edited by John R. Searle. Oxford: Oxford University Press.

———— 1975. Logic and Conversation. In *Speech Acts*, edited by Peter Cole and J. Morgan. Syntax and Semantics, 3. New York: Academic Press.

———— 1978. Further Notes on Logic and Conversation. In *Pragmatics*, edited by Peter Cole. Syntax and Semantics, 9. New York: Academic Press.

———— 1981. Presupposition and Conversational Implicature. In Radical Pragmatics, edited by Peter Cole. New York: Academic Press.

———— 1982. Meaning Revisited. In *Mutual Language*. Edited by N. Smith, 223-243. London: Academic Press.

Halbertal, Moshe, and Avishai Margalit. 1992. *Idolatry*. Translated by Naomi Goldblum. Cambridge: Harvard University Press.

Hallo, William W. 1982. Cult Statue and Divine Image: A Preliminary Study. In *Scripture in Context II: More Essays on the Comparative Method*, edited by William W. Hallo, James C. Moyer, and Leo G. Perdue. Pittsburgh, PA: The Pickwick Press.

Hampshire, Stuart. 1995. A New Way of Seeing. Review *Looking at Giacometti* by David Sylvester. *The New York Review of Books* 42 (July 13): 46.

Haran, Menahem. 1959. The Ark and the Cherubim: Their Symbolic Signifiance in Biblical Ritual. *Israel Exploration Journal* 9:30-38, 89-94.

———— 1985. *Temples and Temple-Service in Ancient Israel*. 1977. Reprint, with new preface and corrections. Winona Lake, Ind.: Eisenbrauns.

———— 1988. Temple and Community in Ancient Israel. In *Temple in Society*, edited by Michael V. Fox. Winona Lake, Ind.: Eisenbrauns.

Hasel, Gerhard F. 1991. *Old Testament Theology: Basic Issues in the Current Debate*. 4th ed. Grand Rapids, Mich.: Eerdmans.

Hawkes, Terence. 1977. *Structuralism and Semiotics*. Berkeley: University of California Press.

Hendel, Ronald S. 1988. The Social Origins of the Aniconic Tradition in Early Israel. *Catholic Biblical Quarterly* 50, no.3:365-82.

Hirsch, E. D., Jr. 1967. *The Validity of Interpretation*. New Haven: Yale University Press.

———— 1976. *The Aims of Interpretation*. Chicago: University of Chicago Press.

Hofstadter, Douglas R. 1979. *Gödel, Escher, Bach: An Eternal Golden Braid*. New York: Basic Books.

Holladay, John S. Jr. 1987. "Religion in Israel and Judah Under the Monarchy: An Explicitly Archaeological Approach." In *Ancient Israelite Religion: Essays in Honor of Frank Moore Cross*, edited by Patrick D. Miller, Jr., Paul D. Hanson, and S. Dean McBride. Philadelphia: Fortress Press.

Iser, Wolfgang. 1979. *The Act of Reading: A Theory of Aesthetic Response*. Baltimore: Johns Hopkins University Press.

Jackendoff, Ray. 1983. *Semantics and Cognition*. Cambridge: MIT Press.

———— 1987. *Consciousness and the Computational Mind*. Cambridge: MIT Press.

———— 1992. *Patterns in the Mind: Language and Human Nature*. New York: Harvester Wheatsheaf.

Jackendoff, Ray and David H. Aaron. 1991. Review Article, *More Than Cool Reason: A Field Guide to Poetic Metaphor*, by George Lakoff and Mark Turner (Chicago: Chicago University Press, 1989). *Language* 67, no.2:320-38.

Jacobsen, Thorkild. 1970. *Toward the Image of Tammuz and Other Essays on Mesopotamian History and Culture*, edited by William L. Moran. Cambridge: Harvard University Press.

———— 1976. *The Treasures of Darkness: A History of Mesopotamian Religion*. New Haven: Yale University Press.

———— 1987. The Graven Image. In *Ancient Israelite Religion: Essays in Honor of Frank Moore Cross*, edited by Patrick D. Miller, Jr., Paul D. Hanson, and S. Dean McBride. Philadelphia: Fortress Press.

Japhet, Sara. 1989. *The Ideology of the Book of Chronicles and Its Place in Biblical Thought*. Translated by Anna Barber. Frankfurt am Main and New York: Verlag Peter Lang.

Jaynes, Julian. 1976. *The Origin of Consciousness and the Breakdown of the Bicameral Mind*. Boston: Houghton Mifflin.

Jensen, Adolf E. 1966. *Die getöte Gottheit*. Stuttgart: Urban-Bücher / Taschenbücher.

Kaiser, Otto. 1983. *Isaiah 1-12: A Commentary*. Translated by John Bowden. 2d ed. The Old Testament Library. Philadelphia: Westminster Press.

Kaufman, Stephen A. 1974. *The Akkadian Influences on Aramaic*. Assyriological Studies, 19. Chicago: University of Chicago Press.

Kaufmann, Yehezkel. 1937-56. תולדות האמונה הישראלית (*Toledot HaEmunah HaYisraelit*). 8 vols. in 4. Tel Aviv: Hatsa'at Mosad Bialik.

———— 1960. *The Religion of Israel: From Its Beginnings to the Babylonian Exile*. Translated and abridged by Moshe Greenberg. Chicago: University of Chicago Press.

Keel, Othmar 1977. *Jahwe-Visionen und Siegelkunst: Eine neue Deutung der Majestätsschilderungen in Jes 6, Ez 1 und 10 und Sach 4*. Stuttgarter Bibelstudien 84-85. Stuttgart: Verlag Katholischer Bibelwerk.

———— 1978. *The Symbolism of the Biblical World: Ancient Near Eastern Iconography and the Book of Psalms*. Translated by Timothy J. Hallett. New York: Seabury Press.

Kittay, Eva Feder. 1987. *Metaphor: Its Cognitive Force and Linguistic Structure*. Oxford and New York: Oxford University Press.

Knohl, Israel. 1995. *The Sanctuary of Silence: The Priestly Torah and the Holiness School*. Minneapolis: Fortress Press.

Korpel, Marjo Christina Annette. 1990. *A Rift in the Clouds: Ugaritic and Hebrew Descriptions of the Divine*. Münster: Ugarit-Verlag.

Kosko, Bart. 1993. *Fuzzy Thinking: The New Science of Fuzzy Logic*. New York: Hyperion.

Kugel, James L. 1981. *The Idea of Biblical Poetry: Parallelism and Its History*. New Haven: Yale University Press.

Lakoff, George. 1987. *Women, Fire, and Dangerous Things: What Categories Reveal About the Mind*. University of Chicago: Chicago Press.

Lakoff, George, and Mark Johnson. 1980. *Metaphors We Live By*. Chicago: University of Chicago Press.

Lakoff, George, and Mark Turner. 1989. *More Than Cool Reason: A Field Guide to Poetic Metaphor*. Chicago: University of Chicago Press.

Lambert, W. G. 1985a. The Pantheon at Mari. *Annales de Recherches Interdisciplinaires*. *MARI*, 4, 525-39.

———— 1985b. Trees, Snakes and Gods in Ancient Syria and Anatolia. *Bulletin of the School of Oriental and African Studies* 48:435-51.

———— 1993. Donations of Food and Drink to the Gods in Ancient Mesopotamia. In *Ritual and Sacrifice in the Ancient Near East: Proceddings of the International Conference Organized by Katholieke Universiteit Leuven, 17-20 April 1991*, edited by J. Quaegebeur. Leuven: Orientalia Lovaniensia Analecta; Leiden: Uitgeverij Peeters and Departement Oriëntalistiek, Katholieke Universiteit.

Lappin, Shalom. 1981. *Sorts, Ontology, and Metaphor: The Semantics of Sortal Structure*. Berlin and New York: W. de Gruyter.

Lemche, Niels Peter. 1985. *Early Israel: Anthropological and Historical Studies on the Israelite Society before the Monarchy.* Supplement to Vetus Testamentum, vol. 37. Leiden: Brill.

———— 1988. *Ancient Israel: A New History of Israelite Society.* Biblical Seminar, 5. Sheffield: Sheffield Academic Press.

———— 1994. Is It Still Possible to Write a History of Ancient Israel? *Scandinavian Journal of the Old Testament* 8, no.2:165-190.

Levenson, Jon D. 1975. Who Inserted the Book of the Torah? *Harvard Theological Review* 68:203-33.

———— 1981. From Temple to Synagogue: 1 Kings 8. In *Traditions in Transformation: Turning Points in Biblical Faith*, edited by Baruch Halpern and Jon D. Levenson. Winona Lake, Ind.: Eisenbrauns.

———— 1987. The Sources of Torah: Psalm 119 and the Modes of Revelation in Second Temple Judaism. In *Ancient Israelite Religion: Essays in Honor of Frank Moore Cross*, edited by Patrick D. Miller, Jr., Paul D. Hanson, and S. Dean McBride. Philadelphia: Fortress Press.

———— 1993. *The Death and Resurrection of the Beloved Son: The Transformation of Child Sacrifice in Judaism and Christianity.* New Haven: Yale University Press.

Levinson, Bernard M. 1997. *Deuteronomy and the Hermeneutics of Legal Innovation.* Oxford: Oxford University Press.

Lewis, Theodore J. 1996. The Identity and Function of El/Baal Berith. *Journal of Biblical Literature* 115, no.3:401-23.

Lindblom, J. 1962. *Prophecy in Ancient Israel.* Philadelphia: Fortress Press.

Loretz, Oswald. 1990. *Ugarit und die Bibel: Kanaanäische Götter und Religion im Alten Testament.* Darmstadt: Wissenschaft Buchgesellschaft.

Mac Cormac, Earl R. *A Cognitive Theory of Metaphor.* Cambridge, Mass.: MIT Press, 1985.

Matthews, Victor H., and Don C. Benjamin. 1991. *Old Testament Parallels: Laws and Stories from the Ancient Near East.* New York: Paulist Press.

Mazar, Amihai. 1990. *Archaeology of the Land of the Bible 10,000 - 563 B.C.E.: An Introduction.* The Anchor Bible Reference Library. New York: Doubleday.

McCarter, P. Kyle, Jr. 1984. *II Samuel.* Anchor Bible Commentary. Garden City, New York: Doubleday.

McCarthy, Dennis J. 1963. *Treaty and Covenant: A Study in Form in the Ancient Oriental Documents and in the Old Testament.* Analecta Biblica, 21. Rome: Pontifical Biblical Institute.

———— 1965. Covenant in the Old Testament: The Present State of Inquiry. *Catholic Biblical Quarterly* 27:217-40.

McFague, Sallie. 1983. *Metaphorical Theology: Models of God in Religious Language.* Philadelphia: Fortress Press.

McKenzie, John L. 1968. *Second Isaiah.* Anchor Bible Commentary. Garden City, New York: Doubleday.

Mendenhall, George E. 1954. Covenant Forms in Israelite Tradition. *Biblical Archaeology* 17:50-76.

———— 1973. *The Tenth Generation: The Origins of the Biblical Tradition.* Baltimore: Johns Hopkins University Press.

———— 1987. The Nature and Purpose of the Abraham Narratives. In *Ancient Isra-*

elite Religion: Essays in Honor of Frank Moore Cross, edited by Patrick D. Miller, Jr., Paul D. Hanson, and S. Dean McBride. Philadelphia: Fortress Press.

Mettinger, Tryggve N. D. 1979. The Veto on Images and the Aniconic God in Ancient Israel. In *Religious Symbols and Their Functions: Based on Papers Read at the Symposium on Religious Symbols and the Functions Held at Abo on the 28th-30th of August 1978*, edited by Haralds Biezais. Scripta Instituti Donneriani Aboensis, 10. Stockholm: Almqvist & Wiksell International.

———— 1982a. *The Dethronement of Sabaoth: Studies in the Shem and Kabod Theologies*. Coniectanea Biblica, Old Testament Series, 18. Lund: CWK Gleerup.

———— 1982b. YHWH Sabaoth: The Heavenly King on the Cherubim Throne. In *Studies in the Period of David and Solomon and Other Essays: Papers Read at the International Symposium for Biblical Studies, Tokyo, 5-7 December, 1979*, edited by Tomoo Ishida. Winona Lake, Ind.: Eisenbrauns.

———— 1988. *In Search of God: The Meaning and Message of the Everlasting Names*. Translated by Frederick H. Cryer. Philadelphia: Fortress Press.

———— 1990. The Elusive Essence: YHWH, El, and Baal and the Distinctiveness of Israelite Faith. In *Die Hebräische Bibel und ihre Zweifache Nachgeschichte. Festschrift für Rolf Rendtorff zum 65. Geburtstag*, edited by Erhard Blum. Hamburg: Neukirchener Verlag.

———— 1995. *No Graven Image? Israelite Aniconism in Its Ancient Near Context*. Coniectanea Biblica, Old Testament Series 42. Stockholm: Almqvist & Wiksell.

Milgrom, Jacob. 1990. *The JPS Torah Commentary: Numbers: The traditional Hebrew text with the new JPS Translation*. Philadelphia: Jewish Publications Society.

Miller, J. M. 1991. Is It Possible to Write a History of Israel without Relying on the Hebrew Bible? In *The Fabric of History: Text, Artifact, and Israel's Past*, edited by Dianna Vikander Edelman. Journal for the Study of Old Testament, Supplement Series, 127. Sheffield: Sheffield Academic Press.

Miller, Patrick D., Jr., 1985. Israelite Religion. In *The Hebrew Bible and Its Modern Interpreters*, edited by Douglas A. Knight and Gene M. Tucker. Philadelphia: Fortress Press.

Miller, Patrick D., Jr., and J. J. M. Roberts. 1977. *The Hand of the Lord: A Reassessment of the "Ark Narrative" of 1 Samuel*. Johns Hopkins Near Eastern Studies. Baltimore and London: Johns Hopkins University Press.

Morgenstern, Julian. 1942-44. The Ark, the Ephod, and the Tent of Meeting. In 2 parts. *Hebrew Union College Annual* 17:153-266, 18:1-52.

Mowinckel, S. 1961. *Das Thronbesteigungsfest Jahwes und der Ursprung des Escatologie. Psalmen-studien 2. Reprint, 1921-24.* Amsterdam: P. Schipers.

Murphy, Gregory L. 1996. On Metaphoric Representation. *Cognition* 60:173-204.

Nehamas, Alexander. 1985. *Nietzsche: Life as Literature*. Cambridge: Harvard University Press.

Nelson, Richard D. 1981. *The Double Redaction of the Deuteronomistic History*. Journal for the Study of the Old Testament, Supplement Series 18. Sheffield: Sheffield Academic Press..

Neusner, Jacob. 1988a. *The Incarnation of God: The Character of Divinity in Formative Judaism*. 2d printing. South Florida Studies in the History of Judaism, 63. Atlanta: Scholars Press.

———— 1988b. Is the God of Judaism Incarnate? *Religious Studies* 24: 213-238.

———— 1996. *The Presence of the Past, the Pastness of the Present: History, Time, and Paradigm in Rabbinic Judaism*. Bethesda, Md: CDL Press.

———— 1997. *Paradigms in Passage: Patterns of Change in the Contemporary Study of Judaism*. Lanham, Md: University Press of America.

———— 1998. *The Theological Grammar of the Oral Torah*. 3 vols. Oakdale, New York: Dowling College Press.

Nietzsche, Friedrich. 1979-84. *Werke*. 5 vols. Karl Schlechta, ed. Frankfurt am Main: Ullstein Materialien.

Noppen, Jean Pierre van, S. de Knop, and R. Jongen, comps. 1985. *Metaphor: A Bibliography of Post-1970 Publications*. Amsterdam and Philadelphia: J. Benjamins Publ. Co.

Noppen, Jean Pierre van, and Edith Hols, comps. 1990. *Metaphor II: a Classified Bibliography of Publications 1985-1990*. Amsterdam and Philadelphia: J. Benjamins Publ.Co.

Ollenburger, Ben C. 1985. Biblical Theology: Situating the Discipline. In *Understanding the Word: Essays in Honor of Bernhard W. Anderson*, edited by James T. Butler, Edgar W. Conrad, and Ben C. Ollenburger. Sheffield: Sheffield Academic Press..

Olyan, Saul M. 1988. *Asherah and the Cult of Yahweh in Israel*. Atlanta: Scholars Press.

Oppenheim, A. Leo. 1977. *Ancient Mesopotamia: Portraits of a Dead Civilization*. Rev. ed., completed by Erica Reiner. Chicago: University of Chicago Press.

Otto, Rudolf. 1943. *The Idea of the Holy: An Inquiry into the Non-Rational Factor in the Idea of the Divine and Its Relation to the Rational*. Translated by John W. Harvey. Rev. ed. London: Oxford University Press.

Patrich, Joseph. 1990. *The Formation of Nabatean Art. Prohibition of a Graven Image among the Nabateans*. Leiden: E. J. Brill.

Patzig, Günther. 1969. *Aristotle's Theory of the Syllogism. A Logicophilological Study of Book A of the Prior Analytics*. Translated by Jonathan Barnes. Dordrecht: Reidel; New York: Humanities Press.

Peckham, Brian. 1993. *History and Prophecy: The Development of Late Judean Literary Traditions*. New York: Doubleday.

Peirce, Charles Sanders. 1960. The Icon, Index and Symbol. In *Collected Papers*, vol.8. Edited by Charles Hartshorne and Paul Weiss. Cambridge: Harvard University Press.

Pinker, Steven. 1984. *Language Learnability and Language Development*. Cambridge: Harvard University Press.

———— 1994. *The Language Instinct*. New York: W. Morrow & Co.

Postgate, J. N. 1990. Archaeology and Texts: Bridging the Gap. *Zeitschrift für Assyriologie* 80:228-40.

Pritchard, James B. ed. 1969. *Ancient Near Eastern Texts Relating to the Old Testament*. 3d ed. with supplement. Princeton: Princeton University Press.

Rad, Gerhard von. 1962-65. *Old Testament Theology*. 2 vols. Translated by D. M. G. Stalker. New York: Harper & Row.

Ramsey, Ian. 1963. *Religious Language: An Empirical Placing of Theological Phrases*. London: S.C.M. Press.

Rendsburg, Gary A. 1996. Biblical Literature as Politics: The Case of Genesis." In *Religion and Politics in the Ancient Near East*, edited by Adele Berlin. Bethesda: University Press of Maryland.

Richards, I. A. 1936. *The Philosophy of Rhetoric*. London and New York: Oxford University Press.

Ricoeur, Paul. 1970. *Freud and Philosophy: An Essay on Interpretation*. Translated by Denis Savage. New Haven: Yale University Press.

———— 1974. *The Conflict of Interpretations*, edited by Don Ihde. Evanston: Northwestern University Press.

———— 1976. *Interpretation Theory: Discourse and the Surplus of Meaning*. Fort Worth: Texas Christian University Press.

———— 1977. *The Rule of Metaphor: Multidisciplinary Studies of the Creation of Meaning in Language*. Translated by Robert Czerny, with Kathleen McLaughlin and John Costello. Toronto: University of Toronto Press.

———— 1979. The Metaphorical Process as Cognition, Imagination, and Feeling. In *On Metaphor*, edited by Sheldon Sacks. Chicago: University of Chicago Press.

Rubenstein. Jeffrey L. 1995. *The History of Sukkot in the Second Temple and Rabbinic Periods*. Atlanta: Scholars Press.

Ryles, Gilbert. 1949. *The Concept of Mind*. London: Hutchinson's University Library.

Sadock, Jerrold. 1979. Figurative Speech and Linguistics. In *Metaphor and Thought*, edited by Andrew Ortony. Cambridge: Cambridge University Press.

Samely, Alexander. 1992. Scripture's Implicature: The Midrashic Assumptions of Relevance and Consistency. *Journal of Semitic Studies* 37:167-205.

Sarna, Nahum M. 1986. *Exploring Exodus: The Heritage of Biblical Israel*. New York: Schocken Books.

Saussure, Ferdinand. [1916] 1974. *Course in General Linguistics*, edited by Charles Bally and Albert Sechehaye, with Albert Reidlinger. Translated by Wade Baskin. London: Fontana.

Schacht, Richard. 1983. *Nietzsche*. London and New York: Routledge.

Schauber, Ellen, and Ellen Spolsky. 1986. *The Bounds of Interpretation: Linguistic Theory and Literary Text*. Stanford: Stanford University Press.

Schmidt, Brian B. 1996. The Aniconic Tradition: On Reading Images and Viewing Texts. In *The Triumph of Elohim: From Yahwisms to Judaisms*, edited by Diana Vikander Edleman. Grand Rapids: Eerdmans.

Searle, John R. 1969. *Speech Acts: An Essay in the Philosophy of Language*. London: Cambridge University Press.

———— 1979. Metaphor. In *Metaphor and Thought*, edited by Andrew Ortony. Cambridge: Cambridge University Press.

———— 1995. *The Construction of Social Reality*. New York: Free Press.

Seow, C. L. 1989. *Myth, Drama, and the Politics of David's Dance*. Atlanta: Scholars Press.

Shepard, Odell. 1993. *The Lore of the Unicorn*. Reprint, 1930 ed. New York: Dover.

Shibles, Warren A. 1971. *Metaphor: An Annotated Bibliography and History*. Whitewater, Wis.: Language Press.

Silva, Moisés. 1983. *Biblical Words and Their Meaning: An Introduction to Lexical Semantics*. Grand Rapids, Mich.: Zondervan.

———— 1990. *God, Language, and Scripture: Reading the Bible in the Light of General Linguistics*. Foundations of Contemporary Interpretation, 4. Grand Rapids, Mich.: Zondervan.

Smith, Mark S. 1990a. *The Early History of God: Yahweh and the other Deities in Ancient Israel*. San Francisco: Harper & Row.

————— 1990b. Solar Language for Yahweh. *Journal of Biblical Literature* 109, no.1:29-39.

Smith, Morton. 1971. *Palestinian Parties and Politics That Shaped the Old Testament*. New York: Columbia University Press.

Solan, Lawrence M. 1997. Learning Our Limits: The Decline of Textualism in Statutory Cases. *Wisconsin Law Review* no.2:235-81.

Soskice, Janet Martin. 1985. *Metaphor and Religious Language*. Oxford and New York: Oxford University Press.

Sperber, Dan, and Deirdre Wilson. 1986. *Relevance: Communication and Cognition*. Cambridge: Harvard University Press.

Sternberg, Meir. 1985. *The Poetics of Biblical Narrative*. Bloomington: University of Indiana.

Sweetser, Eve. 1990. *From Etymology to Pragmatics*: Metaphorical and Cultural Aspects of Semantic Structure. Cambridge: Cambridge University Press.

Talmon, Shmaryahu. 1997. The Signification of שלום and its Semantic Field in the Hebrew Bible. In *The Quest for Context and Meaning*, edited by Craig A. Evans and Shemaryahu Talmon. Leiden: Brill.

Tarski, lfred. 1983a. The Concept of Truth in Formalized Languages. In *Logic, Semantics, and Metamathematics: Papers from 1923 to 1938*. Translated by J. H. Woodger. 1956. Oxford: Oxford University Press.

————— 1983b. Some Methodological Investigations on the Definability of Concepts. In *Logic, Semantics, and Metamathematics: Papers from 1923 to 1938*.

Taylor, Mark C. 1984. *Erring: A Postmodern A/theology*. Chicago: University of Chicago.

Thompson, Thomas L. 1974. *The Historicity of the Patriarchal Narratives: The Quest for the Historical Abraham*. Berlin: Walter de Gruyter.

————— 1992. *Early History of the Israelite People: From the Written and Archaeological Sources*. Leiden: Brill.

————— 1995. A Neo-Albrightean School in History and Biblical Scholarship? *Journal of Biblical Literature* 114, no.4:683-98.

————— 1996. The Intellectual Matrix of Early Biblical Narrative: Inclusive Monotheism in Persian Period Palestine. In *The Triumph of Elohim: From Yahwisms to Judaisms*, edited by Diana Vikander Edelman. Grand Rapids, Mich.: Eerdmans.

Tigay, Jeffrey. 1987. Israelite Religion: The Onomastic and Epigraphic Evidence. In *Ancient Israelite Religion: Essays in Honor of Frank Moore Cross*, edited by Patrick D. Miller, Jr., Paul D. Hanson, and S. Dean McBride. Philadelphia: Fortress Press.

Tracy, David. 1975. *Blessed Rage for Order: The New Pluralism in Theology*. New York: Seabury Press.

Traugott, Elizabeth Closs and Mary Louise Pratt. 1980. *Linguistics for Students of Literature*. San Diego: Harcourt Brace Jovanovich.

Tsevat, Matitiahu. 1965. Studies in the Book of Samuel (§IV): YHWH Seba'ot. *Hebrew Union College Annual* 36:49-58.

————— 1969-70. God and the Gods in Assembly. *Hebrew Union College Annual* 40/41:123-37. Reprinted in *The Meaning of the Book of Job and Other Biblical Studies: Essays on the Literature and Religion of Hebrew Bible*. New York: Ktav Publishing House; Dallas: Institute for Jewish Studies, 1980.

———— 1988. The Prohibition of Divine Images according to the Old Testament. In *Wünschet Jerusalem Frieden*, Edited by Matihias Augustin and Klaus-Dietrich Schunck. Collected communications to the 12th IOSOT Congress, Jerusalem, 1986. Bieträge zur Erforschung des Alten Testaments und des Antiken Judentums, 13. Twelfth IOSOT Congress: Jerusalem 1986. Frankfurt am Main: Verlag Peter Lang.

Urbach, Ephraim E. 1975. *The Sages: Their Concepts and Beliefs*. 2 vols. Translated by Israel Abrahams. Jerusalem: Magnes Press.

Van Seters, John. 1976. Oral Patterns or Literary Conventions in Biblical Narratives. *Semeia* 5:139-54.

———— 1983. In *Search of History: Historiography in the Ancient World and the Origins of Biblical History*. New Haven: Yale University Press.

———— 1992. *Prologue to History: The Yahwist as Historian in Genesis*. Louisville: Westminster/John Knox.

———— 1994. *The Life of Moses: The Yahwist as Historian in Exodus-Numbers*. Louisville: Westminster/John Knox.

Vervenne, Marc. 1996. Current Tendencies and Developments in the Study of the Book of Exodus. In *Studies in the Book of Exodus*. Edited by Marc Vervenne. Leuven: Leuven University Press.

Volz, Paul. 1912. *Das Neujahrfest Jahwes*. Tübingen: Mohr.

Weinfeld, Moshe. 1972. *Deuteronomy and the Deuteronomic School*. London: Oxford University Press.

———— 1978a. Divine War in Ancient Israel and in the Ancient Near East (in Hebrew). In *Studies in the Bible and Ancient Near East Presented to Samuel E. Loewenstamm on His Seventieth Birthday*, edited by Yitzhak Avishur and Joshua Blau. Jerusalem: Rubinstein's.

———— 1978b. 'They Fought from Heaven': Divine Intervention in War in Ancient Israel and the Ancient Near East (in Hebrew). *Eretz Yisrael* 14 (H. L. Ginsberg Volume): 22-30.

———— 1986. Divine Intervention in War in Ancient Israel and in the Ancient Near East. In *History, Historiography, and Intepretation: Studies in Biblical and Cuneiform Literatures*, edited by Hayyim Tadmor and Moshe Weinfeld. Jerusalem: Magnes Press.

———— 1991. *Deuteronomy 1-11*. The Anchor Bible. Garden City, New York: Doubleday.

Weitzman, Steven. 1997. *Song and Story in Biblical Narrative: The History of a Literary Convention in Ancient Israel*. Bloomington: Indiana University Press.

White, Hayden. 1973. *Metahistory: The Historical Imagination in Nineteenth-Century Europe*. Baltimore: Johns Hopkins University Press.

———— 1974. The Historical Text as Literary Artifact. *Clio* 3, no.3: reprinted in Hazard Adams and Leroy Searle, eds. *Critical Theory Since 1965*. Tallahassee: Florida State University Press, 1989: 395-417.

Wittgenstein, Ludwig. 1975. *Philosophical Remarks*. Edited by Rush Rhees, from unpublished writings. Translated by Raymond Hargreaves and Roger White. Oxford: Basil Blackwell.

———— 1977. *Remarks on Colour*. Edited by G. E. M. Anscombe. Translated by Linda L. McAlister and Margarete Schättle. Berkeley: University of California Press.

——— 1980. *Remarks on the Philosophy of Psychology*. 2 vols. (Bilingual edition, from MSS 229 and 232, May 1946–October 1947). Translated by G. E. M. Anscombe and edited with G. H. von Wright. Oxford: Basil Blackwell.

——— 1982. *Last Writings on the Philosophy of Psychology*. Edited by G. H. von Wright and Heikki Nyman. Translated by C.G. Luckhardt and Maximilian A. E. Aue. Chicago: University of Chicago Press.

Wolfson, Elliot R. 1994. *Through a Speculum That Shines: Vision and Imagination in Medieval Jewish Mysticism*. Princeton: Princeton University Press.

——— 1996. Iconic Visualization and the Imaginal Body of God: The Role of Intention in the Rabbinic Conception of Prayer. *Modern Theology* 12 no.2:137-62.

Zadeh, Lofti Asher. 1975. *Fuzzy Sets and Their Applications to Cognitive and Decision Processes*. New York: Academic Press.

Zaidman, Louise Bruit, and Pauline Schmitt Pantel. 1992. *Religion in the Ancient Greek City*. Translated by Paul Cartledge. Cambridge and New York: Cambridge University Press.

Zimmerli, Walther. 1959. Das zweite Gebot. In *Festschrift Alfred Bertholet zum 80. Geburtstag gewidmet von Kollegen und Freunden*. Edited by Walter Baumgartner, 550-60. Tübingen: J.C.B. Mohr.

INDEX OF NAMES AND SUBJECTS*

* I wish to express my gratitude to Mr. Joel Allen for assisting with the proof-reading of the manuscript and for preparing the Index of Biblical Citations. I also wish to thank Ms. Toni McGuire for her assistance with the Index of Names and Subjects.

INDEX OF SCRIPTURAL REFERENCES

THE BRILL REFERENCE LIBRARY
OF
ANCIENT JUDAISM

The Brill Reference Library of Ancient Judaism *presents research on fundamental problems in the study of the authoritative texts, beliefs and practices, events and ideas, of the Judaic religious world from the sixth century B.C.E. to the sixth century C.E. Systematic accounts of principal phenomena characteristic of Judaic life, works of a theoretical character, accounts of movements and trends, diverse expressions of the faith, new translations and commentaries of classical texts – all will find a place in the* Library.

1. Neusner, J. *The Halakhah. An Encyclopaedia of the Law of Judaism.* 5 Vols. 2000. ISBN 90 04 11617 6 *(set)*
   Vol. I. Between Israel and God. Part A. ISBN 90 04 11611 7
   Vol. II. Between Israel and God. Part B. Transcendent Transactions: Where Heaven and Earth Intersect. ISBN 90 04 11612 5
   Vol. III. Within Israel's Social Order. ISBN 90 04 11613 3
   Vol. IV. Inside the Walls of the Israelite Household. Part A. At the Meeting of Time and Space. ISBN 90 04 11614 1
   Vol. V. Inside the Walls of the Israelite Household. Part B. The Desacralization of the Household. ISBN 90 04 11616 8
2. Basser, H.W. *Studies in Exegesis.* Christian Critiques of Jewish Law and Rabbinic Responses 70-300 C.E. 2000. ISBN 90 04 11848 9
3. Neusner, J. *Judaism's Story of Creation.* Scripture, Halakhah, Aggadah. 2000. ISBN 90 04 11899 3
4. Aaron, David H.; *Biblical Ambiguities.* Metaphor, Semantics and Divine Imagery. 2001. ISBN 90 04 12032 7
5. Neusner, J. *The Reader's Guide to the Talmud.* 2001. ISBN 90 04 1287 0 *(In preparation)*
6. Neusner, J. *The Theology of the Halakhah.* 2001. ISBN 90 04 11219 2 *(In preparation)*

ISSN 1566-1237